SUNRISE

SUNRISE

The remarkable rise and rise
of the best-selling
Soaraway Sun

LARRY LAMB

PAPERMAC

First published by PAPERMAC
a division of Macmillan Publishers Limited
4 Little Essex Street, London WC2R 3LF
and Basingstoke

Associated companies in Auckland, Delhi, Dublin, Gaborone,
Hamburg, Harare, Hong Kong, Johannesburg, Kuala Lumpur,
Lagos, Manzini, Melbourne, Mexico City, Nairobi, New York,
Singapore and Tokyo

ISBN 0-333-51070-4

A CIP catalogue record for this book is available from
the British Library

Photoset by Rowland Phototypesetting Limited
Bury St Edmunds, Suffolk

Printed in Great Britain by
Richard Clay Ltd, Bungay, Suffolk

To Joan, with whose help
all things are possible

Contents

Introduction and Acknowledgements

When Rupert Murdoch took over *The Sun* published by the International Publishing Corporation in November 1969, it was the Cinderella of Fleet Street.

It is now by a considerable distance the best-selling daily newspaper in the English language.

Like it or loathe it, one cannot ignore it.

How was it done?

How could a new newspaper, born into what was widely regarded as a dying industry, not only survive and flourish, but become instrumental in putting many of its rivals back on the path to prosperity?

I have for years resisted the temptation to try to answer these questions, mainly because I was afraid the whole thing would look like – or, indeed, might become – some kind of ego-trip. For years I tried to persuade someone else to write the story. Eventually, Rupert Murdoch persuaded me that I should do so.

If the personal pronoun appears a lot in these pages it is only because I was there. The story of *The Sun* of the seventies is very much my own story. But the hero of *Sunrise* is not Larry Lamb, or even the significantly more heroic figure of Mr Rupert Murdoch. It is the newspaper itself. For a newspaper is a living thing. The best ones develop a personality of their own.

Before we embark upon the story, I must point out that this is no way an 'official' history, and that no one has attempted in any way to influence what I have written.

I must also give credit to all those people who have given so freely of their time to make it possible.

In particular, I would like to thank my wife, Joan, whose objectivity as a newspaper historian is suspect only because of her wholly irrational affection for the author; my daughter, Jacquie, who copes with the mysteries of the mighty word processor and my own execrable handwriting with the same unflagging good humour, and those of my friends and colleagues who shared in the work.

They will forgive me if I do not list them all.

Some, however, must be mentioned.

Both Brian McConnell and Henry Russell Douglas made copious contemporaneous notes, not all of which have survived my many moves.

Should you chance upon a felicitous phrase in these pages, however, it is probably one of theirs.

Arthur Brittenden, Philip Wrack, Graham King, Mike Nevard, Frank Nicklin, Beverley Goodway, Brian Horwite and Tony Rees have all contributed generously from their personal memory banks.

I would also like to acknowledge my debt to Rupert himself, and to his Managing Director at Wapping, Bill O'Neill, for making the company's resources available unconditionally to everyone carrying out research on my behalf.

This then, warts and all, is the story of *The Sun* – the greatly daring, bosom-baring, caring, sharing, scintillating Soaraway *Sun*.

It is a story told with affection and pride.

CHAPTER ONE

A Night to Remember

For me 16 November, 1969 was the longest day.

I went to my office in Bouverie Street shortly after dawn, taut as piano wire, and filled with a kind of savage energy. I left it shortly before dawn the next day, totally exhausted, in a mood of black despair.

For the launch of the new *Sun*, which I had vowed to make the best-selling daily newspaper in the English language, had been an unmitigated disaster. So much so, that as we drove home with *The Sun*'s new owner, Rupert Murdoch, and his wife Anna, she suggested, not entirely frivolously, that they would be better off driving straight to Heathrow and going home to Australia.

There were many reasons for the heart-breaking chaos of that first, dreadful night. Because of the speed with which we launched, we were grievously under-rehearsed. Only a handful of the people involved in that first issue had experience of tabloid newspapers. And since most of them had been working for the old *Sun*, owned by the International Publishing Corporation (and known as 'King's Cross' after that company's august chairman) until forty-eight hours earlier, we had no rehearsals, no dummy run, of any kind. The first practice copies we got into type became the first issue. We sold them.

Most of my journalists were the rump of the old IPC team from *The Sun*'s former headquarters in Endell Street. That is, they were in many cases those to whom IPC, who also owned the Mirror Group and the *People*, as well as many magazines, had not offered suitable alternative employment. Some of them made no secret of the fact that they had joined us in the confident expectation of another pay-off when the paper collapsed, as everyone said it would, in weeks rather than months. A few of them are there to this day, and still somewhat surprised to find themselves gainfully employed.

I had eighty-five journalists in all, plus a handful of key personnel I had recruited myself from other sources. Few of them had any experience of the kind of newspaper we had in mind. Even fewer of the people in the Composing Room, where type was set and assembled, had any experience of tabloid make-up.

The result was that the paper was more than three hours late – a disastrous production delay rendered even more critical by the fact that, alone among popular newspapers at that time, we were printing in only one centre, London, and endeavouring to reach the whole of the British Isles from London railheads by breakfast-time the next day.

Down in the machine room, where most of the huge old rotary presses had for years been operated only once a week, to print the broadsheet *News of the World*, things went from bad to worse. When Anna Murdoch pressed the button to start the print run, nothing happened. Inexperienced press crews had been responsible for a series of technical hitches which took many more vital minutes to sort out.

Incredibly, when I took my wife, Joan, down to the machine room to witness the button-pressing ceremony, I found the door barred by one John Addey, a public relations man who had been doing some work for Rupert, and who insisted that I couldn't go in because I was not on his guest list. After all, I was only the Editor. I prefer not to remember what I said to him. Suffice it to say that we were swiftly admitted. On reflection, it would perhaps have been better had we not been, so depressing was the experience.

Nothing improved as the night wore on. At a 'celebration' party in the Chairman's office a senior print union official was sick in a wastepaper-basket. Another was stopped by a security man in a corridor with a bottle of Johnny Walker Black Label in each pocket of his raincoat. Rupert's face – and, I suppose, my own – grew grimmer and greyer as the building's innumerable clocks ticked on.

When we did eventually get copies of the paper, having missed all the trains to Scotland and most of the North, just about everything seemed to be wrong with it. Just about everything on the surface, that is. It was visually crude, sloppily presented, and virtually uncorrected. But even then, somewhere beneath the blanket of despair, I had a gut feeling that there could be merit in its very crudeness; that there could be lurking in those forty-eight amateurish tabloid pages the kind of rawness, the kind of life and vigour which had for so long been lacking in the complacent, deep-piled corridors of Fleet Street.

Apart from that gut feeling there was only one cheerful incident the whole night through. From time to time messengers would march through the office shouting out a car number, and saying that the police wanted the vehicle moved. It meant nothing to me in the general hurly-burly and I took no notice. Not until we left the office next morning, that is, when I suddenly realised it was *my* car number.

Early in the day I had parked my shiny new company Daimler a few yards down the block, outside the *Daily Mail* building. And I had parked it – inadvertently, I swear – directly under a *Daily Mail* loading chute, thereby effectively sealing off a significant proportion of a rival newspaper's production facilities.

The saga of the Soaraway *Sun* had begun, for me, only a few weeks earlier with a telephone call to my office in Manchester. I was then Northern Editor of the *Daily Mail* – and, ironically, in London at the time for consultations with my London Editor, Arthur Brittenden.

I was in Arthur's office when I got a telephone call from

my secretary, Jean. Having discreetly ascertained that we were not being overheard, she said that 'a Mr Murdoch' wished to speak to me, and had left a London number. She knew as well as I did who he was.

Murdoch at that time had gained control of the *News of the World*, after a dramatic takeover tussle involving Robert Maxwell. Speculation was rife about his future plans. Most observers were agreed that he would not for long permit his vast press-room – with twenty-four units, capable of turning out a total of well over 5,000,000 copies a night – to continue to be idle for six nights a week. One did not have to be prescient to guess why he wanted to talk to me. I resisted the temptation to call him from London, went home to talk to my wife, and rang him the following day.

He did not beat about the bush. He doesn't, very often. 'I am trying to buy Cudlipp's *Sun*,' he said. 'If I don't get it, I shall be starting a new newspaper anyway. I shall be looking for an Editor. Can you have dinner with me tomorrow?'

Hugh, now Lord, Cudlipp, was at that time Editorial Director of IPC and architect of the terminally sick Endell Street *Sun*. His chairman, Cecil King, once observed of him that Hugh was a first violin rather than the leader of the orchestra. Between them, they had poured many millions into the new successor to the old *Daily Herald* newspaper, which now boasted that it was 'born of the age we live in'. There were few people in the industry who believed that anyone could make a success of a project after this formidable team, with their virtually unlimited resources, had failed.

Oddly, and arrogantly, enough, I did believe it, mainly because I had spent ten years under Cudlipp at the *Daily Mirror*, IPC's flagship, as a sub-editor, and in a variety of junior executive positions, and I thought I knew where they were getting it wrong. So I said yes to Rupert.

'Savoy Grill?' he suggested.

'That's fine by me,' I said. 'But if there is any element of

4

secrecy involved, from your point of view, it would be asking for trouble. I know that John Junor [Editor of the *Sunday Express*] and Bob Edwards [Editor of the *People*] are often there on Saturdays.'

'Right,' said Rupert. 'Rules, Maiden Lane. Eight o'clock.'

I was there on time, and sipping a dry martini (very dry, straight up, lemon twist) when he walked in. We had no difficulty recognising each other. I bought him a Scotch and soda. He, too, was fond of martinis, he said, but they kept him awake.

We ate lobster. 'Green,' said Rupert, which I gathered was Australian for fresh, and drank Pouilly Fumé, after I had opted for something 'light and white and dry'. It was just as well I did. We had three bottles. Rupert also called for a second round of lobster. I began to realise that this amiable Australian was formidable in more ways than one.

I suppose one would say that the conversation was animated. Certainly never again did I find Rupert so willing to listen for so long. Indeed the entire editorial policy of *The Sun* for years to come was to be based on this first conversation.

I was full of ideas about the kind of newspaper which had a chance of success in what was thought to be already an over-crowded market. Basically, it would be what the *Daily Mirror* used to be – strident, campaigning, working-class, entertaining but politically aware, a thorn in the flesh of the Establishment in its many guises.

The *Mirror*, years before, had fulfilled this role brilliantly. But it had developed a soft underbelly – largely, I suspect, because Hugh Cudlipp, for all his Welsh radical drum-beating, and he was a brilliant drum-beater – had a yearning for respectability. As the *Mirror* grew more and more 're-spectable', so did it move further and further away from its readers.

What I regarded as one of Hugh's sillier ideas was 'Mirror-scope', a four-page pullout in the centre of the paper reserved for 'serious and literate' material, laid out in a calculatedly up-market fashion. Apart from any other consideration this, I felt, was to insult the readers' intelligence. Serious and literate material should have a place in any newspaper. It is not necessary, nor, indeed, is it sensible, to gather it together and effectively label it 'serious and literate'. Much of the same sort of error had been made with the Endell Street *Sun*.

In 1964 Hugh had commissioned a massive piece of market research by the learned Dr Mark Abrams – 'The Newspaper Reading Public of Tomorrow'. I have kept a copy in my desk ever since as an awful warning. For Dr Abrams concluded, in effect, that Britain was rapidly becoming a middle-class nation – in his own phrase 'a nation of steak-eating weekenders' – and that a huge new market of middle-class readers was waiting to be tapped. Nothing could be further from the truth.

Yet the IPC *Sun* appeared to be based entirely upon this nonsensical proposition. It sold something like 3,000,000 copies on Day One, following a massive promotional campaign, perhaps 2,000,000 on the second day – and hurtled rapidly downhill thereafter.

For the fact is, of course, that there was no such mass market as the one envisaged. It is easy to see how the academic Dr Abrams leapt to the conclusion that increased income and increased leisure time would lead to substantial movement between social classes. It is not so easy to understand why Cudlipp, a shrewd, clever and essentially popular journalist for whom I had, and still have, a high regard, allowed himself to be taken in.

Taken in he certainly was. For the newspaper he produced, based so firmly upon the market research, was, like most such products in publishing, so smooth, so laid-back, so iffy and butty, as to be totally devoid of character. Even if the huge pool of customers at whom it was presumably aimed had existed – and it didn't – they would have had no good reason to buy it. It is still a mystery to me why Hugh allowed it to happen. He should have known better.

I said much of this to Rupert and much more in the same vein. It swiftly became apparent that we had very similar ideas.

'What do you think of the City?' asked Rupert.

'They get away with murder,' I replied. 'Business reporting in the UK is appallingly sycophantic. City editors have long forgotten whose side they are on.'

'Would you have a gossip column?' he asked.

'No,' I replied. 'Gossip is only effective if it has an element of malice. Bland gossip is boring. We should be neither boring nor malicious.'

'Are you keen on sport?' he wanted to know.

'I have to be,' I said. 'The customers are.'

'Could you operate effectively printing in London only?'

'Yes,' I answered.

As a former Northern Editor I was only too well aware that national newspapers in the UK wasted a fortune duplicating the entire operation in Manchester. Multi-centre printing, I explained, made sense only if regional centres could be regarded largely as print shops, supplied with editorial and advertising material from central office by facsimile transmission. At that time the print unions simply would not permit faxing of pages. In Manchester I had had all the necessary machinery – shrouded in dust-covers.

The close questioning went on for hours. Gradually I began to feel less tense. I guessed I was getting most of the answers right.

After dinner, at Murdoch's suggestion, we strolled through Aldwych to the *News of the World* office, where the presses were thundering away, and had a look at the first edition. Not knowing how much of the paper Rupert himself had been responsible for, I made what I hoped were sensible suggestions for minor changes later on, and we drank a glass or two of whisky.

'This is the position then,' said Rupert. 'I have a short list of seven or eight people. I will be in touch with you again in a week or two, when I have seen them all.'

I thanked him, and accepted his offer of a lift to my hotel, The President. It was 2 a.m.

I called my wife, as I had promised to do, and said that I had enjoyed the meeting, would be tempted to take the job if it was offered, and I would be back on the first available train. As soon as I had put the phone down it rang.

'Rupert here,' said my new acquaintance. 'Bugger the short list. Can you come round to my house in Sussex Square at nine o'clock?'

I was greeted by his wife, holding their baby daughter, Elisabeth. Anna smiled warmly, and said that Rupert would appear shortly.

'He doesn't waste much time does he?' I ventured.

'No,' said Anna. 'Not much.'

When Rupert came we did the whole deal – salary, company car, terms and working conditions – in five minutes flat. He made a few notes – Heads of Agreement – on a scribbling pad, and we shook hands.

I'm not sure what the notes said, because I never got a copy. But that sheet of paper was the only contract I ever had, or needed. The only thing I tried to insist upon was that I would be responsible only to the Chairman. I had seen too many editors struggling vainly to please managing directors who knew little or nothing of the creative process. I never did get that undertaking in writing. But I never got seriously hampered by managers either. Rupert kept his part of the bargain. In my experience he usually does.

There was one other point we discussed before I left to catch my train to Manchester. Could I, I asked, engage a deputy of my own choosing? The man I had in mind, I said, was Bernard Shrimsley, a former *Mirror* colleague who was then Editor of the *Liverpool Post*.

Rupert grinned mischievously. 'He was the next guy on the list,' he said.

I never did find out quite how that list was compiled. Rupert is said to have confided in fellow directors that he asked a dozen friends in the business for the names of people they would recommend as Editor of a new daily paper, and rang me first because my name was the only one to appear on every list. The story deserves to be true. Whether it is or not, had I been unavailable on that fateful Saturday I have no doubt he would have seen Bernard first – and this might have been a very different sort of book.

When I left Sussex Square I telephoned my wife: 'Change of plan', I said. 'We're moving.' We lived at that time in Bramhall, a Cheshire suburb some eight or ten miles from Manchester. Most trains from London to Manchester stopped near by at Stockport – where Joan was waiting with the car when I stepped off the train a few hours after leaving Sussex Square.

I was tremendously excited. So, too, bless her, was my wife. No doubts. No recriminations. No questions about the wisdom of leaving a good job for what might turn out to be a non-job.

She behaved exactly as she had done when I left the *Daily Mirror* in London only eighteen months earlier. She put the house on the market and cheerfully started to roll up the rugs.

There were, of course, people who did not think it a wise move. Chief among them was Arthur Brittenden, who received my resignation with dismay, and at first declined to accept it.

An embarrassing period followed. At length, I agreed under pressure to meet Arthur and the then Managing Director of Associated Newspapers, Mr Marmaduke J. Hussey, for dinner at one of our favourite London restaurants, the White Tower in Percy Street, Here they both tried very earnestly to dissuade me from making the move – especially when they learned that no written contract existed between myself and Mr Murdoch.

Finally Duke – later Managing Director of Times Newspapers and now, of course, Chairman of the BBC – played his trump card. They had been delighted with my work in Manchester, he said, and they had it in mind to offer me the Editorship of the struggling *Daily Sketch* in a few months' time. In the circumstances, he was prepared to make that offer immediately.

I had been toying with my food all evening, sick at heart at having to keep saying no to two friends who sincerely believed that they were acting in my interests. The latest proposition made the situation even more difficult. And it became more difficult still after dinner when, over champagne in Duke's Chelsea home, he threw in another inducement. Lord Rothermere was eager to deal personally with my contract as *Daily Sketch* Editor, he said, and had asked that I fly down to his home on the Riviera to discuss it. The debate went on deep into the night, and I felt more and more churlish as it continued. But I had done a deal, and I never seriously considered going back on it. I subsequently wrote to Lord Rothermere explaining my position and received a charming reply.

For the next few weeks I tried conscientiously to carry out my duties in Manchester, dashing to London on days off to see Rupert, whilst he brought pressure to bear upon Lord Rothermere for my early release. His Lordship was generous about that, too, as, ultimately, was Bernard Shrimsley's employer, Sir Alec Jeans.

So we were free to join Rupert towards the end of October. By this time the deal with IPC had been struck. Rupert paid a trifling sum for the paper which was ultimately to topple the *Daily Mirror* from its lofty perch and produce profits in excess of £1,000,000 a week.

Instead, as part of the deal, he undertook to buy an agreed amount of newsprint from Reed, the IPC's paper-making group. 'What the hell, we'll need it anyway,' he said.

The Mirror Group, for their part, were anxious merely to unburden themselves of King's Cross – though King himself had been ousted in a palace revolution some months earlier. Their last issue was to be on 15 November, our first on the 17th.

I was overwhelmed with the enormity of this task, in view of the time and talent available, and I went to Rupert with a somewhat cowardly proposition. Could we, I said, ask IPC to continue to print for us, on contract and at their plant, in *The Sun*'s existing broadsheet format, for a further month, whilst our own people and machinery were being brought to a more advanced state of readiness?

Could I produce a newspaper at all in the time available? asked the Chairman.

'Yes, I suppose so,' I said uncertainly.

'Will it be better than the existing *Sun*?'

'Yes, I think so.'

'Will it be better than the *Daily Sketch*?'

'Yes, I hope so.'

'Right,' said Rupert. 'We go on the 17th. From here. From Bouverie Street. And we go tabloid.'

In the frenetic period which followed I paid a couple of flying visits to Manchester to see my family. And thereby hangs a tale.

One Saturday afternoon Bernard Shrimsley and I had been lunching with Rupert at the Savoy, and the talk went on late into the afternoon, until Bernard and I had both missed our scheduled trains home. 'Don't worry,' said Rupert. 'Take my car. I won't be needing it this weekend.'

This was an alarming prospect, and clearly a test of some kind. I had never driven a Rolls, and Rupert's had been parked in a particularly inaccessible corner. Needless to say there was no sign of the doorman when we emerged, blinking, on to the Savoy forecourt. Rupert gave me the keys, and sat in the front passenger seat.

Ever so gently, scarcely daring to breathe, I eased the monster out of its lair, turned it round, remembering to keep on the right (the Savoy forecourt is, to my knowledge, the only road in London where one drives on the right), and lurched like a demented duck into the traffic stream on the Strand.

We dropped Rupert in Park Lane – he fancied a walk in the park – and headed north. So far so good.

But the Rolls had not finished with us yet. When we stopped for petrol on the M1 neither Bernard nor I knew where the filler cap was. When we found it we didn't know where the key was. And when the needle on the (pre-digital) pump eventually started spinning as though there was no tomorrow, we both realised with dismay that we were rather short of cash. We scraped up enough by the skin of our teeth, by now watched with mounting suspicion by the petrol station manager as well as the pump attendant, and sped off, presumably leaving them wondering whether or not to call the police.

This time Bernard was driving. Somewhere north of Watford Gap we ran into fog.

When he, stating the obvious, observed that it was getting thicker, I said with an asperity designed to mask my growing alarm, that if he maintained his present speed there was at least no danger of our being hit from behind. After that we proceeded more sedately to Manchester Airport, where we found a hire car to take Bernard through the murk to his home in Southport, hoping his wife would have enough money to pay the bill, and I crept warily through the suburbs to Bramhall.

Next morning I was awakened by noises from outside, and saw to my alarm that the Rolls, in the driveway, was swarming with children. My son, Nick, then aged eight, had found the keys and the control which activated the electrics – without, happily, starting the engine – and had recruited every child in the neighbourhood to help him play with his new toy. Seats and windows moved up and down, the roof opened and closed frenetically, lights flashed, horns tooted. As I struggled to open the window to shout, my wife, who had been busy in the back garden, rushed round and shooed them away. Fortunately no damage was done.

I left on Monday before dawn, feeling much more at home with the monster, hurtled down the motorways with great confidence and at great speed, and parked the car outside the office in Bouverie Street before even Rupert had arrived for work. That car was later to figure in a dramatic murder case – one which had a profound effect upon my own life, as well as that of the fledgling *Sun*.

I made my next trip home by train – and it was on this trip, on the way back to London, that I created the famous red masthead, since copied in English language newspapers from Fiji to the Costa Brava, with the aid of my young daughter's felt-tipped pen kit, then something of a novelty, on the back of a used envelope. We had asked our advertising agents, Hobson Bates, to submit a number of designs, but I didn't like any of them. They were all too sophisticated. I was seeking something with maximum impact in a very small space. If the masthead was to be white on red, as I wished, the lettering would need to be unusually thick, so as to achieve the maximum density for the surrounding red ink. I drew something close to what I wanted. Ultimately the talented Vic Giles, Art Editor of the old *Sun* and the new, prepared the finished artwork from my sketches.

As recently as 1988 the design was the subject of an interesting copyright action when News Group, publishers of *The Sun*, sought an injunction to prevent its use by Robert Maxwell's Mirror Group in a series of 'knocking copy' advertisements. The *Mirror* contended that the copyright belonged not to *The Sun*, but to me. I refused to join in the action against the *Mirror* as requested by *The Sun*'s lawyers, but I happily bequeathed the copyright to my former employers for the sum of £1. The *Mirror*'s advertisements were discontinued.

As D-Day approached, we were joined by an increasing number of people. Henry Russell Douglas, ex-Oxford, ex-submariner, and former leader writer of the *Liverpool Post*, came south, strongly recommended by his old boss, Bernard, to become a key member of the launch team. Anthony Shrimsley, brother of Bernard, came to head up the political staff. Joyce Hopkirk, later to star with publications as varied as *Cosmopolitan*, the *Daily Mirror*, the *Sunday Times*, *Elle* and *She*, came to see us with an impressive list of a hundred feature ideas and talked her way into a job. And my former Chief Sub-Editor from Newcastle, Norman Baitey, left the editorship of the *Newcastle Sunday Sun* to take part in the great adventure. We recruited Brian McConnell from the *Mirror* as News Editor, Nick Lloyd – subsequently to become Editor of the *News of the World* and the *Daily Express* – as a Features Executive, and a handful of Fleet Street's chronic unemployed, some of whose drinking habits had made them almost unemployable. We needed them as much as they needed us. On the whole, they did not let us down.

When we suddenly realised that we were drowning in paper I asked the *News of the World* management for secretarial assistance. A pert young lady from Gravesend, on the casual list of the print union, SOGAT, was dispatched to help us on a temporary basis. She was the now legendary Marian Davison, so 'temporary' that she became my personal secretary, and the Queen Bee of the entire editorial organisation for many years, and secretary to my successor as Editorial Director, Peter Stephens, for many years after that. But it was always clear that the bulk of the staff were going to have to come from Endell Street, and that, in the nature of things, they were not going to be available to us until after the IPC *Sun* had set on 15 November.

We let it be known that we would welcome applications from all of them. One, from the Sports Editor, Frank Nicklin, said tersely: 'I am Sports Editor of *The Sun*, 46 and still ambitious. Yours sincerely.' He was hired. So were most of the others, much to Norman Baitey's disgust.

Norman had been asked to interview candidates, and grade them A B C or D. He scored 80 per cent Ds – but we hired them just the same. One, the Deputy Features Editor, was jazz drummer Mike Nevard, now Editorial Director of the Globe Magazine Company in Palm Beach, Florida. He was to become an invaluable colleague, but at interview he failed to do himself justice. He wrote to me immediately afterwards asking if he could have another go. Of course he could!

Some – a mere handful – did not write, including two I would have dearly liked to have. They were Clement (now Sir Clement) Freud, who wrote on food and rugby football, and TV critic Nancy Banks-Smith. Clement later accused me of having excised from the newspaper all 'consciously fine writing', meaning, presumably, his, and gave me clearly to understand that he would have been willing to join us, but felt he should have been asked. Nancy Banks-Smith went to the *Guardian*, where her work continued to delight me for years afterwards.

One of the very few people who wanted a job and didn't get one was an old colleague of mine from *Daily Mirror* days, Ted Castle, husband of the formidable Barbara. Ted had been based in Parliament as a sort of special adviser – a link between the paper and its close contacts in the then Labour government. He did not write regularly for the paper, and his former colleagues, some of them quite senior, felt that he was more concerned with the image and welfare of the Labour Party than that of the newspaper which paid his salary. We had no use for such a contact, and I told him so, as an old friend, as gently as possible.

Unfortunately he took this badly and went around telling

everyone who would listen that he had refused to work for us because we were planning a scruffy, down-market paper with no interest in politics. I ignored the stories, until he was directly quoted in the London *Evening Standard* as saying that he could no longer work for *The Sun* 'as it has now become'. As it had not, at the time, 'become' anything at all, I became incandescent with rage, and dashed off a letter to the Editor of the *Standard* which said that the decision that Mr Castle would not work for us had been mine, not his.

I have since regretted that letter. I think, with the benefit of hindsight, that it was unworthy, and that it would have been more generous to allow him to perpetuate this minor myth. My only excuse is that I was under considerable strain at the time, and fiercely determined that, whatever they said about me, no one would slander *The Sun* with impunity.

We had an exciting time when, within a day or two of the launch, Norman was free to move to London on a permanent basis, and I was seeking fresh temporary accommodation. We asked Tony Rees, an Australian journalist who had been doing some administrative work for us, to book us into a 'modest' hotel. There could scarcely have been a more modest hotel than the one he found. Presumably bemused by its Mayfair address, he had booked us into a positive flea-pit. He redeemed himself on the spot by somehow smuggling us both, with our luggage, through a service entrance out into the street and into the Hilton. I reasoned that it would be some time before the Hilton bill landed on Rupert's desk. Fortunately, when it landed, it landed on mine.

Tony subsequently booked me into another flea-pit – a rented house near Putney Bridge owned by zither-playing Shirley Abicair. I'm not suggesting that Shirley had fleas, but her cats had. After fumigation I stayed there for some months, first with Bernard and later with my family.

Meanwhile, from base camps in Bouverie Street and the

Hilton, we continued our frantic search for staff of all kinds. Many newspapers, especially the *Daily Mirror*, paid huge sums to persuade key personnel to stay put.

'I'm afraid I can't join you, Larry,' said one old friend, Fergus Linnane. 'They have tied a bag of gold around my neck.'

Rumour had it that another old colleague whose work I greatly admired, *Mirror* Woman's Editor, Felicity Green, had earlier been offered a directorship after letting it be known that I had asked her to come and see me in Manchester. She was certainly promoted as a result of that invitation – to Executive Women's Editor of the group.

We took to using the Waldorf for interviewing people because of its proximity to our own and other offices, and it became a standing joke in the Street that anyone seen there with any of my executives could confidently expect a big rise. There was an even bigger premium if they were seen with me. Some old colleagues even called to invite *me* for a drink there in the hope that the news would get back to their offices.

On one occasion a knowledgeable observer would have spotted three separate interviews taking place in the Waldorf bar at the same time. At one end I was talking to a *Mirror* executive I hoped to recruit. A few feet away Tony Shrimsley was deep in conversation with a Parliamentary correspondent, also from the *Mirror*. And still further away Brian McConnell was trying hard to lure a big byline reporter away from the *Daily Express*.

We didn't get any of them. But we greatly advanced their careers.

So we interviewed many people. But as we have seen our striking rate was not good. The pundits were unanimously predicting catastrophe, and anxious wives were persuading even the most adventurous of newspapermen that it would be folly to join us.

Hugh Cudlipp, it was said, having got rid of King's Cross,

held a sigh-of-relief party at the Café Royal at which the table decorations were dead sunflowers. He said openly that he gave us six months to live. We thought of responding with cracked mirrors, but we didn't have the time.

We eventually went into battle with fewer than a hundred people in the editorial department. The *Express* and the *Mirror* had more than four hundred, most of them in London, and the *Mail* was not far behind.

It was a far, far smaller staff than I had hoped for, lacking key people in many areas. Just how small it was we were shortly to find out as I led my already battle-weary troops into the trenches for the first hundred days.

CHAPTER TWO

The First One Hundred Days

It is hard to believe, after all this time, that the Soaraway *Sun*, which has dominated the popular newspaper market in Britain for the past twenty years, grew out of the chaos which existed in Bouverie Street in 1969.

Chaos there certainly was. We were grafting a seven-days-a-week operation on to a totally inadequate weekly newspaper organisation geared solely to producing the *News of the World*. And matters were not helped by the fact that we were greatly resented by many of the *News of the World*'s clerical and administrative staff, some of whom had worked a three- or four-day week for years.

Pre-Murdoch, for much of the time Bouverie Street was a backwater. The *News of the World* had no serious rivals, and there was little whip-cracking in any department.

After Murdoch – and, more particularly, after Sunrise – things were very different, and the manifold weaknesses in the organisation were quickly apparent. For instance, because no one at the *News of the World* had ever worked on Sundays, no one thought we might need cashiers on duty on that day. Many of the staff were casual and had to be paid on the day. Reporters being dispatched to far-flung places needed cash advances.

The telephone switchboard, which in any case was totally inadequate for our needs, carried only a skeleton staff. The canteen wasn't fully operational. As most restaurants in the Fleet Street area also closed on Sundays, and the pubs which were open were not then as food-conscious as they are now, this was quite a serious matter, and led to a great deal of unrest.

If the Duty Editor or the Production Manager complained to me I have to confess that I used to spirit them off to the Savoy for lunch. But it was not a solution I felt I could properly apply to several hundred hungry print workers. It took months, with much shouting and desk-banging, to convince the *News of the World* management that on a daily newspaper, Sunday was a normal working day.

A mere seventy-two hours before launch day, no one had thought where we were to seat close to a hundred extra journalists. When we did think of it the indefatigable Tony Rees was sent out to buy a hundred desks and a hundred chairs. 'Make them small ones,' said Rupert, 'or there'll be no bloody room.' Small ones they were – and there was still no bloody room.

Out of earshot of the Chairman, I exercised an editor's privilege and told Tony I wanted an exception made in my case. I like big desks. I got one.

Sharing with Tony the burden of the very real physical problems involved in setting up an office in the twinkling of an eye was the then Deputy Editor – later to be Editor – of the *News of the World*, C. J. 'Tiny' Lear. He was seconded to us as an administrative assistant, and worked wonders. Among other things he persuaded the GPO to install an emergency switchboard, and numerous extra lines, in a matter of days.

The result was a telephonic jungle in which, for a time, the newspaper had a variety of different numbers. But at least we started to get a percentage of our calls, which was an improvement on none at all.

We had another crisis over typefaces. In 1969 computerised photosetting was no more than a dream in Fleet Street, and type was set in hot metal, on a Linotype machine with a keyboard, or, in the case of some larger sizes, by hand.

I had thought the *News of the World* range of typefaces both limited and old-fashioned, and quite unsuited to the kind of newspaper we had in mind. So we ordered a whole new batch of type for headline purposes in a face known as Tempo, which was made in Chicago, and strongly favoured by my deputy, Bernard Shrimsley.

Having ordered it, I forgot it – until a few days before the launch when I was horrified to discover it hadn't arrived. After frantic cabling and feverish experiments with unsuitable alternatives, it was delivered with forty-eight hours to spare.

We still had our problems. For instance we could not, initially, write a Page One headline with more than three letter Es because in the largest size available that was all we had.

There were many stories at that time about Europe, and the EEC. Neither the word nor the initials were popular with me. Both have two Es, leaving only one to play with.

Fortunately, Greece was not at that time seeking admission to the EEC. That headline would have been impossible. We didn't care much for girls called Eve, or, for that matter, Elsie (as in Tanner). 'Elsie engaged', for example, has one E too many.

Extra letters could easily have been manufactured internally. But since the print union involved decided this was outside the range of their normal duties they demanded a special bonus for *all* their members – as opposed to the handful concerned. We declined.

The photoset equivalent of that family of typefaces is still *The Sun*'s basic headline style. Like the masthead, the layout built around it has been copied by tabloid newspapers world-wide. But these physical difficulties, acute though they were, seemed trivial by the side of some more fundamental problems.

The morale of much of the staff was appalling. Many of the people from Endell Street were either dejected and dispirited, or noisily cynical. A substantial proportion felt they should have been offered jobs within IPC. As we have seen, we were resented by many of the *News of the World* back-up staff, who, like some of our own recruits, made no secret of the fact that they were looking forward to the time, which they were convinced would be not far distant, when the infant *Sun* died from natural causes, and they could resume their part-time idyll.

We had interminable union troubles. The National Union of Journalists' Endell Street chapel (office branch) had been very active on the old *Sun*, and had involved itself in all sorts of ways in affairs which I, as Editor, and Murdoch, as proprietor, regarded as none of their business. So whilst a handful of us – including, to their eternal credit, a fair proportion of people from Endell Street – were toiling for twelve, fourteen and sometimes sixteen hours a day to get the paper out, there were others who spent their time in permanent corridor talking-shops, bleating about the admittedly difficult conditions, or forming deputations to wait outside my office with lists of complaints.

Much of the trouble came from former specialist reporters. I have always been wary of specialists, though in some areas – in Parliament, for example – one cannot do without them.

On the old *Sun* there had been twenty-seven. Twenty-seven people with unnecessary private offices and underused secretaries. And though all of them had been told that specialisation in Bouverie Street would be cut to the absolute minimum, and there would be no private secretaries except for senior executives, that didn't stop them whining about it when they arrived.

I believed then, and I believe now, that many newspaper 'specialisations' are not only unnecessary but can be a positive handicap, in that specialists become too close to their subjects, form little clubs of their own, and tend to forget that they are in the business of disclosure. And, of course, once they have acquired the distinction of a title of some kind, they feel entitled to refuse to work outside their immediate area of specialisation, and are therefore chronically underemployed.

When I got to bed after the horrors of launch night I had been awakened, it seemed to me almost immediately, by a telephone call from Rupert. On the way home we had discussed various ways of tackling the immediate problems, and reluctantly decided, among other things, to reduce the scheduled paging for Day Two from forty to twenty-four. The Chairman had now changed his mind. 'We'll *make* the bastards do it,' he said. 'I don't care how long it takes.'

Wearily, I agreed. All my own newspaper experience had led me to believe that however bloody-minded the unions, the amount of work produced grew in direct proportion to the amount demanded. From then on it became an article of faith with me to stretch the Murdoch rubber band to the utmost, to drive the production machine much harder than it wanted to be driven, to do more changes than were strictly necessary and to push all deadlines to the absolute limit. I reckoned that if I got two-thirds of what I asked for I would be getting 90 per cent of what I needed.

Slowly, grindingly, astonishingly, it started to work. Production times on Day Two were far from good, but better. After two or three weeks the 'stone-hands' – who assembled type in page form – were getting more accustomed to tabloid disciplines, broadsheet-trained sub-editors were learning to count every word, and everyone knew where the lavatories were. And the sale – we had reckoned to inherit around 650,000 paying customers from IPC – was comfortably over the 1,000,000 which Murdoch had bravely guaranteed to advertisers.

Things were still chaotic, of course. And shortly before Christmas Rupert and Anna had to return to Australia to cope with a crisis at the antipodean end of the empire.

Rupert had recruited, as a sort of elder statesman to keep

an eye on the shop, Alick (later Sir Alick) McKay, an Australian who was an old friend of his father's and a retired Advertisement Director of IPC. Appallingly, early in 1970 Alick's wife Muriel was kidnapped and murdered – a bizarre crime which horrified the nation. Clearly, Alick was quite incapable of work at this time. Production Director Harry Cole was at home suffering from nervous exhaustion, and I was doing just about everything, including, on one occasion, ordering paper and ink.

Harry Cole was known to the editorial staff as the Abominable No-Man, because everything we asked for he said was impossible. This was more than a little unfair. Harry, a sound technician, had spent most of his working life in the womb-like surroundings of the *News of the World*, where routine had been honed to perfection by years of doing the same thing at the same time, week after week after week. It was not his fault that his secure little world was invaded by a crowd of lunatic, noisy outsiders, trained in tougher schools, and eager to work seven days a week, and he found himself genuinely bewildered.

He felt it wiser to tell us at the outset that something couldn't be done rather than to tackle the project and fail. I understood his dilemma, and felt for him. His unavoidable absence from duty, when both Rupert and Alick were away, helped to make January 1970 one of the most traumatic periods of my life.

Our production problems remained massive. Night after night we missed trains. Night after night we got the wrong editions to the wrong places. The people in South Wales must have been very puzzled by our apparent obsession with Tyneside football. In Bradford, in my West Riding home territory, we missed the local delivery service on twenty-seven days in the month. And the sale went up, and up, and up.

Said a bewildered Australian director, George Viles, a tough old ad-man from Sydney: 'The Brits will walk over broken bloody glass to buy the bloody thing.' And they did.

Towards the end of February 1970, after the first hundred days, the estimated daily sale was more than 1,300,000 copies – twice that which we had inherited. Furthermore, we felt we had almost certainly lost many of those old *Sun* readers, many of whom had been weaned on the old TUC-dominated *Daily Herald*, and many of whom, around Britain's Celtic fringes, were now beyond our reach because we couldn't get to them from London in time.

Just why was *The Sun* such an instant success, in spite of its problems?

We had some highly professional people doing a highly professional job. We spent a lot of money on television advertising. We were pretty good, as the critics were fond of saying, at what is nowadays called tit and bum – and racing – though topless ladies on Page Three had not yet become institutionalised.

But of course, we were much more than that. The most important reason, I think, was that however enormous the task, we were determinedly setting out to be what we said we would be.

Let me quote from the leading article which we published on Day One, and which expresses much of my own journalistic philosophy.

Welcome to the new *SUN*. You are going to like it. A lot of talent and a lot of enthusiasm have gone into its making. And a lot of faith. On Page One of this newspaper, every day, you will see the slogan 'Forward with the People'. It is not original. But we make no apology for it. Because that is what we believe in. That is the way ahead.

Today's *Sun* is a new newspaper. It has a new shape, new writers, new ideas.

But it inherits all that is best from the great traditions of its predecessors.

The Sun cares. About the quality of life. About the kind of world we live in. About people.

We will never forget YOUR place in *The Sun*. This newspaper will not be produced for the politicians or the pundits. It will be produced for you.

That is why we want you to join this young, new, virile campaigning newspaper.

To join it now, on Day One. To grow with it and enjoy life with it.

We want you at all times to feel a part of *The Sun*. To rejoice at our achievements. To be downcast by our own disappointments. To tell us when we have done well, or badly. We want *The Sun* to be the people's newspaper.

Let us go forward together.

I doubt if I would want to alter a word of that – or of the even clearer statement of our aims and intentions which we published at the end of Week One:

This has been an astonishingly successful first week for the new *Sun*. Thank you. We promised we would produce a paper for the people, not the pundits. And the people have responded. Magnificently.

The pundits have responded too. Predictably. They like to fit things into pigeonholes. They have been whipped into a froth of anxiety by a paper that will not be pigeonholed.

That is why they say *The Sun* has no principles. No views of its own. They are wrong. It is not *The Sun* that does not know where it stands. Today we say where we stand on a number of major issues. And, as promised, we will not curry favour.

The Sun has already condemned the barbarity of corporal punishment. It is even more strongly opposed to capital punishment. Not because of the ghastly, archaic trappings of black cap, condemned cell, pinions, rope and drop. But because *The Sun* believes capital punishment is wrong.

. . . *The Sun* is on the side of youth. It will never think that what is prim must be proper . . .

It believes that the only real crime is to hurt people.

★   ★   ★

About Europe, the British people have been told too little.
But it seems likely that when we know more *The Sun* will be
FOR entering Europe.
*Because Britain is a trading nation. Because in the long run only
through trade can these islands support 60 million people.*
The Sun has no party politics. It tries to judge political issues
as they arise. On their merits.
That is what the pundits will not believe. And cannot forgive.
The Sun is a radical newspaper. That is to say it believes in
change for the better. But not in change for change's sake.
Above all, *The Sun* is on the side of the people. We make no
apology for saying it again.
We are not going to bow to the Establishment in any of its
privileged enclaves. Ever.
. . . Do we really strike you as a paper with no opinions?
Stay with The Sun. *You'll
be glad you did.*

They did stay with us. And to judge from my ever-swelling
post bag, they *were* glad they stayed. Because *The Sun* was
– and still is – as unpredictable as it is irrepressible. In those
days it *refused* to be pigeonholed. Because we acknowledged
what many journalists were at that time anxious to forget –
that the basic interests of the human race are not in philosophy, economics or brass-rubbing but in things like food
and money and sex and crime, football and TV. But we did
not deal with these things to the exclusion of all others.

There were many critics in those early days who made
the mistake of confusing bold headlines and big pictures
with irresponsibility. They were the ones who believed that
a dull newspaper must be a worthy one, and regarded
interminably long stories as reporting in depth when they
merely represent reporting in width.

The new *Sun* prided itself on carrying all the news that
was significant. On being a vehicle of information as well as
a vehicle of entertainment.

Lord Longford said the secret was 'Antipodean Erotica'.
The Press Council attributed *The Sun*'s success to 'a mixture

of sex and punchy radicalism'. At the same time Sir Keith (now Lord) Joseph was telling the House of Commons: 'Page two of *The Sun* (then the editorial page) is a very important page for the whole of this country.'

I think they were *all* right, except that the erotica was home-grown. We tried hard to be the complete newspaper, to be significant as well as irreverent.

Irreverent *The Sun* certainly was and is. God forbid that it should ever become respectable.

Early in 1970 the *Financial Times* columnist Sheila Black, who ironically was married to *Daily Mirror* Editor, Lee Howard, generously reported that the new *Sun* had 'a soaraway, crest-of-the-wave feeling'. It sure did. We worked at it. Day after day. Night after passion-filled night. We were grateful to Sheila for the Soaraway *Sun* label – which *The Sun* still carries with pride.

In the early days we packed everything into the paper that could be packed in. In Week One we carried a long serialisation of Jacqueline Susann's then very daring novel *The Love Machine*, interviews with the Prime Minister, Harold Wilson, and with Britain's most brilliant soccer star, George Best; pictures of nude girls – from the back – at Mick Jagger's swimming-pool; cartoonists – the incomparable Paul Rigby, and the brilliant, engagingly erotic young Posy Simmonds. We introduced soccer wall-charts, and a readers' 'Best Buy' service we called 'Get Set'.

If any idea had worked well anywhere else we stole it. If it hadn't been tried we tried it. If it couldn't be done we did it. If we had an idea on Friday for a series we would blurb it in Saturday's week-ahead column before a word had been written. If the *Mail* or the *Express* or the *Mirror* dared to carry a blurb on Friday for a series scheduled for the following week we would launch a sizzling spoiling operation on Saturday. Feature ideas raised at morning conference were frequently in print by the evening.

Thus we hit and sustained for weeks – months, years –

a high note of creative hysteria, fuelled by increasingly optimistic circulation forecasts, and the occasional measured dose of Murdoch whisky. Rupert tended to disapprove of drinking in the office. In my office, anyway. We shared many a bottle in his.

I defended the practice stoutly on the ground that the people I invited in were usually those who had already spent eight or ten hours at their desks. They not only deserved a drink, they needed one.

Furthermore, when they were drinking in my office after the first edition had gone to press, there was only ever one topic of conversation – the paper. Many of our best ideas came at these sessions, when the pressures of the day were receding a little.

Rupert joined us occasionally. Sadly this tended to be counter-productive, since many of my colleagues were greatly in awe of him, and became much less spontaneous in his presence. His contributions, when he made any, were well meant but not usually helpful. We tended to hope he would forget having made them.

Not in the first hundred days, but some years later, after he moved to New York, Rupert used to visit us occasionally. It was always what we used to call a 'stimulating' time.

One Friday, after what had been for all around him a particularly exhausting visit – Rupert seemed as fresh as ever – he said goodbye to us all and left for Heathrow. Because I had some writing to do, a modest Friday night party was launched in the office of the then Deputy Editor, Arthur Brittenden (how he came to join us will be explained in due course). Arthur had borrowed from my secretary, Maid Marian, some particularly elegant, and rather large, whisky glasses.

As the drink started to flow in earnest the door opened. Rupert had missed his plane, and returned to the office. Told that I was in my office he stormed down the corridor. 'Let them drink my whisky if they must,' he raged, 'but must they drink it out of bloody plant pots?' Overall, he had little cause for complaint, and by that time, to be fair, he didn't complain much.

From the end of the first hundred days it had been abundantly clear that Sunrise was not going to be swiftly followed, as the pundits had unanimously predicted, by Sunset. High Noon, perhaps, would have been more appropriate.

At the end of two hundred days, in June 1970, the outlook was even brighter. I was then able to tell a lunch-time meeting of the Institute of Public Relations:

'No one now thinks we can be safely ignored. No one now thinks we will close in six months – or six years. I am happy to tell you that according to the latest estimates our average sale for the first six months of the newspaper's existence will be in excess of 1,500,000 copies a day.

'Advertisement revenue is increasingly buoyant, and, unlike some of its long-established competitors, the newspaper is firmly in the black.'

It has been very much in the black ever since. So much so that it was for some time the biggest single money-spinner in what is now the biggest communications empire the world has known.

CHAPTER THREE

The Murder of Muriel McKay

On 29 December 1969 Muriel McKay was kidnapped. It was a moment unique in criminal history. It was the first kidnapping for ransom in Britain for nearly 800 years. It was the moment Muriel McKay's fate was sealed. And it happened at precisely the moment the fledgling *Sun* was itself struggling for life.

To this day there is not a shred of evidence to show what happened to Muriel's body. There was a gruesome, and much-canvassed theory that it had been fed to pigs. But there was no evidence.

As we have seen, kidnap in the United Kingdom had been and continues to be, an extremely rare crime. Scotland Yard were unused to dealing with it. So were the Press. Mistakes were made on both sides. There was a mind-boggling deluge of wisdom after the event.

But it is now generally accepted that publicity can heighten the risk to the hostage who is being held to ransom, and a pact which is, in effect, a conspiracy of silence has since been introduced between the Yard and newspaper editors if a kidnap occurs. They ask the Press to keep quiet until the victim is free, or dead, and editors, unanimously in my experience, agree to do so.

Apart from tennis, not a great deal happens in Wimbledon, a residential area seven miles south-west of Central London. But it was from their suburban home here that Muriel McKay was snatched and never seen again. Her killers never told how, or when, or where.

Mrs McKay was warmly judged by everyone who met her to be a modest, charming lady. She was fifty-five years old. The Trinidad-born brothers Arthur and Nizamodeen Hosein were sentenced to life imprisonment for her murder. Although originally he desperately yearned to know what had really happened to his wife, eventually when talking with friends the devastated husband, Alick, often sought to try to convince himself that soon after she was abducted from their home in Arthur Road, his beloved Muriel must have died suddenly from natural causes, perhaps a heart attack, so that the kidnap brothers were left with nothing to ransom.

Ironically, Muriel McKay's kidnappers never intended her to be their victim. The target was Anna Murdoch, wife of Rupert. But the Murdochs were in Australia. An off-the-cuff remark by Mr Murdoch may have cost the life of his deputy's wife, and conceivably saved the life of his own. 'While we are away,' said Rupert to Alick, 'by all means use the Rolls.' He was not to know that the brothers Hosein had their eyes on the Chairman's blue Rolls-Royce, registration number ULO 18F – the car I had myself borrowed for a trip to Manchester only weeks before.

Some time before 29 December they lay in wait in Bouverie Street until Alick was leaving his office, then they followed the car. Because the Murdochs were away, the trail took them to Wimbledon. And the scene was set, in a case of mistaken identity, for Muriel McKay to die.

From the moment on the 29th when Alick arrived home and found that his wife had vanished he knew that she must have been taken against her will. There were others, both police officers and Pressmen, who were more cynical.

To be fair to those who got it so badly wrong, it is not reasonable to assume that everyone who cannot immediately be found must have been kidnapped. Police and Press checked ships on their way to Australia. They checked airports. They checked with friends and acquaintances, convinced there must be a more logical explanation than kidnap. Perhaps something no more out of the ordinary than a family quarrel. Only Alick knew such armchair detective theories to be nonsense, and for him it was not only a frustrating but a desperately harrowing time.

'For God's sake,' he would ask me wearily, 'why do people still think Muriel has just run away?'

It fell to me to do what I could to help my friend and colleague Alick in his ordeal. At the same time I had to continue to edit *The Sun*, still only a few weeks old.

I had myself only days before moved my family, complete with dog, rabbit, guinea pig and goldfish to the totally inadequate house at Putney Bridge. I had no home. I had found no schools for the children. I was working all day every day, and deep into the night. But my problems were trivial alongside Alick's.

So every day, on my way into the office, I went to Arthur Road to see him, to hold his hand. Often I called there again on the way home. I wept for him, and bled for him.

Often, in the house in Arthur Road, I met policemen who were working on the case. In the early days, some of them made it quite apparent that they regarded the problem as a purely domestic issue. It took several days to persuade them to take the matter seriously. Though there were policemen who were ultimately to suggest that their failure to get to the kidnappers in time was due to *The Sun*'s having revealed too much about what was happening (of which more later), the fact was that it was at least a week before some of the detectives involved gave up the idea that she had gone off of her own accord. I know, because I talked to them during each of these seven days. I also know, for the same reason, that it was at least a week before Alick himself was cleared of suspicion.

What *had* happened on the night of 29 December?

Alick was driven home in the Rolls. He arrived at 7.45 p.m. and was astonished to find the front door unlocked.

Usually it was kept on a chain, a chain that had been fitted after a burglary some months earlier. Immediately worried and distraught, and instantly aware that something quite dreadful must have happened, he called the police.

Five hours later the kidnappers made their first approach. Their first words were: 'Tell Mr McKay it is the M3, the Mafia.' A detective listened on an extension. The caller went on: 'This is the Mafia Group Three. We are from America. Mafia M3. We have your wife. We tried to get Rupert Murdoch's wife. We could not get her, so we took yours instead.'

Then, more chillingly: 'Have one million pounds by Wednesday night or we will kill her.' In the next few weeks there were to be another eighteen phone calls from the kidnappers. The second warned Mr McKay against calling in the police and said a letter from his wife was on the way. Next day, it landed on the doormat. It was clearly written under duress and said:

> 'Alick, Darling, I am blindfolded and cold. Please do something and get me home. Please co-operate or I cannot keep going. I think of you constantly and have kept calm so far. What have I done to deserve this treatment?'

Arthur Hosein's fingerprints were on that letter.

For eight days there was a frightening menacing silence. Then Stafford Somerfield, Editor of the *News of the World*, received a letter which said Mrs McKay was being treated by a doctor from abroad. It repeated the ransom demand for £1,000,000 and said that if her husband did not co-operate she would be 'disposed of'.

In later calls the kidnappers refused to tell Alick if his wife were dead or alive. He told them he had simply not got the kind of money they were talking about and suggested an initial payment of £20,000.

I cannot imagine why people behave so badly when a family is in such distress, but while public sympathy was in the main overwhelming, a great number of phone calls to the McKays, newspapers and police were from cranks and hoaxers, including sick heavy-breathers who would telephone and then say nothing.

The story of just how the Hosein brothers were caught and brought to trial has been told many times. But this is the story of *The Sun*. And the effect of the crime upon myself, and the newspaper, was devastating.

As the reader will have gathered, I was stretched to the point of exhaustion. At the same time, since we were only six weeks old, and struggling for circulation, some of the policemen involved – not, I think the most senior ones – were initially of the view that the whole operation was some kind of sick publicity stunt.

When it became clear that this theory was nonsense, some unofficial spokesmen at Scotland Yard took to suggesting to their newspaper contacts that I was hampering police inquiries by publishing confidential information I had acquired as a friend of the family. In fact, recognising the dangers inherent in the situation, I had given the most explicit instructions to my News Desk that we were not to publish any – repeat ANY – details of the case which were not available to all newspapers by way of the Press Association wire service.

This did not stop certain Scotland Yard detectives, striving desperately to explain away the Yard's own lethargy and ineptitude, from whispering the charge to anyone who would listen. Some time later, after the Hosein brothers had been sent down, the *Sunday Times* published a story about the case based entirely upon this calumny, though it was the exact reverse of the truth.

In the fashion of *Sunday Times* 'in-depth' reporting at that time, they made no attempt to talk to me, or to Alick. I was boiling with rage about it. My immediate instinct was to sue – and the very best legal advice was that I could expect to gain a great deal of money.

On the other hand, there was Alick. He was back on duty, but had aged dramatically. He was not wholly recovered from his ordeal in the witness box. For him, the matter was as closed as it was ever likely to be. Since the tragedy, we had become very close friends. Ultimately, I decided that I could not create a situation where the whole grisly story might have to be gone through again.

I did not feel this way when, many months later, Reader's Digest published a book containing a story about the case which was yet again based upon allegations made by detectives seeking to explain away their own inadequacies, and about which, yet again, I had not been approached, presumably in case the truth spoiled the story. The author said, in effect, that I had let down Alick and betrayed our friendship for the sake of being first with the news.

The office received a review copy of the book. I complained immediately to the publishers, who promptly agreed not to release it. Then, foolishly, they began to distribute it in the United States, in South Africa, and, of all places, in Australia. Quite what made them think I would not get to hear of a book about Muriel McKay published in Australia I cannot imagine. As it happened, within days of publication, journalists in Sydney and every other State capital were queueing up to tell me about it.

I promptly instructed solicitors to sue for defamation in the State of New South Wales, and to engage top counsel. In due course, I flew to Sydney for the hearing. The solicitors had identified three distinct libels. The judge ordered one of them to be struck off, on a technicality which I failed to understand. But on the other two, the Reader's Digest company were found guilty as charged, and I was awarded $20,000, with costs.

Rupert Murdoch gave evidence on my behalf. He told the court that it was ridiculous to suggest that I had no reputation in Australia to be damaged, as the defence had claimed, that the London *Sun* was already a legend among

English-speaking journalists world-wide, and that in any case I had worked for weeks at a time with all his Australian companies.

Surprisingly, Alick's son, Ian McKay, also gave evidence. I had been involved with him in several sharp exchanges in January 1970, about his own habit of making unguarded comments to representatives of other newspapers, though I was content, on this issue, to let others lead the pack. However, he said that at no time had Alick, or the rest of the family, thought that I had betrayed any confidences or behaved in any way improperly, and that, I had, indeed, been totally supportive, putting his mother's safe return above all other considerations.

This court case, however, was by no means the end of the story. Reader's Digest chose, incomprehensibly, to me, since the case could scarcely have been more clear-cut, to appeal. And when the Appeal Court of New South Wales turned them down they appealed to the Federal Appeal Court, which is, for practical purposes, the highest court of appeal in the Commonwealth of Australia.

Years later, when I had left News International and was working in Perth, for Robert Holmes à Court ('Hacca' to his friends, and his enemies), this appeal, too, was dismissed, and at last I got my $20,000, tax-free, as libel damages are, together with the interest it had earned in the building society account where my solicitors had thoughtfully placed it. They told me that, had I lost, I was up for a breathtaking $250,000 in costs, which would have ruined me.

Whilst all this was dragging on, I had consulted Rupert's New York lawyer, Howard Squadron, about the book's having been published in South Africa and the United States, stressing that I was not seeking punitive damages, but merely a retraction. In due course he reported that the company had agreed to release to all news agencies a statement withdrawing the accusations to which I objected, apologising for having made them, and to pay $5,000 to a charity of my choice.

'Thanks, Howard,' I said. 'Now what about your own bill?'

'Don't worry about it, Larry,' he replied. 'The charity of your choice is the Distressed Jewish Lawyers' Association.'

It is necessary to refer to the trial of the Hosein brothers only briefly. After a series of lower court appearances they stood in the dock together at the Old Bailey on 14 September 1970, at the start of a sixteen-day trial which, as crime reporter Norman Lucas was to write later, was to be marked by 'outbursts and interruptions such as are rarely witnessed in a British court of justice'.

Lucas went on: 'Nizamodeen cried and Arthur shouted. The police were accused of lying and of violence, the judge of partiality and racial prejudice and the trial had to be adjourned more than once for Nizamodeen to recover his composure and Arthur his temper.'

The prosecution was led by Attorney-General Sir Peter (now Lord) Rawlinson, himself once a newspaper lawyer, who later acted for me in a libel case against *Private Eye*. Alick, the prosecution's first witness, appeared to be unsteady on his feet as he entered the witness box, but he gave his evidence clearly enough, and betrayed little of what he was feeling. When I saw him that evening, he was distraught, and had clearly been greatly upset by the ordeal.

But much has already been written about the McKay case, and much doubtless, remains to be written. We are concerned only with its effect upon *The Sun*. As we have seen, not only was Alick himself *hors de combat* at a critical stage, but on police advice, and for the best of reasons, Rupert delayed his own return to the UK.

When Alick returned to the office he was still not capable of making an effective contribution, and no one expected him to do so. But we encouraged him to return, in the belief that the office environment might at least help to take his mind off his terrible tragedy. I made a practice of popping downstairs to the directors' floor – Mahogany Row – when the first edition was well under way, to report on the day's happenings.

Alick did not want to know about the day's happenings. Night after night, week after week, he insisted upon going over and over the whole dreadful story. I listened. It was all I could do to help.

Ultimately, he was to meet and marry the beautiful Beverley Hylton, widow of impresario Jack Hylton, former Miss Victoria and former girlfriend of the legendary Australian cricketer, Keith Miller. He shared with Beverley several years of happiness. But initially, he was inconsolable.

At times, in the early years – even, for a short time, before Alick's tragedy – we had no effective Managing Director. One Jack Worrall, a provincial newspaper manager from a subsidiary company based in Worcester, was *in situ* when the paper was launched. I thought he was totally out of his depth and that he failed to concern himself with our problems. Rupert held the title himself, jointly for a time with friend and confidant Paul Hamlyn, who had a substantial investment in the company. But there was often no one in management to whom to turn on a day-to-day basis.

For a while, we had Neville Hopwood, who Rupert had recruited from the bureaucracy at the Newspaper Publishers' Association. Neville was no newspaper manager, though he tried his best to *edit* the paper from time to time. Once, when I had a major industrial crisis brewing, I telephoned his home to be told by his wife: 'Mr Hopwood is not to be disturbed on Sundays.' Wow! Never on Sunday is not a good creed for a newspaperman. Neville did not last long. Like many before him, and others to come, he found the Bouverie Street nettles too big to grasp.

Ultimately, Advertisement Director Bert Hardy emerged as the strongest candidate for the top manager's job and was made Chief Executive. He ranks in my book as one of the best managers I have worked with – strong, supportive, forward-looking and always eager to encourage the creativity upon which, in the end, newspapers depend.

When Bert left News International, Rupert surprisingly repeated the Jack Worrall experiment by recruiting George Welsh, who at that time ran the Worcester company. George was willing enough, but I thought he never understood the national newspaper scene, and ultimately, following illness, made way for Bruce Matthews, a gravure printing expert from Melbourne who had been Chairman of Rupert's colour printing subsidiary, Bemrose of Liverpool, and waiting quietly in the wings for the big job to fall into his lap. He performed splendidly, and was the mastermind behind the great Wapping coup which was to change the course of newspaper history in the United Kingdom. The Wapping project, ironically, had initially been the brainchild of Bert Hardy.

All this is diversionary stuff, arising from my attempt to show just what a problem it was to run a newspaper with a globe-trotting Chairman who called himself Managing Director and a Deputy Chairman whose mind was, sadly and inevitably, on other things.

There were a couple of books written about the McKay murder. One is *Murder in the Fourth Estate*, by reporters Peter Deeley and Christopher Walker, who both worked for the *Observer* at the time. The other, to which we have referred earlier, was by Norman Lucas, then Crime Reporter of the *Sunday Mirror*, a man known to have close contacts at the highest level at Scotland Yard. Both are competent pieces of reportage, albeit not always precise in matters of detail.

When the police arrived at the house in Arthur Road on 29 December, for example, they did not find me, as Deeley and Walker report, ensconced with a reporter and a photographer. I went there alone, as a friend, because Alick had called to say Muriel was missing, and he was desperately worried.

But we all know that, in matters of which we have personal knowledge, reporters rarely get it wholly right. That is because they, and their informants, are human. It is not, as so many newspaper critics seem to think, part of a giant conspiracy to mislead.

CHAPTER FOUR

Sun People Get Around

The success of *The Sun* was not my triumph, or Rupert Murdoch's. Nor was it primarily due to Promotions Director Graham King, brilliant though he was.

Our success cannot properly be attributed to superb marketing, though that was undoubtedly a factor, and it most certainly was not due to massive expertise in the areas of production and distribution. We did not possess such expertise.

Let us pin the medals firmly where they belong: on the chests of a small but dedicated group of editorial enthusiasts, knowledgeable, skilled, and tireless in their pursuit of our declared aim to do better than anyone else that which we set out to do. A handful of them are still with the newspaper in its new home at Wapping. Some are scattered throughout the Murdoch empire. Several, having left the fold, have gone on to do great things in the wider world. I am intensely proud of all of them.

Let us start with Bernard Shrimsley, former Northern Editor of the *Daily Mirror*, former Editor of the *Liverpool Post*. He is lean and cerebral, with a biting wit. A perfectionist who drove production managers – and accountants – to drink because of his insistence on 'improving' stories and pages long after they were due away.

I asked him to edit the paper for a while in the seventies, when, wearing my other hat as the company's Editorial Director, I seemed to be spending more time in Australia or New York than in Bouverie Street. Since he was editing, it seemed only fair to call him Editor, which we did. One of his more notable innovations was the new style of 'agony aunt' column, then splendidly written by Claire Rayner. Such columns are nowadays among the best-read features in scores of newspapers around the world.

Bernard writes for relaxation. And he tells the following story of a meeting with his accountant, some time after the publication of his first novel, *The Candidate*:

'I have to tell you', said the accountant, 'that your earnings as an author last year amounted to one pound seven and tuppence-halfpenny. *The net position, however, is not so rosy!*'

Bernard, as we have seen, was in the trenches from Day One. So was his brother, Tony, who died, sadly, long before his time, of cancer in November 1984, when he was Director of Communications at Conservative Central Office.

Tony, who, like myself and, for that matter Rupert Murdoch, once had distinctly socialist leanings, wrote a book about the first hundred days of Harold Wilson's first Labour government. He led *The Sun*'s political team with great flair. His personal output, in terms of words in the paper, was prodigious. He, too, was from the *Mirror* stable.

A furious Hugh Cudlipp, on hearing that Tony planned to join us, seemed to regard his decision as a personal affront. He is alleged to have cried: 'If there is another Shrimsley in our midst, let him leave now.'

Bernard was worried that there might be thought to be some degree of nepotism in our hiring of Tony. Rupert and I had no such anxieties. We were, of course, at pains to ensure that Tony dealt directly with me in matters concerning salary and expenses and the other perquisites of office, and that I, and not Bernard, rewrote his work when it needed rewriting, which was not often.

For some years Tony shared with Henry Russell Douglas the task of writing leaders for *The Sun*. Some of them were memorable. Some, I think, actually did sway governments, though not as much as some politicians believe. We published a book of them in 1977. Tony, if he was still alive, would have been rightly proud to see how well they have stood the test of time.

Henry Douglas was another great stalwart in the early days, turning his hand cheerfuly to any task. He is a big man in every sense of the word, with a big heart, a big appetite, a big family (five children), and a magnificently well-stocked mind. Ultimately, because of his capacity to spot a libel a hundred miles ahead of the semi-housetrained young barristers we engaged to perform that duty, we made him the group's Legal Manager. As a journalist, however, he was of great value to me in the early days, uncomplainingly switching his attention from leaders to think-piece features in elegant, cultured prose, draft speeches for myself and the Chairman, and detailed briefings ahead of difficult meetings or television interviews.

Norman Baitey came to us from Newcastle, where, years earlier, he had been my Chief Sub Editor. I asked hm to lunch at my home in Bramhall one Sunday in October 1969, to discuss the proposition that he should join *The Sun* as an Assistant Editor. He drove through the night from Tyneside after his last edition had gone to press. I drove from London, where I had been closeted with Rupert on the Saturday, my day off from the Manchester *Daily Mail*, and for much of Sunday morning. Norman beat me to it, but only just. His car bonnet was still warm when I pulled into the driveway behind him. Lunch was just about ready. By the time we went to bed, I had another recruit.

Norman was not dearly beloved in Bouverie Street, except by me and a handful of close colleagues. He set high standards, and he was not skilled at sugaring pills. At one time, the chapel passed a resolution saying that they wouldn't work with him, which hurt him deeply. But it made no difference to the newspaper. His duties as a 'Prodnose' Assistant Editor, constantly on the lookout for traps and snares and imperfections in original copy and in type, could be, and were, carried out perfectly well without his having to appear on the editorial floor. I felt rather cowardly about asking him to keep a low profile. But I would have got no thanks from anyone, least of all Norman, had I risked closing down the paper at that time on that issue.

News Editor Brian McConnell was a *Mirror* man. He was on holiday in Spain when he heard we were trying to contact him, and talked his way on to a fully booked aeroplane to Heathrow by feigning illness. Would he join us? Yes, please. He did not have an executive background, but both Bernard and I remembered him as a tremendous worker, with a profound knowledge of the business and what was probably the fattest contacts book in Fleet Street. He found the job – with limited staff, limited funds and limited organisational experience – backbreakingly difficult. But he stuck at it through countless anguished hours, and he tortured and bullied the News Desk into an efficient machine against all the odds. We owe him a great debt.

From Endell Street came Frank ('Four Rows of Teeth') Nicklin, of whom we have heard and will hear more, Ray Mills, a tough, loyal and uncompromising Chief Sub Editor who later became Northern Editor of the *News of the World*, and Mike Nevard. We have seen how Mike came to join us. What he didn't tell us at the time was that he was also in line for the job of Features Editor at the *Evening Standard*. He decided, rightly as it turned out, that ours was the more exciting of the options on offer, even though the job I offered him was the somewhat lowly one of Features Executive – one of three such appointments. I had already decided not to appoint a Features Editor, and that Bernard would be in direct charge of that department for the time being.

We did not set out deliberately to achieve results through what is now known as creative tension, but I suppose that is the way it worked. Mike, in fact, became Features Editor within a very short time. Of the other two Features Executives, Nick Lloyd, who came from the *Sunday Times*, worked his way steadily through the ranks to the Editorship of the

News of the World and beyond. Bill Smithies left us for the *Observer*.

Mike, whose journalistic zest was matched only by his passion for jazz and rock, helped to put the pop into *The Sun*'s snap-crackle-and-pop. His knowledge and love of all kinds of popular music quickly made *The Sun* the favourite daily reading of many thousands of young people who shared his enthusiasm. He was born into jazz and journalism. His grandfather was a printer's reader, and his drumming father saw himself as the Kentish Krupa. By the age of seven, Mike was playing drums and writing for his local paper in Ashford, Kent.

Starting grammar school in 1939, a week after war was declared – which was precisely when I started at my own grammar school in Yorkshire – Mike got one afternoon of tuition a week. Evacuated to Oxfordshire, he produced his first tabloid – drawing and writing it in an exercise book – and selling it to his parents for pocket-money. Later, when he wanted extra cash, he produced a Special Issue.

At fifteen he became a reporter on the *Kentish Express*, dodging doodlebugs. Between reporting, he was running a jazz club and staging appearances by bands like those of Vic Lewis, Tito Burns and Ray Ellington. His life's ambition was to work for the *Melody Maker*, produced by Odhams Press. He achieved his ambition at the age of twenty. But, he has written, 'Life for me really began when I was hired by Larry Lamb to work for the Murdoch *Sun*.'

Mike was an excellent Features Editor, and an intensely loyal colleague. He quickly built up a powerful team. Incredibly, three of them, all Assistant Features Editors, had only one eye – Mike Terry, Jerry Holmberg and Eric Grimshaw. Says Mike: 'I used to have this nightmare where a CID man on a murder hunt would come into the office and say he wanted to question a one-eyed features executive. And I would say: "Which one? We have three." And he wouldn't believe me.'

We were also fortunate enough to acquire from Endell Street the vastly experienced Unity Hall, now, of course, a prolific novelist. Unity, who had been a news reporter way back, did not take too kindly to the idea of going back 'on the road'. She did it nevertheless, with absolute professionalism and great good humour, and it was not long before we were able to find for her a more suitable executive/writing role.

Joyce Hopkirk also played a major part in *The Sun*'s success. She was a former news reporter from Tyneside, who had switched to magazine work and was now seeking fresh fields to conquer. We made her Women's Editor.

The Women's Department dealt primarily, but by no means exclusively, with fashion, cooking, slimming, knitting and so on. They also seemed to have most of the best, and certainly the most daring, ideas for series about matters explicitly sexual. Sex was not a subject which we had ever planned to neglect. It was, however, the women on the staff who persuaded us that the readers could never get enough of it.

Joyce ran her department with skill and charm, and a steely determination to keep mere males in line. The major part played by women in *The Sun*'s success was largely due to her efforts.

Two other newspaper people of rare quality had been with us from the beginning – cartoonists Paul Rigby and Posy Simmonds. Australian Paul had been recruited by Rupert, and dragged away from the sunshine of his native Perth. He was a superb draughtsman, and a complete professional. When I told him, at our first meeting, that I wanted to see three or four sketches each morning before deciding on the day's topic, he was clearly taken aback. That obviously was not the way he had worked for the *Perth Daily News*. There he merely delivered the finished article at the scheduled time, having discussed it with no one. He was far from pleased with my own proposal. But from that day on he never mentioned it. Not to me, nor, so far as I am aware, to Rupert, to whom he might well have appealed. He simply turned up on time, with a batch of ideas and sketches, and delivered the finished version of the one we had agreed upon at or before the appointed hour. We became, and remain, good friends.

During his time with us Paul drew many great cartoons. The one I remember most vividly, which we published on 15 April 1970, concerned the American astronauts Jim Lovell, Fred Haise and John Swigert. Their spacecraft had run into serious trouble on the way back to Earth, and there was grave concern for their safety. Paul's drawing, across seven columns, had the Apollo 13 surrounded by every known kind of flying machine from the dawn of flying history. And the caption – his own – read: 'Come on, fellers, you can make it!' It brought tears to my eyes – and, I suspect, to the eyes of some even more cynical newspapermen. Make it, of course, they did, splashing down safely in the Pacific within the target area.

Posy Simmonds was every bit as professional. Shortly before launch day she had published a modest little book about the antics of a cartoon bear called simply 'Bear', who was becoming a bit of a cult figure. This was drawn to my attention by some of the girls Joyce was busy recruiting. I found it very funny, but I doubted whether I could use Bear, who was an exceedingly lecherous animal, in what was to be a family newspaper. In particular, I was worried about one of his sidekicks, Rabbit, who always carried an enormous carrot, for reasons which escape me for the moment. Not for the first time, or the last, I allowed myself to be persuaded that I was hopelessly old-fashioned, and Posy was hired.

As far as I was concerned, Posy never hit a wrong note. Since her work was not topical, we saw her rarely. From time to time she dropped a batch of pocket cartoons in the front hall, and vanished again. There were always enough, and to spare. We could reject a couple from time to time –

though we did so rarely – but we never ran short. Once, when she actually came into the office, I plucked up sufficient courage to ask her why she wore huge sun-glasses with lenses which seemed to be two or three inches across. 'Because they make me look like an old Rolls-Royce,' she said.

Posy subsequently branched out in all sorts of directions. Her work now appears regularly in the *Guardian*, the *Spectator*, and elsewhere. But how I regret the passing of Bear!

Of course, there were many people who joined *The Sun* *after* launch day who played a significant part in its success. My former editor, Arthur Brittenden, rendered redundant by the merger of the *Daily Mail* and the *Daily Sketch* in 1971, made a brief and disastrous foray into commerce – actually into the video business, which was a good idea whose time had not yet come – and then wrote to Rupert seeking work. Rupert referred him to me. As I had formerly worked for Arthur, and we had by no means always seen precisely eye to eye, this was a potentially embarrassing situation. But the paper was growing rapidly, still chronically understaffed, if not always in numbers at least in terms of executive expertise, and I could not afford to let Arthur slip through my fingers. I invited him to join us as an Assistant Editor, and he readily accepted. We never had the slightest problem thereafter.

Years later he was to write to me:

I never forget the first moment you took me into the newsroom – the night you had given me the job. I looked around the floor – there must have been around a hundred people – and I recognised almost everyone. It was an extraordinary experience, like having all your Fleet Street past reappear before you.

. . . People I had fired in a previous incarnation queued up to shake hands and welcome me. I was hugely touched. What I was to learn was that there *was* a great fund of good fellowship at *The Sun*, because by then there were no office politics at executive level. Fleet Street generally was riddled with them. But at *The Sun* there was such a compact team that there wasn't time for idle gossip or playing silly games. All one's time was spent working.

The Sun had for many months after it was launched, far fewer staff than any other comparable paper. And it paid off. One kept one's head down, and got on with the job.

As you will remember, we all worked much longer hours than our opposite numbers on any other paper. Executives were in by 10 to 10.30 a.m., sometimes earlier. We would be at the office for a minimum of twelve hours. Your system involved a team of three, including yourself, who shared out the responsibility of being in charge of the newspaper late at night – a sort of Duty Editor. When it was my turn I would aim to get home in time to make a midnight call to the Night Editor who, by that time, had seen the first edition of the opposition papers.

There would be decisions to be made on which, if any stories, the others had got were worth following up, and whether anything had happened which you should know about. So it was often 2 a.m. before I got my head down. At 7 a.m. there was the thud of the morning newspapers coming through the letter-box, all of them to be read.

Often we would work for two or three weeks without a break and then have a weekend off. But no one seriously jibbed. There were very few complaints. It was all tremendously stimulating and exciting and satisfying. And the executive team were all great friends – happier with one another than with anyone else.

Some months before Arthur joined us, the *Mail–Sketch* merger had given me the opportunity to pluck another plum from Associated. *Mail* News Editor Ken Donlan, who had been my News Editor in Manchester, was also on the redundancy list. And I wanted him. I was in the somewhat remote island of Eleuthera in the Bahamas, when I heard that the *Sketch* was to close, and I sent an immediate message to the office: 'If Donlan jobless tell him on no account to accept another post until I get home.'

The way I came to be sunning it in Eleuthera is a story in itself. Some weeks earlier Rupert had gained a controlling interest in London Weekend Television. At the same time, *The Sun*'s sale rose above two million copies a day for the first time. We ran the following leader to celebrate the occasion:

> On Thursday of this week, sales of the non-stop *Sun* for the first time topped 2,000,000. This means that in just 15 months, since *The Sun* was transferred to its present management, an ailing newspaper has been transformed, with your help, into the greatest success story in modern publishing history.
> This success story will continue. Two million, for us, is the beginning, not the end. Happily, people who buy *The Sun* once tend to go on buying it . . .

Rupert received this news one Friday evening at LWT, where he was celebrating, with his wife Anna, another kind of triumph, and he invited Joan and me to join them there. Many hours and much champagne later, in the house in Sussex Square, he had one of his not infrequent brainstorms. He was due to fly to Australia on Sunday, for the launch of a new publication, a Sunday version of his up-market national daily, *The Australian*, the newspaper which I was one day to edit. And apropos of nothing at all he said: 'You'd better come with me, Larry.'

I could feel my wife doing instant calculations about clean shirts and lightweight suits. For my part, I was both flattered and excited. But I did make a token protest. Joan and I had taken only one very brief holiday in fifteen months, and I had promised to take her to the Bahamas in a month's time.

Without turning his head, Rupert reached over his shoulder and plucked an airline timetable from the shelf. 'That's easy,' he said after a moment or two. 'You leave Sydney on Qantas round-the-world flight QF2 via the

Pacific, on Friday, Joan takes QFı westbound from London the next day, and you will be in Nassau within minutes of each other.'

We were. I was waiting on the tarmac when QFı touched down. The next day, we took a Pan Am jet to Rock Sound, Eleuthera. Eleuthera was a tiny island, at that time little developed. The Rock Sound airstrip, built by Pan Am solely for the tourist trade, was the most modern amenity it had to offer. Communications were appalling. Thus, when we were safely installed in our resort bungalow in the woods, a quarter of a mile from the hotel complex, we were, we thought, pretty well incommunicado.

Not at all. At breakfast-time on Day Two a heavily sweating messenger trotted up the track. He didn't quite have a forked stick, but that was the impression he gave. 'There's a Mr Murdoch on the telephone for you, sir,' he said. 'You can take it at the poolside.' The messenger was fitter than I. The long jog back to the hotel pool must have taken all of five minutes. Unsurprisingly, contact had been lost.

The telephone system on Eleuthera at that time was pretty primitive. It involved a radio tower, and much furious winding of handles. I booked a call to Rupert, by then, I knew, back in London, and settled down to wait. Joan and I spent the next few days by the poolside. Every time we made contact, we were cut off before the conversation had ended, before any decisions had been made. Each time I booked another call to Rupert, and he to me. Among the things I learned, almost a sentence at a time, as the days wore on, was that Rothermere was about to close the *Daily Sketch* and merge it with the *Daily Mail*. I also learned that the Editor of the combined newspaper was to be David (now Sir David) English of the *Sketch* rather than Arthur Brittenden of the *Mail*, and that, in general, *Sketch* people seemed to be being preferred for the top jobs. It seemed to me that Donlan might well, therefore, be available. So that, in a rather large nutshell, is how we came to recruit Ken Donlan. How we tackled the combined *Sketch–Mail* under the redoubtable David English, we shall see.

Meanwhile, who else? Some of our very best people, ironically, came from IPC's training school in the West Country. They included David Montgomery, the quick-witted Ulsterman who ultimately became Editor, first of the *News of the World*, and then of *Today*, Philippa Kennedy, later to join me at the *Daily Express* where she became Chief Feature Writer, and Hilary Bonner, who is now the *Daily Mirror*'s Show Business Editor.

I persuaded my old chum Dick Parrack, from Newcastle way back, to leave the Editorship of the Thomson evening in Hemel Hempstead, the *Evening Post*, to join us as Editorial Manager. Peter Stephens, later to succeed me as Editorial Director, came to us from Newcastle.

My close friend Philip Wrack, for years the one-man backbone of the London *Evening News*, came to us when that newspaper was merged with the *Evening Standard*. Philip, whom we subsequently made Deputy Editor of the *News of the World*, nursed no fewer than ten Editors through their teething problems in that most difficult of all roles and was loyal to all of them.

Though the paper was running fairly smoothly within a year or so, with most key positions satisfactorily filled, I was still conscious of a shortage of 'back bench' executives. The 'back bench' of a morning newspaper is rather like the bridge of an aircraft carrier. It consists of a team of production-oriented senior journalists, under the command of the Night Editor (the Officer of the Watch) whose duty it is to keep the ship on course whilst supervising the smooth loading, take-off and landing of aircraft (in our case, news, sport and feature pages) in strict rotation, and to the best of their ability, strictly to time.

I knew from long ago that the *Daily Mirror* had the best back bench in Fleet Street. Any one of their top three people, I thought, would enormously strengthen my own team. So, without much hope, I approached the three of them. Fergus Linnane, who long before had been bribed to stay with the *Mirror* because it was known that he was a friend, Roy Pittilla, another old colleague, and Vic Mayhew, a cheerful extrovert known to his friends and his enemies, with good reason, as Mayhem.

I interviewed them all within the same hour on the same day. Maid Marian instituted an elaborate system of entry and exit involving several sets of back-stairs in order that they should not meet. I hoped I might get one of them. To my astonishment, all three accepted an invitation, couched for obvious reasons in the vaguest terms, to join *The Sun*'s back bench.

It was the most spectacular piece of poaching in Fleet Street's history. Apart from strengthening my own team immeasurably, it dealt a severe blow to *Mirror* morale. Not only had they lost key people, but it was now apparent to everyone that we were here to stay. No longer would anyone fear to join us, in case the paper should not survive. We had 'arrived' long ago, among the newspaper reading public. This coup indicated that we had at last arrived in Fleet Street.

There are some other groups of *Sun* people deserving of more than a passing mention. Since KRM – Keith was his father's name – never hesitated to rob Peter to pay Paul, I was often called upon to supply staff for foreign adventures. *The Sun* was not only the cash-flow centre of the Empire. It was the talent pool.

When our then modest profits were beginning to burn a hole in his pocket, Rupert launched the *National Star*, in the good old US of A, as a rival to the mass-circulation weekly, the *National Enquirer*. Since only the merest handful of American journalists were willing to talk to us, let alone join us, we staffed it with people from London and Sydney. I took my very best people across the Atlantic for that launch – and some of them, including the irreplaceable Mike Nevard, stayed there.

I lost even more people when Rupert, in due course, acquired the *New York Post*. *The Sun*'s present editor, Kelvin MacKenzie, I sent there for a time to widen his experience. At one stage the entire back bench of the *Post*, the only evening newspaper in the world's greatest city, was staffed by *Sun*-trained Limeys.

The traffic was not all one way. In Australia, a few News Ltd executives began to see that the company's world-wide activities could be of direct value to them. People identified as having unusual talent, and destined for high office, were sent to us for weeks or months at a time for training. Some of the candidates I identified myself, after a talent-spotting tour Down Under.

Ron Richards, who at the time of writing is in charge of all Murdoch enterprises in the State of Queensland, was one such. John Hartigan, now Editor of the *Sydney Daily Telegraph*, also spent some time with us. So did Marty Dougherty, who became Editor of the *Sydney Daily Mirror*.

At the time I saw 'group-think' – a publishing philosophy conditioned by the fact that we operated on three continents – as very much the way ahead. Rupert, obviously, also thought internationally. So did the then Finance Director, Mervyn Rich. Sadly, few other directors, from the UK, the US or Australia, quite grasped the concept. Many of them still don't. And the group never became really integrated in any meaningful way except financially. Be that as it may, *Sun* people, within or without the Murdoch empire, have occupied, and still occupy, key positions in newspapers around the world. I like to think they were well trained.

CHAPTER FIVE

Women in The Sun

The Murdoch *Sun* was the first newspaper clearly to recognise the obvious truth that every other reader is a woman. Not only that, we were in tune with the new mood of *feminine* feminism, as opposed to militant feminism, which crossed the Atlantic in the early seventies, long before the opposition knew it was happening.

From Day One we addressed ourselves to women in a direct and, I hope, non-patronising fashion. And we did not do so merely because we knew that women, especially in the North, controlled the purse strings, and often decided which newspaper the family would buy. We wrote not only about clothes, slimming, knitting and babies, cleaning and cooking, though we neglected none of these things. We addressed our female audience on matters across the whole spectrum of human interests: on love and marriage, on matters emotional and matters political, on men and money, sex and sin, sport and crime. And we constantly invited our women readers to tell us what they thought about the service, and what improvements in it they would like to see.

That we were successful in our appeal to women, especially young women, was due largely to the advice we received from the women on the staff. We had many excellent female journalists. A group of them, led by Joyce Hopkirk, I organised into a separate department we called Pacesetters. This was, I suppose, a sort of female ghetto, and I am not sure I would dare to plump for the same sort of arrangement in these more enlightened days.

At the time, however, it worked like a charm. The Pacesetters' women had pages of their own to fill – we called
them 'the pages for women that men can't resist' – but were
expected to contribute ideas and finished articles to the
general features section.

I hired a woman caption writer at one time – Patsy
Chapman, now Editor of the *News of the World* – and we
even had, for a while, a woman racing tipster. Patsy taught
me a lesson in her very early days on *The Sun*. When I
bumped into her in the corridor one day she drew my
attention to a story in that morning's paper in which a
woman was described as 'an ordinary housewife'. I agreed
that the phrase should never have appeared, and ordered
that it should not appear again.

I had certain anxieties at the start about Pacesetters and
women's departments and women's pages in general. And,
after all, we did not have pages labelled Men Only. The
women on the staff talked me out of this view. They felt
that there were topics essentially of interest only to women,
and that few women would feel they were being patronised
because the newspaper had a section specially for them. It
is interesting to note that some newspapers in the United
States and elsewhere which abandoned women's pages under
pressure from the bra-burning brigade, have since returned
to them.

It was very quickly clear that the Pacesetters plan – we
had copied the title from the IPC *Sun* – was a winner.
Their office became a creative hothouse. Joyce's schedule at
conference was often as long as the news list. The big
problem became not an ideas shortage, but a shortage of
people to write them up – the very reverse of what had
become the norm in Fleet Street.

Pacesetters even helped out in the betting department. In
her first year Joyce, confidently backing her knowledge of
women – and men – tipped the winner of the Miss World
contest. 'I bet this year's winner will be a blonde,' she wrote.

57

'Watch out for Miss Austria.' Miss Austria, twenty-year-old photographic model Eva Rueber-Staier, was elected, and the lucky punters picked up odds of 12–1.

The Sun was so good at these games – punting and talent-spotting – that when, in 1972, they tipped Miss Australia, and she won, Murdoch's critics accused the paper and Mecca, the contest organisers, of having fixed things between them. *Sun* punters, who picked up odds of 16–1, didn't really care. But for the record, it wasn't a fix. Just good judgement.

I have always liked working with – indeed, being with – women. And I had always believed, when I had worked on male-dominated newspapers, that the industry as a whole needed many more women in high places. I have never taken much to 'stag' parties, or male-only functions of any kind. And I have certainly never sought to surround myself exclusively with male executives. Apart from smelling better, it seems to me, women tend to work harder. They are often more receptive to change. And they are not short of stamina. Women who can handle a couple of toddlers efficiently cannot be short on stamina. Women who can handle a couple of toddlers *and* a demanding *second* job are nothing short of miracle-workers.

But it would be silly to pretend that there are not problems involved in hiring women journalists, especially on morning newspapers. On the *Daily Mail* in Manchester I had sought long and hard for women news sub-editors – the subs' desk being traditionally a male preserve. When I found them, I found it impossible with a clear conscience to roster them on late duty, which in those days would have meant turning them out on to the back streets of Manchester, and the mercies of the all-night bus service, at 2 or 3 a.m. So they tended to find themselves permanently on day shifts. The men didn't complain. The women did. They sought an equality of opportunity which I found it hard to give them.

So it was with night reporters. On *The Sun*, we had only

a couple on duty after midnight. If one of them was a woman, which of them was the Night News Editor to send if we had, say, a particularly brutal rape-and-murder case in the East End? As I said, the women never sought special privileges for themselves. It was just that men – including myself – found it impossible to bring ourselves to treat them as they wished to be treated.

There was another problem on the subs' table. As a sub-editor myself, I had frequently felt like bursting into tears when a tough chief sub rejected my third or fourth attempt at a headline when there were only seconds to go to close-copy time. Occasionally, women subs, being somewhat more emotional, actually *did* burst into tears. There is nothing to be ashamed of in tears. But because of them, chief subs became increasingly reluctant to drive their women subs too hard.

In spite of all this, I never wavered in my belief that we needed more women in journalism. Now I was in a position to put the theory into practice, and I set out to do so. Once I even got myself into trouble with the Equal Opportunities Commission who complained that an advertisement I had placed asking specifically for female staff, in a bid to redress what I saw as an unacceptable degree of imbalance, was unfair to men, and constituted illegal discrimination.

The Sun was breaking new ground in all directions in the early seventies, and most of the more daring innovations were suggested by women. We wrote frankly about things like masturbation, menstruation and pre-menstrual tension, cancer of the breast and cervix and other medical problems which were simply not talked about at the time. We readily gave advice on complex sexual problems – but we made sure it was written by experts. At the same time as we pursued these deadly earnest subjects with deadly earnestness we strove to maintain an air of bubbling eroticism. Even the problems page was fun in *The Sun*.

I think it is probably fair to say we were the first popular newspaper to move into consumer journalism in a big way. South African-born Val Hudson (Little Val, the Shopper's Pal) became our prices and quality watchdog, and very good at it she was. She was also capable of fine humorous writing – a rare quality.

Soon after Val joined us she decided that she wanted to start a family, and made no secret of the fact that she was trying to get pregnant. We encouraged her to write about this, at first in a serious sort of fashion. But Val saw the whole thing as a joke, and sent herself up remorselessly, even inviting the readers to send in any hints or tips which might help her achieve her objective. She was deluged with suggestions, not all of which were printable. In one hilarious article Val described in detail how she and husband Robin Corbett (later a Labour MP) had taken to sleeping with bricks under the foot of the bed in order to prevent any seepage of that fluid which is vital to procreation.

Our first Fashion Editor was Deirdre McSharry. She and Joyce made an immediate decision that the fashion pages were to have as much appeal for men as they did for women. They never needed any encouragement to make it happen. Deirdre later followed Joyce to *Cosmopolitan*, and later still into the Editor's chair at that magazine.

Almost all *Sun* women went on to do great things. Unity Hall became Women's Editor of the *News of the World*, and author of what is probably the most widely read agony column in the world, even allowing for those which are syndicated in the United States. Claire Rayner was already well known when she joined *The Sun* – but she was much more so when she left. Again, for that kind of column to appear in a daily newspaper was something of a journalistic first. It was swiftly copied, first by the *Daily Mirror* and later the *Daily Star*.

Some agony aunts nowadays complain that they are being forced to invent problems because the letters they get are not sufficiently erotic for their editors. I never asked Claire, or anyone else, to do this, and I don't know whether she did or not. But there was certainly no shortage of eroticism. Some of the letters which I know to be genuine were breathtakingly frank. It never ceased to amaze me how so many people are prepared to be utterly explicit about their sex lives in letters to newspapers. Perhaps it is just because they *are* letters to newspapers. It is possible to regard one's daily newspaper as a friend, and I like to think most of our readers did, but a letter to Claire might be easier to contemplate than a face-to-face encounter with, for example, a marriage guidance counsellor.

Sun writer Sally Ann Voak was the first mass-market daily paper columnist to write regularly about slimming, and the virtues of a proper diet. Nina Myskow, who wrote for us on pop, and Margaret Forwood, on television, are now household names. Wendy Henry, who became the first woman to edit a national newspaper, the *News of the World*, and later edited the *People*, worked first on *The Sun*. Judy Wade and Jean Ritchie have made names for themselves as authors.

Bridget Rowe, who joined us as Assistant Editor, Features, now edits *Woman's Own*. Jo Foley, one of Joyce's successors in Pacesetters, later edited the *Observer* magazine, and subsequently, *Options*. There were many more. I enjoyed working with them all, and I am proud of their achievements. And if I have forgotten anyone who deserves to be remembered, I beg her forgiveness. There were so many.

CHAPTER SIX

The Circulation War:

Up the greasy pole

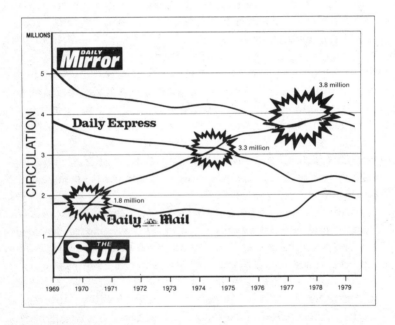

Soon after we first met, Rupert told me that he thought we could pass the *Daily Mirror* in five years. Alarmed by the implication that I would somehow have failed if we didn't achieve this target, I suggested that ten years would be more realistic. In fact, it took eight. The lines on the graph crossed in the second half of 1977, for which period, ironically, we had no audited figures. So we did not claim to have passed them until March 1978.

Had it not been for the wrecking tactics of a handful of cretinous lemmings in the print unions, we would have done it far sooner. They seemed to take a crazy delight in dragging their supine followers ever closer to the edge of the abyss into which Murdoch was eventually to push them. He is not the kind of man to take pleasure in anyone's discomfiture. But I suspect he was willing to make an exception in their case.

Long before we overtook them the *Daily Mirror* had fulfilled the Chairman's impish prophecy that they would get to 4,000,000 before we did. They fell below that figure, from a proud 5,000,000 at the time of *The Sun*'s launch, in the second half of 1975. It was much later, in June 1978, before we topped 4,000,000 on a daily basis, though we had exceeded that figure from time to time on special occasions. There were many milestones along the way.

After only a hundred days the paper boasted: 'Meet Britain's liveliest centenarian. Today *The Sun* is 100 issues old. There won't be a telegram from Buckingham Palace. But there will be close on 4,000,000 guests at the party. Our readers. The people who count.'

We were not selling 4,000,000 copies after a hundred days, of course. Whenever a newspaper wishes to inflate its achievements in circulation terms, it talks about readers rather than copies sold. Since we reckoned that each copy was seen by at least three people, 4,000,000 was a modest claim. Because after a hundred days we were selling more than one and a half million copies a day. This was a formidable achievement.

The last period for which audited figures were available for the Endell Street *Sun* showed a circulation of 950,000. But that was for January to June 1969. It is no secret that the newspaper had been deliberately run down in the second half of the year. Our best calculation was that we might have inherited a theoretical 650,000 buyers on Day One. But we lost many of those because we simply couldn't get to them, and many more because they decided immediately that the Murdoch *Sun* was not for them. It is hard to blame them. The first issue must have come as a severe culture shock to readers weaned on the old *Daily Herald*. So the truth is that we had put on a firm 1,000,000 copies a day in the first hundred days.

It was an incredibly eventful period. In the early days many newsagents were reluctant to stock the paper. Many more kept it under the counter for fear of offending *Mirror* representatives, because Mirror Group Newspapers constituted a big slice of their bread and butter.

All *The Sun*'s editorial staff, and their wives and girlfriends, were issued with forms on which to report any newsagent they came across who did not display the paper – and to record what he had said when challenged. They were also told to move the paper up in the racks outside newsagents' shops, and to make sure that it was not covered by any other newspaper.

In the early summer of 1970, drained to the point of exhaustion, I took myself off to Saint Tropez for three days' rest. Early in the morning, on our first day in the elegant Byblos Hotel, we were awakened by a messenger with an 'urgent' telex. It was the previous month's circulation figures. I did not dare tell my wife I had asked for them, and put the incident down to an excess of zeal on the part of Bernard Shrimsley. The figures indicated that we were selling 1,750,000 copies a day. By January to June 1971 we were up to 2,000,000. From June to December, the audited figure was over 2,500,000.

We topped 3,000,000 in the second half of 1973, then struggled a little. We put on a trifling 400,000 the next year, and nothing at all in 1975, mainly because of industrial disputes which cost us many millions of copies. But 1976 saw us comfortably over 3,500,000 and 1977 closer to 4,000,000, which we achieved in June of the following year.

The Sun marked all these milestones with characteristic

bombast. On 9 March 1970, we boasted: 'UP, UP and UP goes the sale of the Soaraway *Sun*. On Saturday it leapt past a staggering 1,500,000. This is an increase of more than 600,000 copies in just 94 issues – an achievement without parallel in recent publishing history.' In fact *The Sun* was being uncharacteristically modest. The 600,000 increase was based upon the old *Sun*'s last audited figure, for January–June, 1969, of 950,000. But of course we didn't inherit anything like that number.

The next major milestone came in February 1971. 'The non-stop *Sun* tops 2,000,000' we cried on Page One, in white on black. At 3,000,000 we were back to the old UP, UP and UP routine. Yet again we boasted of the most spectacular publishing success of our time.

When we passed the *Mirror* we devoted half the front page to a series of white on black headlines which read: 'We made it, *Sun* lovers. Top of the Pops. The Soaraway *Sun* is the best-selling daily newspaper in Britain – and that's OFFICIAL.'

When the sale finally topped 4,000,000 every day for a month, in June 1978, we got even more excited. 'You're on the winner' we shouted. 'Your Soaraway *Sun*, Britain's best-loved daily paper, continues to stride ahead of the rest.'

It is interesting to reflect that, long before this milestone was reached, the down-market *Sun* had more AB readers – that is, up-market and well-heeled ones – than *The Times* and the *Guardian* combined. The newspaper's appeal was extraordinarily wide-ranging.

Indeed, at one time I was inclined to think that there must be no fewer than 4,000,000 chauffeurs in the United Kingdom, since everyone I seemed to be meeting told me that he saw the paper regularly because his chauffeur always bought it. This does not quite explain the number of photographs taken by enterprising freelances which showed ultra-AB readers catching the ten o'clock City special from

Sevenoaks buying *The Sun* and concealing it in the *Financial Times*.

Of course, from an advertiser's point of view, it was very expensive to reach our AB readers. Not every advertiser is seeking a mass audience. Clearly, we did not sell a lot of space to Sotheby's. And the full-page car ads, when we started to get them, did not usually come from Rolls-Royce.

Cover price increases rarely had any effect on the newspaper's progress. Sometimes, indeed, the promotional packages we put together to cushion such increases actually put the sale up. Once, cheekily, I announced on Page One that the paper was 'Still only 7p' on the day on which it went up to 7p. Not only did I not receive a single complaint, but we actually got letters congratulating us on holding the price down!

The climb up the greasy pole was tremendously exciting. Circulation Manager Brian Horwite remembers: 'I recall a wholesaler in Maidstone saying *The Sun* could not survive more than six months because it couldn't attract sufficient advertising. Another wholesaler, in Herne Bay, said: "That bloke in your telly adverts couldn't sell newspapers on London Bridge."

'In our TV promotions – it must have been in 1970 – the actor in the commercials was Chris Timothy. He could pack more words into thirty seconds than anyone else. Graham King, the Promotions Director, is reported to have said: "If that man takes a breath I'll fire him." And when this guy from Herne Bay said that to me, I said: "Great. You *remembered* the ad. That's the idea."

'In those days each newspaper exchanged sales figures on a monthly basis. It was surprising to us that *The Sun*'s immediate opposition didn't react to our success. Certainly today if *The Sun* is successful in promoting, the opposition immediately use TV, radio, posters and so on, to offset any gains that we make.

'But in those early 1970s some opposition dailies certainly

gave us the impression they didn't believe our sales figures. We enjoyed tremendous increases month after month. I'd exchange sales figures – and we'd, say, gone up 100,000 – and they'd laugh. I thought, "Why are they laughing?" because it was true. They really didn't comprehend that we were racing ahead, and it took the *Mirror* months and months before they reacted. When the *Daily Mirror* did react – and they were the Number One, I think they thought they were invincible – once they realised they were losing sales to *The Sun*, they carried tons of publicity. But they couldn't stop the momentum of *The Sun* which obviously at the time appealed to all new buyers of newspapers and many of the readers of opposition dailies. In eight years, I think it was, *The Sun* was Number One. Ron Cotton – the Circulation Director of the Mirror Group at the time – did telephone me, though, to offer us congratulations.

'Working for *The Sun* in those early days was exhilarating, but it was absolute chaos distribution-wise, as we were only printing in London. Any delay resulted in many copies missing trains. The alternative was to send these supplies by road, obviously arriving much later in various parts of the country, and *The Sun* had to be distributed after all the other newspapers. Our circulation reps spent many months at various rail stations or at pre-planned collection points to deal with those supplies sent by road, arranging the necessary emergency distributions.

'It's not much good having the best paper in the country and not having it available when the readers want it. Despite this serious adversity, sales still continued to rise. We'd get people phoning complaining that the paper was unavailable, but those readers continued to be loyal and therefore it was obviously very clear that *The Sun* was the paper that the public wanted.

'Those days were memorable, they were really exciting times.'

One of the more spectacular jumps in circulation (over

500,000 copies between the first six months of 1971 and the second half of the year) coincided with the demise of the *Daily Sketch*. David English, when Editor of that newspaper, had said of the one I had the honour to edit, 'There is nothing new under *The Sun*.'

Quite so. But the circulation of the *Daily Sketch* slumped from 871,000 at the time the Murdoch *Sun* was launched to 764,000 a year later – and the rate at which it was shedding readers was increasing daily.

Early in 1971, Lord Rothermere decided that enough was enough, and the *Sketch* had to close. Murdoch immediately saw himself as the White Knight rushing in on his charger to save it. Hence his telephone call to me on Eleuthera. 'I'm thinking of buying the *Sketch*, Larry,' he said, when we eventually made contact. 'What do you think?'

He had to wait a while to know what I thought, because at that point we were cut off. By the time the link was re-established at least I knew what I thought. 'It would be folly,' I said. 'There isn't room for another pop tabloid. If you want to make it middle-market it will struggle against the *Mail* and the *Express*. The middle market isn't all that big. And if you can be patient for six months I promise you we'll get them all anyway.'

Because of the vagaries of the telephone system this conversation was spread over several days. Whilst it was going on Rupert was busy talking to Sheila Black on the *Financial Times*. He was then approaching his fortieth birthday. 'I'm thinking of giving myself a birthday present, Sheila,' he said. 'I'm thinking of buying the *Sketch*.' Sheila didn't think any more of the idea than I did. Indeed, I think the only person who might have thought it a good idea would have been Lord Rothermere himself. When Rupert finally said 'no,' the *Daily Sketch* was killed, and merged with the *Daily Mail* under the Editorship of David English. At the same time, the *Mail* became tabloid.

The *Sketch* had been 'killed' by rumour more often than

almost any other newspaper. It had always refused to lie down. Indeed rumours of its death had always, like those of Mark Twain's demise, been grossly exaggerated. It was originally a Rothermere/Allied Newspapers publication – as the *Daily Graphic*. It then became the *Daily Sketch* and was sold to Lord Kemsley in 1924. In the Kemsley empire it became the *Daily Graphic* yet again, and then once more found its way back to the Rothermere family (now Associated Newspapers) and in 1959 was renamed the *Daily Sketch*.

As such, it underwent what might have been mistaken for a *Sun* operation, backed by gimmicks, competitions and heavy promotion. Win a Racehorse, Win a Pub, were among its more spectacular operations. The circulation rose, but so did the cost. Retrenchment in costs resulted in reduced sales. And that sale was never to be revitalised in the face of the *Mirror*'s buoyancy from 1961 until the end of the sixties, when recession hit one and all, and *The Sun* began to shine.

But what would happen to the *Sketch* readers? Would they switch to *The Sun*? Or could the *Daily Mail* retain some, most or all of them?

Technically the word tabloid refers only to the shape of the page. But David, in his anxiety to avoid its pejorative connotations, insisted upon calling his new *Daily Mail* a 'compact', and announced that he was reconciled to losing 'the bottom end' of the *Sketch*'s readership.

He lost bottom, top and middle, settling down within months to a figure of around 1,750,000, lower than that of the pre-merged broadsheet *Mail*. And *The Sun* went up and up and up.

We had a lot of fun at David's expense in the early days of the new *Daily Mail* – all of which he took in good part. The Saturday before he launched we filled half of Page One with a noisy blurb for the week ahead: 'Next week in your fun-packed, fact-packed, jam-packed IMPACT compact.'

'Win Vivien Neves,' we shouted, under a picture of Vivien, a spectacularly beautiful model, with a kitten perched less than precariously on her unclothed left breast. But of course we then added: 'For a strictly limited period.' We also introduced a form of *Sun* bingo, a controversial new series, The Baby Trap, '. . . and a whole bagful of fun competitions'.

The Sun kept up the pace for weeks. It was altogether too much to resist for the lost legions of *Sketch* readers, who flocked to our banner in droves. To his credit, David was not to be tempted into mixing it with us. He stuck to his guns, and established for himself a distinct and distinctive niche in the middle market. It was 1977 before its sale exceeded that of the pre-merger *Daily Mail*, and 1978 before it topped 2,000,000, a pinnacle from which it swiftly fell. But it remained, and remains, exactly what it set out to be, a middle-class, middle-market, South-East-oriented tabloid with a good advertising profile and strong woman-appeal.

We have seen what *The Sun*'s success did to Associated Newspapers. What effect did the lusty young newcomer have on the rest of Fleet Street? There were those who suggested that we forced the *Mirror* to lower its sights to compete with us. If they did, they didn't make a very good job of it. I suppose it all depends what one means by 'lower'.

I think the *Mirror* was, and remains, a very worthwhile newspaper. We took advantage of a certain degree of complacency which had set in when they were the unchallenged leaders of the pack, and it took them a little too long to react. Had they gone for us, with all guns blazing, early in 1970, I think we might have found it difficult to survive. But they reacted like the proverbial crocodile on Mogadon. By the time they did wake up, *The Sun* was unstoppable.

Far from causing them to 'lower their sights', however, we had exactly the opposite effect. They ceased to be complacent, began seriously to question some of the things they had been doing badly for years, and developed a much sharper competitive edge.

Indeed, it was not the least of our achievements that all national newspapers, and not just the so-called 'popular' ones, became significantly more competitive in the early seventies. We shook the industry out of its torpor, and persuaded newspapermen everywhere that the industry was not necessarily headed, as so many pundits had been forecasting, into terminal decline.

Though we certainly made the national press more competetive, we didn't do many of them much good. It is commonly thought that we did great damage to the *Daily Mirror*. Some, maybe. But the paper that probably suffered most, if one doesn't count the *Sketch*, whose death was inevitable, was actually the *Daily Express*.

In the years from 1969 to 1979 the *Express* lost 37 per cent of its readers. This disastrous slump led, in part, to the appearance on the field of a new challenger, the *Daily Star*.

It happened like this. Victor (later, Lord) Matthews was appointed to run the ailing Express Group after his own company, Nigel Broackes's conglomerate Trafalgar House, had acquired a controlling interest from Max Aitken, son of Beaverbrook. There was a somewhat unkind joke circulating at the time to the effect that Express Newspapers was the biggest golden handshake in history, because it was purchased primarily to get Victor away from the day to day running of Trafalgar House.

The new chairman found Fleet Street a bit of a handful. Like many of us, he had long cherished a belief that one had only to treat people properly in order to be properly treated, and was dismayed to find that in his new sphere of activity it simply wasn't true.

Battered and bloodied by the unions, and finding himself quite unable to reduce staffing to sensible levels without destroying the business, he came to the fairly obvious conclusion that if he couldn't have fewer staff he would have to have more newspapers, the better to deploy the people he couldn't get off the payroll.

In mid-1978, *The Sun* suffered a ten-day stoppage as a result of one of the unions' periodic bouts of suicidal bloody-mindedness, and the sale of the *Daily Express* shot up. When *The Sun* was back, however, all its readers promptly returned to the fold.

Victor was heard to ask his managing director, Jocelyn Stevens, after a meeting of the Newspaper Publishers' Association, just why it was that these readers had failed to stay with the *Express*. 'Because *The Sun* is not a newspaper. It's all tit and bum and racing,' said Jocelyn, thereby demonstrating, not for the first time, that he didn't understand the situation. 'Very well,' said Victor. 'Let us start a newspaper to compete on these terms.' He also decreed that the new newspaper would be printed in Manchester, partly because he had an even bigger surplus of plant and people in that centre than he had in London, and partly because he hoped to be able to take advantage of *The Sun*'s problems in coping with late sport in the North and Midlands.

Express Editor Derek Jameson, now famous in his new role as broadcaster *extraordinaire*, was drafted in as Editor-in-Chief. He was quoted in the *Observer* as saying that the new paper would be all tits and bums, QPR and roll your own fags. He later said he had been misquoted, and I believe him. Jocelyn Stevens, however, made a point of saying much the same thing, more than once. And Chairman Victor Matthews blithely announced on launch day: 'I wouldn't want to leave the *Daily Star* around my own home – not with a youngster.'

In spite of their too-honest chairman, and other problems, the *Daily Star* did grind out a modest market for itself, and did damage *The Sun*. We fell back well below 4,000,000 and the *Star* at one time achieved a sale of 1,500,000, aided to some extent by our own inability consistently to finish the print order.

The situation was restored, in 1981, after I had left, in characteristic Murdoch fashion. He slashed the cover price by 2p and launched a bigger and better version of the *Star*'s bingo game. A *Sun* sale of 4,000,000-plus was swiftly restored.

The *Star* survives, though it has suffered somewhat, primarily because it soaks up overheads, as Victor Matthews had planned. But it is unlikely to pose a serious threat to *The Sun* or the *Mirror* because its founders totally failed to perceive the essential truth that these two papers were rather more than tit and bum and racing. The truth may be seen more clearly now, and the *Star* is a better newspaper, but I fear it will be forever burdened with the label it chose to stick upon itself.

CHAPTER SEVEN

It's All, All, ALL in the Super, Soaraway Sun

Most journalists are in the business because they like to feel they have a message of some kind. But it isn't the slightest use having a message unless one has an audience. On *The Sun* we regarded it as our top priority to acquire and maintain such an audience. And we did so by *selling* the newspaper, in an uninhibited, unsophisticated way, by any means which came to hand.

The best medium, of course, was television. But we also had the *News of the World*, the best-selling newspaper in the English language. And we launched the initial onslaught, three weeks before blast-off, through the pages of our sister paper in the following manner: 'Watch out for *The Sun*.The new *Sun* will be launched on November 17. The new *Sun* will be your kind of newspaper. *The Sun*. It will be bold, it will be lively, it will be honest, it will never, ever be boring. Watch out for *The Sun*.'

On Sunday, 2 November, the Sunday paper continued: 'Just two weeks to *The Sun*. Britain's newest daily newspaper will be launched on Monday, November 17. *The Sun*. Top class writers, cameramen, cartoonists, are flocking to join *The Sun*. It will be backed by the News of the World Organisation – who already produce the most popular newspaper in the English language. *The Sun*. It will cost just five pence – the same price as an ordinary newspaper. Watch out for *The Sun*.'

On Sunday, 9 November, we continued: '*The Sun* is coming out. Just one week from tomorrow the new *Sun* will be launched. It will be the first genuinely competitive daily newspaper for a generation or more. It will be your kind of newspaper. *The Sun* will be on your side. It will bring you the facts. It will never sit on fences. It will never curry favour. We promise that we shall make *The Sun* the most provocative, the most informative, and the most entertaining daily newspaper in the business.'

There were no specifics because we didn't have any to offer. Just noisy – some would say hysterical – drum-beating. Our advertising agents, Hobson Bates, charged with the duty of producing pre-launch television commercials, were wringing their hands because we couldn't tell them what was going to be in the new paper. We couldn't tell them because we didn't know. But we impressed upon them our view that the one thing we were *not* going to be was boring, and eventually they cobbled up an acceptably professional series of ads on that theme. As soon as we did have specifics, of course, the style changed completely, and the slam-bang commercial burst upon an astonished world.

Before *The Sun*'s launch on 17 November 1969, a new style of promotional thinking was being developed in Australia among various Murdoch publications, mainly the *Daily Mirror* in Sydney. Traditionally, newspaper sales promotion activities had fallen into two categories:

a) Free trial delivery periods, often with the offer of a free gift. This technique hit dizzy heights in the 1930s when salesmen touting home delivery would offer complete sets of Dickens' novels, only to be followed days later by rival salesmen with sets of encyclopaedias.

b) What is called 'generic' or 'image' advertising – the projection of a newspaper's personality to the market-place, increasingly by way of television.

But changing established reading habits was a slow process. Never a patient man, Murdoch did not have much time for these traditional methods of increasing newspaper sales. In the steamy, dog eat dog, fiercely competitive

Sydney newspaper market, necessity begat invention as
the two afternoon tabloids fought tooth and nail for supremacy.

Murdoch's competition in Sydney, ironically *The Sun*,
had a long-established lead and a loyal audience that even
the *Daily Mirror*'s outrageous front pages couldn't shake
free. But the *Mirror* had an enormous fund of ideas. It was
full of surprises. It was a more entertaining paper than its
rival. Why not sell this daily dose of bright, brash and
entertaining journalism to a hitherto neglected market – to
young people, and especially women, who didn't regularly
read a newspaper? And so the composite, or magazine
concept, newspaper television commercial was born.

The technique was to gather the best and brightest stories
and distil them down to a few words of script along with
riveting visuals. Features would be specially written to be
projected on television. A contest would be thrown into the
mix, and perhaps a special money-off offer. What went out
over television was a fast-moving mini-production, usually
a 30-second or 60-second commercial, jammed with good
things to read, to do, to send for, to laugh and marvel at.

The effect of these new-style commercials was immediate
and dramatic. Sales increases could be measured on the day.
In less than a year, the *Daily Mirror* overtook its rival and
surged on to a commanding lead which it held for many
years. The man primarily responsible was a tough, tall,
rangy Australian, Graham King. And Rupert decided that
he was the man to run the Promotions Department in
Bouverie Street.

King said later: 'At the time I was panting for something
new. I had always been an Anglophile, and the London
opportunity was a dream come true. As usual, Rupert
went through his courtship routine, running me around the
Cotswolds in his Rolls-Royce because he knew of my
interest in antiques and historic places. He didn't realise
that he would have had to beat me off with a stick!'

Hobson Bates never quite knew what hit them when Graham swept in. But they responded quickly, and soon developed a creative and productive team which, after a few months, could produce quite ambitious commercials in twenty-four hours, in an industry where several weeks' production time is the norm.

For *The Sun*, production had to be fast – and cheap. By the very nature of things, since the product changes dramatically from day to day, the shelf-life of a newspaper commercial based upon what was in the paper was one, or at best, two days. Furthermore, it could not be made too far in advance lest the listed contents should be overtaken by events.

One of the key elements in the technique we developed is excitement – which is best generated on TV by sheer speed. The words and the pictures flew past so fast that the viewer could hardly take them in, but they were undeniably exhilarating.

We spent weeks searching for a voice that could pump out 180 breathless words a minute, and eventually we came across a young unknown actor working at the Old Vic. He was a gangling, untidy youth with tin-framed National Health spectacles. His name was Christopher Timothy – who, as everyone now knows, was eventually to play the lead in the television series *All Creatures Great and Small*. But in 1970 Timothy was Mr Sun.

We bought him a couple of suits, paid for contact lenses, and put him into harness as our presenter. His voice, at full gallop, could cut through steel; words came out like bullets. When we started getting bags of complaint mail, we knew we had achieved something important. We were getting our message across.

In those days, before electronic editing, videotape commercials had to be made at one go. Within months the team was producing 60-second commercials on the trot, using four cameras racing from one scene to another, rolling in film, cutting in graphics and supers – all without editing. Voice track, music and effects would be added later. A typical commercial would start production with set building and lighting at 6 a.m. and continue through the day until it was in the can around 9 p.m. Shoots that went on until 4 a.m. were not unknown.

Sun commercials became famous. They were impossible to ignore. They reflected and projected the newspaper itself – its breeziness, its frankness and its humour. Despite the pressures, everyone involved in making them had a lot of fun. I would often attend these sessions myself – particularly the ones that went on late at night, after I had got the paper moving, and I never ceased to be impressed by the way Graham marshalled his team, and pushed, bullied, coaxed, cajoled and coerced them unrelentingly until he achieved maximum impact from the material available. For his part, he used to say that *The Sun* was a dream of a paper to promote.

There never was a week when we didn't have the material to make a commercial, if the budget for airtime allowed. There never was a week when we didn't have an imaginative special offer, a new contest, a new series. What Graham found most refreshing, I think, was that senior editorial staff took such a very keen interest in what he was doing.

Journalists are traditionally contemptuous of promotional gimmickry, resenting the space it consumes at the expense of their own golden words, and feeling slightly shamefaced about the concept of a newspaper which actually sells itself, like soap. There was no such atmosphere on *The Sun*.

We bought books, commissioned series, dreamed up offers and competitions, all with an eye on their suitability for television promotion. Everyone was constantly on the look-out for ideas which could be exploited in this way. So Graham was never short of material. Often we packed ten or twelve different items into a single commercial.

Then we evolved the 'theme' commercial – where all

the items in the package, serialisation, features, contests, giveaways and offers were linked to a single theme. Thus, in 'Ooh la la Week', the paper would concentrate on all things French, free weekends in Paris, an evening with Sacha Distel, half-price French knickers, and so on.

Knickers, especially French ones, caused us a lot of trouble with the ITCA, the advertisement 'watchdog' committee of the Independent Broadcasting Authority. They seemed to take the view that there was something obscene in the word, let alone in footage of a pretty girl actually showing them. On one occasion, Graham fought his way clear of a ban by dressing a whole high-kicking chorus line in the knickers we had on offer, claiming that the can-can was an acknowledged art form, and that the ITCA would only succeed in making themselves look silly if they banned it. You can't ban-ban the can-can, we said.

We made sure the whole world knew on those occasions when the ITCA did make themselves look silly. We set out to smash the tradition which existed among advertising agencies, that one did not talk about ITCA bans for fear of offending them. We shouted and screamed about censorship and Old Mother Grundy whenever they stopped us doing anything we wanted to do. Gradually they came to realise that we were much closer to the public pulse than they were, and they banned less and less.

Very early in *The Sun*'s history – before launch day, in fact – we had decided that television was probably the biggest single area of human interest, with one possible exception, which we did not propose to neglect. So we tackled television from the outset in a major way, devoting a far greater proportion of our available space to matters concerning the box than any other newspaper. In the process, we taught the rest of Fleet Street how to stop Saturday being a dead, dead day, when sales were traditionally well down on the average for the week.

We reasoned that since there was no commuter sale on that

day, most casual copies were probably bought by housewives while shopping in the high street. And we further reasoned that, since the cost of *TV Times* and *Radio Times* could well appear steep to those on fixed, low-income budgets, the best Saturday service we could offer was a massively detailed weekend programme guide.

It worked like a charm. We did a big weekend pull-out supplement (lift-out, our Australian colleagues called it) sometimes as big as twelve pages. And Saturday swiftly became our best-selling day. But that wasn't the only way in which we turned television to our advantage.

Whilst the prophets of gloom and doom had been busy saying that television would destroy newspapers, I had been preaching the doctrine that the Press and the broadcast media were complementary rather than competitive. Since one couldn't beat them in getting the news to the customer fast, I thought we should exploit them, by capitalising on the public's interest in everything which appeared on the small screen.

So, whilst other newspapers were deliberately paying scant attention to what they regarded as a rival medium, *The Sun* was equally busy playing up each and every story about television and television personalities. I sometimes wonder if that process may not now have gone too far. But it was extremely effective at the time.

One of the ways in which we bent the box to our advantage was *The Sun* TV Awards. Rupert and I were discussing with Graham King the merits of certain small-screen performers, and Rupert suggested a reader poll to see which were the most popular in a variety of categories. Graham immediately saw an opportunity for free TV time, and we were off on another roller-coaster.

Only weeks later the first awards were presented at a glittering night out in the Banqueting Hall at the Royal Lancaster Hotel. All the winners had been selected by *Sun* readers.

Nyree Dawn Porter won the actress of the year award for her part as Irene in the *Forsyte Saga* series; Edward Woodward was voted top actor; Cilla Black, top female personality; Cliff Richard, top male personality; Tommy Cooper, top comedian. *Coronation Street* was voted the top series; *Steptoe and Son*, top BBC series; and *On the Buses*, top ITV series. ITV's *World of Sport* won the top sports programme award; *World in Action*, the top current affairs programme; and *Blue Peter*, the top children's programme.

There to present the awards was Harold Wilson, the Prime Minister. At that time, May 1970, Britain was poised for the date of the General Election, but the PM would not be drawn, even though the orchestra played throughout the evening 'June is busting out all over'. He did, however, greet Violet Carson, Ena Sharples of *Coronation Street*, who accepted the award on behalf of the cast, by putting his arm round her waist and singing 'Cockles and Mussels'.

The whole performance was televised, giving *The Sun* one whole hour of TV time, and raising £4,000 for charity. The awards became an annual event, and ran for several years.

By the end of 1970 *The Sun* was working hard to recruit a new kind of audience – children. Of course, children generally do not buy newspapers, but their parents do. We found that promotions directed at the young teenage market were more often than not surprisingly successful. Obviously teenagers had influence over their parents, certainly enough to coax them into buying a newspaper in which they were interested.

So evolved one of *The Sun*'s most successful strategies, the 'apron tug'. Aim to interest the children, who in turn would ask, force, blackmail or otherwise inveigle their parents into buying the paper. The long-term benefit for *The Sun* was that this new readership – young parents in growing households – proved to be one of its greatest assets over the next two decades.

Thus while sport was still very much an adult activity so

far as newspapers were concerned, we spared a thought for the younger fry, too. *The Sun* was launched with, among other things, a soccer wallchart. Children got the chart for a few pence – illustrated and full of information, but with a hundred blank spaces on it – and then had to buy *The Sun* each day for the tokens which they clipped out and sent in exchange for the stickers to place in the blank spaces. It was a smash hit, and the first of many charts and albums like it.

The football collecting craze culminated in autumn 1971 with the launch of *The Sun* Football Encyclopaedia and Soccerstamp Album. Soccerstamps were the natural follow-on from stickers and cards, and a set of 500 was designed and printed by the government's postage stamp printing firm, Harrison and Co.

All records were broken. More than 1,100,000 albums were sold for 10p each at newsagents. The paper was swamped with requests for the stamps, and at one stage, 3,000 people were employed to service requests for them. A year later (with requests still coming in at the rate of thousands a day) some 200 million Soccerstamps had been sold. And the effect on *The Sun*'s circulation was dramatic.

At one point the great Soccerstamp craze led us close to disaster. Graham, inventive as ever, launched a side-issue promotion based on faulty stamps. As in the real world of stamps, we claimed the faulty ones had a special value, and offered a £10 prize to any reader who found one.

We had the faulty ones specially printed, of course. And we thought we had the distribution tightly controlled. Until the day the Chairman's Portuguese butler marched in to him at breakfast waving an envelope. 'Mr Murdoch, Mr Murdoch, I am rich,' he cried.

He wasn't rich, but he did have ten faulty stamps, worth £100. Rupert did the frightening sums in his head over the toast and marmalade and the wires started humming.

By lunchtime it was clear that our rules about distribution

of the faulty stamps had been breached on such a scale that there were probably a million pounds' worth in circulation. There was only one thing to do.

'Owing to circumstances beyond our control,' I wrote, straight-facedly, for the next day's newspaper, 'we can no longer offer £10 reward for Soccerstamps printed upside down or faulty in any other respect. Claims already submitted will be honoured. Sorry, folks.'

Astonishingly, it worked. The flood of claims immediately dried to a trickle. We were able to meet not only all those claims in hand, but all subsequent claims, at a total cost of only £20,000. A relatively inexpensive, if somewhat nerve-wracking lesson.

Next in popularity to sports were pets, especially ponies. We discovered that, at some stage of her life, every girl coveted a pony. Working very closely with the RSPCA (to whom we made substantial donations) we hired experts to comb the country, looking for and buying up healthy, well-trained ponies. After experiencing a quite enormous response to competitions in which ponies were the prize (complete with tack, training and a year's free stabling), we packaged a week-long promotion called 'Pony Week' in which several ponies were offered, along with free riding lessons, pony trekking in Wales, and a centrespread wallchart identifying all the horse breeds in the world.

We offered our readers just about every breed there was – palominos, Highland ponies, Shetlands, hacks. We even discovered – in South America – a pair of the extremely rare Fallabellas, horses little larger than a retriever. These were imported, and one of them, christened 'Arabella the Fallabella' was offered as the prize in a pony contest, and won the hearts of millions.

Pony Week was a real winner, and pointed the way to further pet promotions – 'Doggie Week', 'Fishing Week', and perhaps the most contentious of all, 'Pussy Week', which posed a dilemma for the ITCA. 'Everyone knows that pussies are cats,' said Graham. 'And no, we wouldn't prefer to call it Cat Week.'

By the end of 1970, the concept of 'theme' promotion was well established. We would normally run a heavy TV advertising campaign through Sunday and Monday, selling the contents of *The Sun* for the entire week. This way, new readers were persuaded to stay with *The Sun* for at least a week. That, for most of them, was enough. They were hooked.

Everyone from the editorial and promotions departments would contribute ideas – special features, picture ideas, competitions, offers, freebies. Thus 'Romance Week' would feature prize letters from readers about their great romance, or their fantasy romance, Mills & Boon writers would contribute, naughty undies and nighties would be offered, and readers could win trips to romantic places. All theme weeks were tremendous fun.

One week, 'Bath Week', gave *The Sun* an excuse to feature bathtime lovelies through the week, market-testing of bathroom toiletries, special offers of bathtowels, and the chance to win a designer luxury bathroom. This superb prize was won by a man in a tiny council flat. We had to work out how to fit in a bathroom which was twice the size of his living room!

One of the editorial features was 'The True Story of the WC'. The water closet, as most people know, was invented by the eminent Victorian, Sir Thomas Crapper, whose plumbing firm was, until the mid-1960s, an established landmark in the Kings Road in Chelsea. None of this, however, impressed the ITCA, who promptly ruled that the name of Sir Thomas Crapper could not be mentioned, even in an undertone, in any television commercial.

We argued for days. Graham even established that the word 'crap' did not derive from Sir Thomas's name at all, but from the Latin 'crapulous'; it was simply a coincidence. Still we were refused, and the commercial went to air *sans* Crapper. The argument raged for weeks after in the trade press and we were delighted, a month or so later, to have the opportunity to goad the ITCA once more. This was during 'Fishing Week', and for a prize in a fishing competition we secured a week's free trout-fishing on the River Piddle. There is such a river – in fact, there is more than one and the one we chose did harbour trout – but the silly burghers of the ITCA would have none of it. We were not allowed to use the name.

In 1972, with sales sticking a bit, we tried a totally new and ambitious promotional technique, the Big Drop. We planned a sixteen-page tabloid-sized full colour mock-up of *The Sun* in which every story, every picture, was some kind of advertisement for the paper, and every contest and every special offer was open only to those who bought the paper. Entry forms or order forms had to be accompanied by tokens from *The Sun*. And we planned to print no fewer than 13,000,000 copies, and have it pushed through every letter-box in the land free of charge.

The product itself was fine. Every bit as bouncy and colourful as I wished. Bemrose, the group's gravure colour printers in Liverpool, did a magnificent job, technically. But the distribution was a disaster. Many thousands of people wrote or telephoned to complain that they had not received their copies.

And from all over the country came heartbreaking reports of ditches and dustbins filled with hundreds of thousands of bundles. Naïvely, neither ourselves nor the distribution agents had considered the obvious danger that many of the casual staff they employed would simply take the money and ditch the paper.

We thought, in the end, that perhaps only about 70 per cent of copies actually hit the doormats at which they were aimed. Even so, we rated the operation a success. It was much the biggest thing of its kind ever attempted, and it set our somewhat sluggish sales firmly back on the upward track.

We had lots of contests in *The Sun*, with appealing prizes. The Pacesetters Department dreamed up many of the best ideas. We didn't offer many Rolls-Royces, but we got a splendid response to 'Win a year's free tights'. Other big hits in this area were 'Win a year's free baby-sitting', 'Win a year's free groceries' – or petrol, or nappies, or beer. They all pulled them in.

And in the 'Get-Set' area we excelled ourselves. We never sought to make any money from this sphere of activity, though we did make a little. But we offered genuine bargains.

Eventually we had to have a 'Get-Set' department, with three or four people constantly on the look-out for merchandise. They led a hair-raising life, often being required to produce an offer within twenty-four hours. Occasionally, of course, we had a back-fire.

Once we offered bargain wigs, wigs being very much the vogue at the time. Tens of thousands sent for them – and thousands sent them back. Not because of the quality, or the price, but because when they tried them on, their husbands or boyfriends fell about laughing. We learned the hard way that wigs are not a good impulse mail-order buy.

But of all the offers, the most successful, month after month, year after year, were offers of underwear, the briefer the better. We had a pair of knickers designed that would fit into a matchbox. ('Set your man alight.') And we had tremendous success with knickers in a tin.

I had noticed a paragraph in the *Guardian* which said that a small firm in Cheshire was building up a steady business selling tinned knickers to Sweden. I couldn't imagine why. But if the Swedes bought them, I reasoned, why not the Brits? We added an extra refinement. We decided to perfume ours. And we asked Chanel to join us in the great 'Tinned Knicker Adventure'. They refused, snootily. So we simply bought copious quantities of Chanel No. 5 – that which

Marilyn Monroe said was all she wore in bed – and had the ladies on our production line put a drop in each tin.

'The paper's always full of knickers,' grumbled the Chairman. 'Can't you find anything else to put in it?' Indeed we could.

Whilst we were having a lot of fun with offers and contests, a 'good read' – the serialisation of how-to-do-it books, memoirs, and novels – played a vital role in *The Sun*'s successful mix of the predictable and the unexpected.

The television promotion of a book about train robber Ronnie Biggs became a sensitive issue, with a credibility problem thrown in, as there had been claims by other papers that they had the 'genuine' Biggs story. But our story had something the others hadn't – Biggs's fingerprint was on every page. We seized on this and the print, blown up to full screen size, became a memorable graphic in the selling of the story on TV.

To project a serialisation we often dramatised scenes from the book, building sets overnight, hiring lookalike actors and going for the most spectacular action. The commercials for *The Fuzz* and *Gumshoe* – hardhitting cops and robbers novels – went through several teams of stuntmen, recreating fights and brawls and violent action. Sold like that, novels really put on readers.

One memorable serialisation was that of a book called *Rabid*, which was a novel about a couple who smuggled a dog from France to Britain in their yacht. The dog developed rabies and attacked people; worse, the disease spread to other dogs and soon the country was under siege by ravenous killer dogs. I bought the book, and retitled it *The Day of the Mad Dogs*, with a suitably redesigned cover. For the commercial we hired some dangerous-looking but superbly trained dogs which had been used in the film *The Omen*. The commercial began sedately, with a middle-aged couple relaxing in the drawing room of their elegant country home with their two dogs. Suddenly the dogs leapt up and savagely attacked the defenceless couple. We showed close-ups of the dogs' foaming mouths (shaving cream) and bloodied victims. Then followed scene after horrific scene of screaming babies waking in the night, fearful parents, hunters out shooting the mad dogs. As a finale, the last scene showed an expiring victim, sweating and moaning in hospital (we had expert medical advice throughout).

The commercial went out after much argument with the ITCA and IBA, and promptly recorded the biggest volume of complaints that independent television had ever received about an advertisement. Eventually the IBA bowed before the storm, and pulled it off the air at 11 p.m. But *The Sun* positively walked out of the newsagents' shops the next day, and every day that week.

Graham King was a many-faceted character. Whilst he was deeply involved in arguing with the ITCA and working out ways of selling more knickers, he was writing, in his spare time, a scholarly tome on the life and works of Emile Zola. He actually left the organisation in 1974 to pursue a writing career, but has since returned to the fold as Promotions Director at Wapping. He made a tremendous contribution to the success of *The Sun*. We journalists often provided promotional flour and water, salt and yeast. But Graham was the Master Baker.

CHAPTER EIGHT

When the News is BIG it's Big in the Soaraway Sun

On my desk as I write is an issue of *The Sun* newspaper dated 10 January 1989. It has no Page Three girls. It has no kiss and tell stories. The word bonking does not appear at all. Pages 1, 2, 3, 4, 5, 6, 7 and 9 are devoted to one story – a slick, detailed, highly professional account, with spectacular pictures, of the aftermath of a plane crash on the M1.

Through all the drama and the anguish and the heartbreak, the newspaper treads sure-footedly, informatively, sympathetically. Its account is no less comprehensive, though rather better edited, than that of the *Daily Telegraph* of the same date. It illustrates beautifully a point about *The Sun* which needs to be made: whatever else has happened in its brief and turbulent history, it has never lost the knack of rising to the big occasion.

There is no more exciting place to be than a newspaper office when the world seems to be crashing down around one's ears. It is like being at the centre of the universe. The bigger the news, and the faster it flows, the faster the adrenalin flows. I have known nights when we changed the Page One lead on each of five editions, because so much was happening.

More often, the big nights are the nights when one event dominates all else. These are usually disaster nights. In a curious way journalists somehow contrive to divorce themselves from the horror about which they are writing. Thus a good story becomes a 'great' story and a 'tremendous' story as the casualty count goes up. This is not because most journalists are cynical, which they may be, or uncaring, which they certainly are not. It is because quite simply they are aware that they could not do the job properly in the time available if they permitted themselves to get emotional about it.

There were many such drama-packed nights in the early years of *The Sun*. One was the night of the Birmingham pub bombings, 21 November 1974.

The Sun at that time was 'off-stone' – that is, away from the Composing Room on its way to the presses – at 7.15 p.m., and supposedly printing at 8 p.m. At 8.20, bombs exploded in two city centre pubs in Birmingham, the Mulberry Bush and the Tavern in The Town.

News of them – a sketchy paragraph or so indicating explosions and 'some casualties' – landed on my desk at 8.50. It was too late to stop the First Edition. But scenting a major story, we flung the whole editorial machine into top gear. Within five minutes extra reporters and photographers were speeding up the motorway to reinforce our tiny staff in the Birmingham office. The machine room overseer was told to slow down the run and prepare for a slip page; staff enjoying supper breaks in nearby pubs were recalled to the office.

Within ten minutes I had a story saying that fourteen people were believed to have been killed, and several more bombs found. We cleared two columns on Page One, hustled the story in and had it running by 10 p.m. '14 dead as bomb blasts hit city centre' said the headline.

Ninety minutes or so later the Third Edition, from which the Birmingham supplies were normally taken, was sent away ahead of schedule with the story filling the whole of Page One and several inside pages. We had then eighteen dead, and 100 injured, and put a thick black border round the front page. Still later, we changed Page One to nineteen dead – and then again to twenty, by which time the story was filling most of the inside pages.

As picture after picture and thousands more words came pouring over the wires, we threw out more and more routine news and features – and more and more advertising – to make room for them. Among the things we reported, ominously, was that there were groups of people roaming the city streets chanting, 'Kill the Irish'.

Police had found two other huge bombs, one of which had been planted over a giant oil tank at the Ivy Bush Hotel. Mercifully, neither had exploded. With the city's emergency services at full stretch, volunteer taxi drivers formed queues outside the stricken buildings to ferry the injured to hospital. I can recall no other disaster when this happened.

We did not stop updating the story until well after 3 a.m., at which time I sent for the Night Production Manager.

'I want the fifth slip [the very last edition] to go to Birmingham,' I said.

'We can't do that,' he replied. 'All the Birmingham supplies have gone. There are no more trains. And the publisher is quite happy with the edition he has sent.'

'*I'm* not happy with it,' I said. 'Truck in the fifth slip. Change up [that is, change all supplies still with the wholesaler] where there's still time, and top up [replace all copies already sold but not retailed] where there isn't. Blame me for the cost of the truck.'

Having thrown out hundreds of thousands of pounds worth of advertising, and put the entire machine room staff on overtime, I was hardly likely to quibble at the cost of sending a truck to Birmingham.

To their credit neither Rupert nor the paper's first Advertisement Director, Bert Hardy, ever made more than a token protest about the way we flung money about on these occasions. For his part Rupert cared little for the fact that we would almost certainly have lost a packet on the night when the sums were done, provided that we had done the story better than anyone else, and got ourselves talked about. On this night, and many others, we did.

A key figure on many such occasions was Night Editor Roy Pittilla, a former *Mirror* colleague who presided over the 'back bench' of journalistic production executives. Roy was responsible, after a handful of major decisions had been made higher up the chain of editorial command, for selection and presentation, two of the primary journalistic arts. He was also responsible for maintaining a smooth flow of copy to the Head Printer. The Night Editor's role is a demanding one, involving a great many snap decisions. Those who are best at it become progressively more imperturbable as the pressures mount. Roy was one of these. We were fortunate to have him.

There had been an earlier IRA horror bombing on the mainland – on 8 March 1973. Bernard Shrimsley and I were in my car, close to Fleet Street, on the way back from lunch. The time, I have to confess, was 2.42 p.m. Suddenly there was the sound of an explosion, it seemed somewhere behind us, not too far away. 'Hurry back,' I said to my driver. But the traffic was thick, and there was a police roadblock on The Strand, which we had to wriggle around through the back streets.

Eleven minutes later, as we turned into Bouverie Street, there was a second, much bigger explosion, to the east. We later discovered that the first bomb had been planted in a car in Whitehall, the second in a car parked outside the world's most famous court-house, the Old Bailey.

In the two blasts more than 200 people were injured. Some of the injuries were fearful. But amazingly, only one person was killed. The majority of casualties came from the Old Bailey bomb. Because it was the Old Bailey, and because reporters and photographers were in the area in the natural order of things, news and pictures were already starting to flow as Bernard and I rushed into the office.

Within minutes every stand-by reporter and every camera-man in the building was on his way to the Old Bailey. Striking hospital workers rushed back to duty at the nearby hospital, St Bartholomew's, as soon as they heard of the bombings. As it happened, many of them were on the premises, at a union meeting, as the casualties came in.

This time, we had a little more time to spare than we often had. The First Edition, printing on schedule, carried the story not only on the front page, but on the back, which was normally reserved for sport, and several pages inside. Cartoonist Paul Rigby and columnist Jon Akass scrapped the work they had already filed and came up with on-the-day contributions. Page after page carried huge dramatic pictures, graphic reconstructions, maps, and interviews with shocked survivors. We even found time for a leading article, 'This time it's us', making the point that the people in Belfast had learned to live with blasting and maiming. Against London's day of anguish, they could set a thousand days.

It was then, and to some extent still is, the IRA's custom to issue a warning when they were about to explode a bomb in a public place. There were warnings on this occasion. And *Sun* reporters chipped and chiselled away all day at the timings involved, to find out whether or not anyone had been guilty of not taking them seriously. We established that at the Old Bailey there was a delay of thirty-four minutes between Scotland Yard's having received a bomb warning and police moving in to evacuate the area. This was the timetable:

1.56 p.m: A man with a strong Irish accent telephoned *The Times* newspaper and told a secretary: 'There are bombs in three cars.' He gave the locations and car registration numbers.

2.01 p.m: *The Times* telephoned Scotland Yard.

2.34 p.m: Snow Hill police station, a hundred yards from the Old Bailey, was alerted by Scotland Yard.

2.35 p.m: A squad of police was moved into the area and started evacuations.

2.53 p.m. The bomb exploded.

This gave the police less than twenty minutes to try to clear offices, pubs and courts. The streets were still crowded when the bomb blew up.

A mile away in Whitehall, casualties were much lighter. And there they had only a twelve-minute warning to clear the area. The tip-off came at 2.30 p.m. and the explosion at 2.42 p.m.

Page One of *The Sun* the next day, 9 March, carried a big picture of a distraught and blood-spattered victim being led away from the the wreckage of her office and a big white-on-black headline: 'Blitz: 200 hurt, 1 dies, as terror bombs blast the heart of London'. We did not seek to apportion blame for the delayed warning.

Horror of a different kind was to hit London in February 1975, when a crowded rush-hour tube train crashed through buffers into a dead-end tunnel at Moorgate, killing thirty-six people and injuring seventy more, some of whom died later in hospital. There were scores of horrific stories about the crash; of the wounded survivors who waited for rescue for many hours in total darkness; of a nineteen-year-old policewoman who could not be dragged from the wreckage until her foot had been amputated. Asked by approaching rescuers, 'Do you want us to send down one of the girls to keep you company?' she joked, 'I'd rather you sent down one of the boys.'

I was away from London at the time. The newspaper was produced by Bernard Shrimsley. His Page One showed a picture of the policewoman on a stretcher, alongside a shot of another of the last few survivors to be dragged clear, under the heading: 'Out of the Tomb'. I would have been proud to have done it myself. I always selected the stories for, and drew – that is, designed – Page One when I was there, but that was largely a matter of self-indulgence.

The name of Bart's hospital crops up often in Fleet Street stories. When I was a sub-editor on the *Daily Mail*, in 1957,

I was rushed there for treatment with a spike sticking out of my head.

Most newspaper offices at that time used long metal spikes, on a heavy lead base, as an instant 'filing' system for waste paper. Bending down to grab a cigarette from a bottom drawer, I had inadvertently spiked myself right between the eyes.

'Pull it out, pull it out,' I shrieked. No one dared do so. The duty nurse was summoned, and bandaged it tight to my forehead. The duty engineer arrived, with bolt-cutters, and cut off the base. Then I was led, like a unicorn, to Bart's.

I wasn't seriously hurt. The spike had penetrated my forehead, but run up over the frontal bone, close to the skin. A brave junior doctor in casualty pulled it out. And spikes were for ever after banned in Northcliffe House.

Years later I was taken to Bart's again, as near dead as makes no difference, after a massive heart attack in the *Express* building. They performed an emergency bypass with their customary efficiency, and thanks to their care I am fitter now than I was then. The operation was conducted by Gareth ('The Knife') Rees. *Private Eye* said it took nine hours – because it took him eight hours to find my heart.

Not all the big stories of the seventies were stories of disaster. One of the 'good news' stories which gave me greatest pleasure was the safe return to Earth of the intrepid astronauts on Apollo 13, on their way back from a moonshot which nearly ended in disaster.

For five emotion-packed, tear-jerking days and nights in the vast loneliness of Space, the crew of Apollo 13 had coolly tackled crisis after crisis after a mysterious explosion turned their 'routine' mission into a fantastic cliff-hanger. On Friday, 17 April 1970, we filled the front and back pages with a diagrammatic portrayal of the ordeal which the astronauts had faced, and were facing. We called it 'Splashdown

Special' – and boldly forecast, in big type: 'They'll be home by seven.'

At 7.07 p.m. GMT the next day, the severely damaged spaceship splashed down safely in the Pacific bang on time and bang on target, a bare three miles from the waiting recovery vessel the USS *Iwo Jima*. Forty-five minutes later the spacemen, Jim Lovell, Fred Haise and John Swigert, were safely aboard. Signalled Mission Control, from Houston: 'You can have Sunday off.'

We had sent *The Sun*'s man in New York, John Sampson, to Houston, for what we were convinced would be the big celebration party. And we had filled oceans and oceans of space throughout the paper with disposable material for the first edition to make room for every detail of the glad tidings.

Not for the first time I was struck by the massive goodwill and unselfish effort which certain stories engendered among the entire staff. As the story developed, the most bolshie of journalists stood by television and radio sets and tape machines, watching for any angle we might not have, or could develop, and filing without being asked. The most bloody-minded typesetters in the Composing Room set type so fast it made their fingers hot.

In the process department, which at that time was dominated by a handful of covert Marxist wreckers, pictures were made into usable blocks in exactly half the time they had said the day before – and would say again the day after – was the irreducible minimum. The result was that on the second edition, long before any of our rivals were even printing, we had the whole thing buttoned up. 'Amen!' said the Page One headline.

Another 'good news' issue was the marriage of Anne, now Princess Royal, to Captain Mark Phillips of the Queen's Dragoon Guards, a marriage which now, sadly, seems to have gone somewhat astray. We filled the front page with a superb picture of the couple under the heading 'The

Captain's lady'. It was a particularly satisfying day for us.

Nearly a year earlier, in January 1973, we had run an exclusive page lead about the lovers under the heading, in type two inches deep, 'They are in love.' The story was picked up and re-run world-wide. Here at home, however, it was ridiculed. The Palace press office denied it flatly, more than once. Rival newspapers which rang the Palace for information were treated to the usual press office sniggers about the gutter press. Then Anne denied it herself. Then Mark denied it.

'We're just good friends,' he said. 'The only love we share is for horses.'

The dashing Dragoon should have told that one to the Marines. At *The Sun*, we went on forecasting a Royal wedding. And it happened, just as we said it would.

'How could you be so sure when everyone was mocking you?' asked Rupert.

'Let us say that our sources were unimpeachable,' I replied.

We had pages and pages of pictures of the big event, of course. And the sale was up 10 per cent – about the same as for Derby Day.

Big sporting days were always big in *The Sun*. We took the view that on Derby Day, or Grand National Day, or Cup Final Day, more people were going to be talking about these events than anything else. So, unless an event of this kind coincided with really big news of a different kind, we had no hesitation in doing a Page One lead, a back page lead, and often a four-page pullout inside, on the day of the event. The sale always shot up in consequence. Sometimes, on Grand National Day in particular, it approached five million.

A story which surprised me by the intensity of feeling it aroused, inside and outside the office, was the assassination of Beatle John Lennon, shot down by a crazed gunman outside his New York apartment in December 1980. 'They loved him, Yeah, Yeah, Yeah,' said *The Sun*'s Page One headline. And they certainly did.

Though I didn't think I was underestimating the story, I didn't think that Lennon was John F. Kennedy, and I wasn't planning to fill the paper with it. But as the day – 9 December – wore on, I gradually gave it more and more space. Not only was abundant excellent material being filed, but everyone I spoke to – reporters, cleaners, front hall porters – questioned me eagerly about the latest news. Rupert rang from New York to ask what we were doing with the story, which was in itself highly unusual. I was tempted to tell him that we had planned to hold it over for a day or two, but resisted the temptation. In the end, it occupied pages 1, 2, 3, 4, 5, 6 and the centre spread – not far short of the treatment we were to accord to the shooting of Ronald Reagan a few weeks later.

I was in my office, having a chat with Billy Gillespie, Deputy Managing Director, when the news about Reagan came through. The first edition for issue dated 31 March was well under way. It was a quiet night. Then the wire message was dropped on my desk: 'President Reagan shot and seriously wounded. Three aides also hit.' I was never more proud of *The Sun* than I was that night.

Gillespie, an experienced newspaperman but a fairly recent recruit to News International, was to say later: 'I had never seen anything quite so slick. Within three minutes the Editor had killed two features and commissioned two more – on the history of Presidential assassinations and assassination bids, and on the health record of the President. Whilst the Editor was phoning, all the key people came into the office to wait for instructions. He didn't have to call for them. They knew. As the Editor talked, he drew a plan of a new Page One. When I went into the Composing Room, it seemed only a few minutes later, the old Page One had been broken up and type was being assembled under the heading: "Reagan shot" – six inches deep.'

It had indeed. We had that page running within one hour. After two hours, we had turned the whole paper upside down.

Rupert called from New York the next day. 'I know you were the best of the tabloids,' he said. 'Harry told me.' I did not rise to every fly which Rupert cast in my direction, and I did not rise to this one. But it infuriated me none the less.

Rupert had comparatively recently acquired Times Newspapers. 'Harry' was Harry Evans, who had been made Editor of *The Times*. I don't know whether or not we were the best tabloid of the day, but I have no doubt whatever that we were better than *The Times* – and much, much faster.

In fact, at that time everyone in Bouverie Street, those who had toiled in the Murdoch vineyard through the heat and burden of the day, bitterly resented the patronage which was oozing out of *Times* headquarters in Gray's Inn Road. We regarded most of the people there as amateurs. And though I wouldn't choose so to describe Harry Evans I was distinctly unamused by the fact that he and the Chairman were discussing the merits of that day's *Sun* before the Chairman had seen fit to discuss them with me.

The incident was not important in itself. But it was an indication of the very difficult circumstances in which we were working at that time. Rupert, whether from New York or his own office in Gray's Inn Road, seemed to be taking all his editorial advice from people on *The Times*. Since that newspaper, in recent years, had been almost as big a failure as *The Sun* had been a success, and since *Sun* people felt, rightly or wrongly, that it was primarily through their efforts that the Chairman had been able to afford what they regarded as a monumental piece of self-indulgence, there was a great deal of ill-feeling abroad.

Sun staff felt – as I imagine the people in Sydney must have felt when Rupert first came to London – that we were being neglected, milked of his time and attention, starved of cash, and robbed of talent we desperately needed which he switched from Bouverie Street to oil the wheels of his new toy. Relations were particularly bad in the political arena.

I had at that time one of Westminster's most reliable and experienced political correspondents, Walter Terry. And we had for ten years or more had at least as many good people in Parliament as *The Times*. It was particularly galling, therefore, to hear fairly regularly from Gray's Inn Road, that our political stories were rubbish, which meant that the political staff of *The Times* had been unable to stand them up.

It was soon after this that I began to feel that my job on *The Sun* was done. We had toppled the *Mirror*, clawed our way to the top of the heap, played a part, however insignificant, in pointing the nation down a new political path. And it was becoming increasingly clear that Murdoch was beginning to lose confidence in my ability to keep the paper on course.

Certainly he became quite unreasonably critical. When I told him so he reacted, characteristically, by suggesting that I should take six months' leave of absence. 'Think about it over the weekend,' he said. 'Let me know on Monday.' But he rang my home the next day to say: 'I must have your decision. I have schedules to keep.'

Since it was by that time common knowledge that he had already approached my successor, and former protégé, Kelvin MacKenzie, I did not see that I had a lot of choice. And since Kelvin, it was clear, had already been offered the Editorship of *The Sun* – with no nonsense about the role being in any way 'Acting' or 'Temporary' – I did not see how I could possibly return, at any time in the future, without causing universal embarrassment.

So, long before the six months was up, to the great relief of my wife and family, I arranged to meet Rupert for dinner, one Sunday evening in the Savoy, to tell him that I wouldn't be coming back. The parting was amicable, in so far as these things can ever be amicable. He said that he would have been quite happy to keep me on paid leave for another six months or so, or until a suitable vacancy manifested itself within his organisation.

There was no ill-feeling between us, and is not to this day. Years later I was offered, and was happy to accept, a commission to revitalise Murdoch's ailing antipodean flagship, the *Australian*, in the role of Editor-in-Chief. Meanwhile, I joined Mr Robert Holmes à Court in Perth, Western Australia. But that is another story.

Back at *The Sun*, big news nights, of course, did not always involve the unexpected. Sometimes they were totally predictable. At General Elections, for example. Or on Budget Day.

One of the most outstanding production achievements of the year in Fleet Street took place at *The Sun* on Budget Day. Since we printed only in London to supply millions of readers all over the country, we had to be off-stone (editorially complete and ready to go to press) by 8.15 p.m. in the very early seventies – and 7.15 p.m. later on, when the print order became so big that we couldn't complete it in the time available. There were times when the Chancellor did not sit down in the Commons until around 5 p.m. In that incredibly short time page upon page of the newspaper had to be filled, including the Chancellor's speech, tax tables, what all the tax changes meant, a cartoon, a leading article, a Page One headline summing it all up – and so on.

We had a back bench executive, Graham Courtenay, who was the Regimental Sergeant-Major supreme. For days before the Budget he worked on a document which was virtually a string of orders for every member of the editorial staff – from the Editor to the messengers.

Heaven help anyone, myself included, who got out of line. The system was so finely tuned that the paper was printing before 8 p.m. and by 8.30 p.m. was in the offices of all the opposition newspapers. They didn't print until 10.30–11.30 p.m. because, in addition to their London offices, they printed in Manchester and in some cases in Scotland as well, and had nothing like the distribution problems we had. So, not only on Budget nights, but six nights a week the year round, all *The Sun*'s ideas were there to be 'lifted' – or stolen. But steal as they liked they still couldn't stop *The Sun* soaring away.

Of course, we had similar problems on election nights too. I remember writing the headline 'Up The Poll' in the General Election of 1970 *before* the count was anywhere near complete. But it seemed, on the basis of three or four early results, that the pollsters would be confounded, and that Ted Heath was set to topple Wilson. We took a chance. We took lots of chances in those days and we didn't always guess right. When we got things disastrously wrong we told the readers the next day exactly what had happened. Their reaction was invariably sympathetic.

Exciting nights they were, all of them.

CHAPTER NINE

The Think-In:
How the plotting was done

As an Editor, I used to be fond of saying that one could not edit by committee. 'This is not a democracy,' I would say. 'By the time you lot have reached a decision we'll have missed the train to Leeds.' In consequence, I acquired a reputation as something of an autocrat, who went his own way without paying much heed to the views of those around him.

Nothing could be further from the truth. Though editing is inevitably a long process of instant decisions – there are few pending trays in journalism – and I made a great show of being decisive, I frequently displayed much more confidence than I felt. And the decisions I did make, apparently on the spot, often owed much to a deliberately elaborate system of consultation with my senior colleagues. They, not I, worked the ship. I merely helped to steer it.

I kept in touch with views other than my own in a variety of ways. We usually had three editorial conferences a day – one in the morning, to find out what was going on, one in the early evening, to decide on the shape and content of Page One, and one late at night, often over a drink, to discuss the overnight features.

Then we had a weekly 'week-ahead' conference, mapping out a rough programme of non-urgent feature material for the next seven days, all of which we were prepared to dump without ceremony if something better came up. All heads of department attended these conferences, some of their deputies, and sometimes, when they could be spared, representatives of the Poor Bloody Infantry from the front line, the sub-editors' and reporters' desks.

But the keystone of the pattern of talking-shops we established was the biannual policy conference, or 'think-in'. These weekend conferences, held at pleasant country hotels within easy driving distance of London, were of enormous value.

We worked hard – I insisted on three working sessions a day – and played the same way. Thus we acquired long lists of ideas, broad agreement on where we all stood on the issues of the day, which staff and which systems were working well, and so on.

The minutes – usually taken by the Woman's Editor, which shows what a chauvinistic lot we were – often ran to sixty or seventy foolscap pages. The Woman's Editor, not surprisingly, got a great deal of attention on these occasions since she was usually the only woman. Every one of the women who occupied this post over the years was an asset to the newspaper and a joy to work with. On these think-in occasions every one of them behaved beautifully, dressed glamorously, and generally helped us to maintain a fairly civilised atmosphere.

In the evening we had good dinners, drank good wine, played darts at local pubs – and went on talking about the paper. Mr Murdoch's investment on these occasions was repaid a thousand-fold, and think-ins are now a common practice on many newspapers.

Some of ours were the stuff of which legends are made. The first one, only a few weeks after launch night, was held in a scafront pub at Aldeburgh, in Suffolk.

Norman Baitey and I set off late on Friday, having seen the major edition changes safely under way. Bernard Shrimsley, Frank Nicklin and Joyce Hopkirk were a couple of hours ahead of us. We were even further delayed because Norman, in the navigator's chair, took us up the wrong bank of the

River Alde. We arrived very late indeed – and, to our surprise, found the front door unlocked.

Following the only light we could see, and the only noises we could hear, we found all three of our colleagues in the same bed – fully dressed, I rush to add – drinking brandy to keep warm, whilst waiting up for us, and chatting away merrily.

Arriving after midnight they had found a note pinned to the door, clearly not meant for them, which read: 'There are supposed to be some people coming from London. If they look OK let them in.'

The note had apparently escaped the notice of the person to whom it was addressed, who seemed to have gone home, and forgotten to lock up. The proprietor and his wife were not at home. There appeared to be no one else on the premises.

The resourceful Joyce took charge, found and allocated rooms, broke open the bar with a nail file, seized a bottle of brandy and some cigars for her colleagues, and left a note explaining what had happened.

The following day mine host, who had rematerialised overnight, seemed astonishingly unconcerned, and cheerfully brushed aside our apologies. We ate an enormous breakfast before moving into the nice warm lecture room he had prepared for us, to talk ourselves hoarse.

The talk went on all day. At dinner, we were joined in the dining room by a young honeymoon couple, who followed us into the lounge for coffee. Being full of ourselves, and equally full of good red burgundy, we quizzed them mercilessly about their newspaper reading habits and were downcast, but not silenced, to learn that they had never heard of the Soaraway *Sun*.

We then, quite unfairly, engaged them in a fierce argument about the merits and demerits of the popular Press. They did not read national newspapers at all, they told us. Did they not then feel that they were under-informed, we challenged. 'Nonsense,' they said. 'There is radio, there is television, there are local newspapers. We have never felt the need to buy a daily paper.'

Somewhat stung by this, we slapped in supplementary questions in quick succession. How do you know what is going on in Parliament? – From the radio. Are you, as newly-weds, not interested in home-maker articles – on cooking, cleaning, DIY and so on? – There are plenty of splendid articles in women's magazines. Do you not feel a need to know what is going on in the wider world? – No. Don't you think that you would find national newspaper advertising – of supermarket prices, for example, or even honeymoon hotels – helpful in planning your day to day living? – No.

I think we all felt that our pride was at stake – not to mention the reputation of the industry. And we subjected this poor young couple to a positive barrage of propaganda.

Much, much later, out-fought and outnumbered by ruthless professional wordsmiths, they staggered in a bewildered fashion towards the staircase, wishing, no doubt, that they had gone to Benidorm. The ideas we came up with on that occasion set the pattern of the newspaper for the next six vital months, and the pattern for many such weekends to come.

Once, La Hopkirk dragged us to a hotel on the Solent, at Bucklers Hard. As we approached it towards midnight the night sky was lit by torches of flame from oil refineries on the far bank. And when we stepped from the car in the hotel car-park the air was heavy with the smell of oil.

'Where on earth have you brought us?' I demanded.

'It says in the book that the restaurant is excellent,' she replied. It was.

In later years, the task of holding the fort on think-in Fridays was usually left to Dick Parrack, a former colleague of mine on the *Newcastle Journal*. Dick reckoned it could be absolutely guaranteed that towards midnight he would get a call from the Chairman in New York – where it was still only 5 p.m. – saying: 'Where the hell is everybody.'

I had on the wall of my office at that time a most ingenious clock which told the time in every major city in the world simultaneously. It was designed to stop me waking up the peripatetic Rupert – who, in the words of Cecil King, dashed around the world like a demented blue-bottle – in the middle of the night. Unfortunately, I was never able to persuade him that *he* needed one, and he took it as a personal affront if I was not available whatever time he called. He didn't do it on purpose; he just didn't think. And since he had a serious sleeping problem it wasn't any help for me to know what time it was wherever *he* was – which, of course, I always did. I have known Rupert to cross the Atlantic for dinner – and still have time to discover that I wasn't in the office at 10 p.m.

Once, in a remote hotel in deepest East Anglia, we came across Desmond Wilcox, a former colleague of mine on the *Daily Mirror*, and the charming and ubiquitous Esther Rantzen, breast-feeding her baby in a quiet corner of the lounge. Then, as now, these two were very much in the public gaze. They had crept away in secret for a quiet weekend away from it all, and must have felt that the gods were not on their side suddenly to find their rural hideaway full of boisterous Fleet Street journalists. I am glad to say that no one in my party saw fit to make a copper or two by phoning Nigel Dempster, or any other gossip columnist.

One of our most memorable think-ins was at the elegant Chewton Glen in the New Forest. Shortly after our arrival one of our colleagues (who must remain nameless for reasons which will shortly become obvious) received a telephone call to say that his wife had won a car in a sweep. It seemed a good idea for him to buy us all a drink to celebrate. Then we thought we each ought to buy him one. We got to bed in the small hours.

The next day, after breakfast, our colleague failed to turn up for the morning session. There was no sign of him in his room. His bed had not been slept in. By midday he was still missing. Everywhere he might possibly be was thoroughly searched. The hotel management was alerted. Eventually the police were told.

Our friend was found in mid-afternoon, *under* his bed, fast asleep, sheltered from view by the floor-length counterpane hanging round him. It was clear that he had slept there through the night and well into the next day. Why? We never knew why. He didn't remember.

That evening – or rather, late that night – I was approached by an assistant manager who advised me, gently enough in the circumstances, that another member of my party was bowling oranges, off his long run, across the ballroom. 'Is he getting wickets?' I asked, before strolling to the edge of the pitch and persuading the bowler that the light was too bad for further play. The hugely tolerant management charged us only for the oranges – and accepted a further booking eighteen months later.

Over the years the size of the think-in team grew to ten or twelve people, travelling in three or four cars. Sometimes we used to arrange to meet for supper at a restaurant on the way. On one such occasion, in Hampshire, we were astonished to find the door of a restaurant where we had a firm booking slammed in our faces. It transpired that since the booking had been accepted – in my name – the proprietor had learned who we were. And by a most extraordinary coincidence his wife had run away with – of all people – a distinguished member of the News International Board.

No history of the think-in would be complete without reference to the Bear at Woodstock, close by Blenheim Palace. There, on one occasion, I was given a room in a sort of turret near the top of the building. During the night I was awakened several times by the unmistakable cry of a baby. When I mentioned this at breakfast next morning, the duty manager's eyes opened wide. 'But there is no baby in the hotel, sir,' he said.

As you may have guessed, the staff later told us that among the many legends associated with the Bear, an ancient coaching house, was one about a mother and baby who had been murdered in the room I occupied, hundreds of years before.

No, I don't believe in ghosts. And yes, I *did* hear a baby.

At the Lygon Arms in Broadway, in the Cotswolds, where we met more than once, I was allocated a room in a very old part of the building which was reached by a back staircase. Unknown to me and to my colleagues at the time, there was another way into it – through the lecture room which had been allocated to us. It was very illuminating, next morning, to hear my colleagues assembling for the morning session grumbling mutinously at the intense work schedule laid down for the weekend, and my refusal to allow time for a sightseeing trip of the region. After hearing myself described several times as a slave-driver I entered the room, to everyone's great consternation, from my bedroom door and opened the conference by saying: 'Good morning, slaves.'

CHAPTER TEN

Page Three or Bust?

I am neither ashamed nor particularly proud to say so, but I suppose I helped to make Page Three a part of the language. In many ways I now wish I hadn't.

The Sun did not invent the bosom, any more than it invented the permissive society. And thousands of people, including many women, get great pleasure each day from looking at pictures of beautiful girls in a state of undress. Certainly I recall many occasions when the women in my family would discuss, at breakfast, the merits of that day's Page Three girl, without suggesting in any way that they felt women were thereby being exploited.

Even so, I have come to the conclusion, over the years, that there *is* an element of sexploitation involved. And it is undoubtedly true that by handing the pundits this stick with which to beat us we did divert attention from the very many other ways in which we were breaking new ground.

Unlike Ms Clare Short, MP, I would not now wish to ban Page Three girls. I am against most bans as a matter of principle. Nor would I now wish to cover them up. And if we hadn't emancipated the nipple, I'm sure some other paper would have done it before long.

However, I do not like to feel that I was in any way responsible for the current fiercely competitive situation in which the girls in some of our national newspapers get younger and younger and more and more top-heavy and less and less like the girl next door.

This feeling does not, I think, reflect any new-found

puritanism on my part. Nor does it merely reflect the march of time – at least, I hope it doesn't. But in *The Sun* of the seventies we had a firm rule: they had to be *nice* girls. Sleazy pictures were unlikely to see the light of day – not least because Woman's Editor Joyce Hopkirk and her colleagues in the Pacesetters Department had an absolute right of veto.

Not only did my female colleagues have the last word in picture selection, but for a considerable time we had a female caption writer – Patsy Chapman, who was years later to become Deputy Editor of *The Sun* and subsequently Editor of the *News of the World*. In this way we hoped to avoid rugby-club crudities of the 'Whoops, chaps, get an eyeful of these two beauties' variety. To some extent, I think we succeeded. Sadly, the 'rugby club' writers now seem to dominate the caption scene on all those newspapers which carry regular pin-up pictures.

Important though they were to the paper's development – mainly because they got us talked about – I don't think the girls were nearly as significant as was generally supposed. If we left out the Watford dog results the telephone lines ran hot with complaints. To leave out the Page Three girl, which we did from time to time, caused scarcely a ripple. That much having been said, Page Three was tremendous fun.

Contrary to popular belief, regular topless girls were not an ingredient in the editorial mix which got the Soaraway *Sun* off the ground. The evolution of the Page Three girl was a gradual process. In the second issue of *The Sun* the centre spread revealed model Uschi Obermeier's nipples, but Page Three was clean as a whistle.

By Friday of that first week, Page Three almost had a nipple – just a hint of one. On the Saturday, doubt obviously crept in. A half-page pin-up in one edition was fully clothed; in an earlier edition there had been a distinct show of cleavage. On the following Tuesday, nipples were half-seen through a wet shirt.

It was, in fact, a year before the first topless girl appeared on Page Three – a year to the day: 17 November 1970. Which gave *The Sun* every right to introduce its Birthday Suit girl. Her name: Stephanie Rahn. 'We, like our readers, like pretty girls,' read the caption. In the same issue, two nudes were used to illustrate a *Sun* special, How To Pick A Mate. The tradition was established; the Page Three girl was born; the topless pin-up era had dawned.

Many months later whilst I was about my master's business in New York, the girls were moved further back in the paper. But by then Page Three girl was universally understood to mean topless beauty, and everyone soon saw the absurdity of having a Page Three girl on Page Seven.

Many fine photographers contributed to Page Three, including some excellent freelances with international reputations. But the most consistently brilliant was our own Beverley Goodway – who is still clicking away twenty years on. Beverley was a fashion photographer who moved into the Page Three field almost by accident. He started off by doing the odd bikini shot at the end of a fashion session, and gradually realised that his work would gain greater exposure, if that is the right word, if he concentrated on glamour.

'This was a fairly small step for me,' he says. 'I had always been more interested in the model than the clothes. Toplessness seemed of very little consequence, either to me or the girls. Sensuality in pictures tends to come more from the look in a girl's eyes than her precise degree of nudity.

'I learned to flatter models, both to build up their confidence in themselves and their confidence in my ability to photograph them well. I discovered that wet hair often helped to emphasise the shape of a face rather than a bulky style, which tends to hide it.

'I never suffered any flak from the women in my life because of my work. In fact, when I met my wife, in 1971, I took her along to a session with Vivien Neves just to show

her how professional and above-board it all was. It was poor
Viv who found it embarrassing to pose with another girl
looking on.

'I once tried to do a picture of Rita Pennington in the
nude riding a horse into a lake. We hired an elderly and
docile horse and led it to a lake. Almost as an afterthought
we prodded a stick into the lake first to feel the depth. Not
only was it very deep but it had a soft spongy bottom in
which both horse and Rita would have been lost for ever.
We abandoned the shot!

'Once I heard a chap bragging in a pub about his girlfriend
being very beautiful and being a Page Three girl. He said
she had to give up Page Three modelling, however, because
she was being pestered by that lesbian, Beverley Goodway.

'Curiously enough, in the field of topless modelling, some
girls became especially popular because of their long legs.
It was always difficult to make long-legged girls work on
Page Three because of the limitations of space and shape,
but they came off brilliantly on the Centre Spread, especially
on those occasions when you agreed to do it vertically. (To
understand the word 'vertically', in this context, open any
tabloid newspaper at the middle and turn it on end.)

'Two of the most popular girls were Jilly Johnson and
Nina Carter, close friends who had superb figures, lovely
legs and a great sense of humour. They were guaranteed to
liven up the most boring of sessions! Another of the most
popular girls was Gillian Duxbury who was always incredibly
well groomed and had a bottomless wardrobe of erotic
accessories which she wore with an air of total innocence.
They were all very professional.'

For me, the greatest Page Three girl of them all was
Vivien Neves – who once appeared naked in *The Times* in,
of all things, a fertiliser ad. Viv was, and is, gorgeous, though
she now suffers, alas, from multiple sclerosis. Beverley did
not take too many pictures of her, because she acquired a
boyfriend, John Kelly, who was also a photographer, and

reasonably enough reserved exclusive rights for himself. He supplied us with some sensational pictures.

On *The Sun*'s second birthday, in 1971, I asked John for a carefully stunted picture of her which made her look as though she came gift-wrapped, in a see-through plastic box tied with ribbon. He took to the idea immediately. Unfortunately he didn't work all that fast, and he wasn't all that time-conscious. And he didn't start until we were dangerously near close-copy time for the page.

I waited eagerly in my office for the first print as the minutes ticked away. When it landed on my desk it was breathtaking – but I judged it so erotic as to be unusable. My female colleagues, who were usually more daring than I, did not agree.

Four pictures were being developed, I was told. All of them showed Viv on her hands and knees in a pose of a kind we had not previously allowed into the newspaper. I rejected the second print and the third. When the fourth arrived I took a deep breath, decided it was just about decent enough to avoid bringing down the combined wrath of the Chairman and Mary Whitehouse upon my unprotected head, and said: 'Run it.' I don't suppose it would turn a hair nowadays.

Once we got a picture which would at any time have been sensational when Viv was heavily pregnant and posed for us nude in a tin bath, tummy well in evidence. It was a lovely shot of a kind which demonstrated conclusively that there is nothing intrinsically smutty about nudity – and that women really do glow when happily pregnant.

Over the years, we tried every conceivable variation on the Page Three theme. One day I realised that we could get two for the price of one by posing the girls in front of full-length mirrors. Being greatly taken by the success of our early experiments in this direction I commissioned a series of spectacular pictures under the general heading 'The Best Mirror Girls are always in *The Sun*', much to the fury of my old friends at the *Mirror* building in Holborn.

In the same vein, when, under pressure from readers demanding male pin-ups we ran a 'Daily Male' series, we timed it to coincide with the relaunch of the *Daily Mail* as a tabloid, under the heading 'You'll find your Daily Male in *The Sun*'.

At Christmas we posed several girls at a time in tinsel chains and Santa hats and little else. During Test matches we posed them with cricket paraphernalia; during Grand National Week in silks. Well, silk caps anyway. The more the critics jumped up and down, the more popular the feature became.

We launched a Page Three calendar, in full colour, which was an instant sell-out. We marketed Page Three playing cards, with pictures guaranteed to put bridge-playing maiden aunts off their game. And we registered 'Page Three' as a trademark – not that we had any hope of keeping it to ourselves.

When the rival *Star* was launched they carried a series of somewhat crude full-colour topless pictures on Page Seven under the heading 'Starbirds'. But the rest of the world called them Page Three girls – and Page Three is where they eventually ended up.

The *Daily Mirror*, which had published pictures of pretty girls on Page Three for years, found itself torn all sorts of ways. They found it hard to accept that they were being over-hauled in the circulation race for sound journalistic reasons, and preferred to believe that it was all down to toplessness.

This posed something of a problem for them. They couldn't make up their minds whether to stop sneering and copy us or not. First they did, then they didn't. Then they decided on a rather hypocritical compromise. They would print naughty pin-up pictures – suspenders, wet T-shirts, phallic symbols, the lot – but they wouldn't actually uncover the nipple. Nude or not, their pictures never matched the consistent quality of those in *The Sun*. But they were, and are, a great deal more tasteful than Starbirds.

One of the more remarkable things about the history of the Page Three girls is that never at any time did I receive a vestige of a complaint about the behaviour of any *Sun* photographer – or any freelance one – during a nude photo-session. A strong bond of comradeship existed between the girls and the picture-takers, though there was rarely anything sexual in that relationship.

It became commonplace for photographers to tell of models who uninhibitedly asked for their assistance in rubbing out flesh marks left by bra-straps or knicker elastic, or arousing detumescent nipples with a wet face-towel. And the models themselves would come in with ideas for special poses, or props, and discuss their thoughts animatedly with the Picture Editor, Len Hickman, a scholarly, close-to-retirement father-figure who showed a surprising talent for getting the best out of the girls.

Though there was a great deal of fuss made about Page Three by the chattering classes I do not think their indignation was shared by most women – certainly not by the hundreds and hundreds of women who proudly sent us pictures of their daughters.

Few, if any, of these pictures were of immediate use. Natural topless models are a very rare breed. There was a time when we felt there were fewer than fifty who met our requirements on the combined books of all the agencies in London. But from time to time we did get a picture of a stunning girl. Once we were satisfied that Momma was not deceiving us about her age – fourteen, fifteen and sixteen-year-olds were not uncommon, but not acceptable – and that the girl herself was keen, we would arrange a studio session, and invite Momma along. We got some superb pictures, and launched a few careers, in this fashion.

I had very few complaints about Page Three girls except those from totally predictable sources. I cannot recall a single instance of anyone threatening to stop buying the paper if we didn't stop printing topless pictures, though I suppose there must have been some. There were, however, plenty of indications that many women took as much interest in Page Three girls as their men.

Women would write to us on their husband's behalf to ask for pictures of their favourite models as a birthday treat, or to tell us how pretty the girls were. Occasionally, when by accident a story of rape or other male violence towards women appeared on the same page, there were those who suggested that such juxtaposition was not a good idea – and they were usually right. Even so, they tended to write more in sorrow than in anger, because they, like their menfolk, had come to regard the Soaraway *Sun* as *their* newspaper, and to take an almost proprietorial interest in what we were doing.

Had I for one moment had reason to suppose that what we were doing on Page Three was unacceptable to most women I would have stopped it at once. No editor is brave – or foolish – enough deliberately to alienate half his audience.

CHAPTER ELEVEN

The Blockbusters

I don't pretend that we actually invented the technique, but I think *The Sun* was the first daily newspaper effectively to deploy the 'blockbuster' series as a deliberate circulation-builder.

The tactics were simple: buy or create something of significant interest to large numbers of people, spend a lot of money shouting about it on the box – and then run it for several days, structuring the material so that at the end of each day's instalment the heroine is left tied to the railway line with the train approaching. In this way, we reasoned, if by expenditure on television we could persuade the readers to buy the newspaper on one day, the series might hold them for seven or eight. And if we didn't keep them after that, we didn't deserve to.

We kicked off with *The Love Machine*, by Jacqueline Susann, famous for her *Valley of the Dolls*. The idea, I think, came from Anna Murdoch. I wasn't too happy about it to begin with, firstly because Fleet Street history tended to suggest that the serialisation of fiction was rarely successful in terms of reader-gathering, and secondly because the book itself was, by the standards of that time, on the naughty side. I wasn't anxious for the new newspaper to be launched amid a storm of condemnation from irate archbishops.

I was wrong on both counts. Telephone calls, letters from readers and the circulation figures themselves showed that it had been a good idea; the predictable chorus of condemnation served merely, in practice, to bring the newspaper to the attention of many thousands of people who might otherwise never have heard of it.

After this experience, we quickly learned that we could live with hostile publicity. Except in some rather special cases of particular, personal and wounding misrepresentation, we grew to welcome it on the ground that no publicity was bad publicity. Perhaps the most telling example of this basic truth was the story of Ronald Biggs, the Great Train Robber and escapee.

It began on Maundy Thursday, the newspaperman's traditional holiday, the day before Good Friday when no papers were then published in England and Wales. Murdoch had arrived at a *Sun* journalists' party in a dive bar behind Oxford Circus and told me that Ronald Biggs, the robber, on the run from the police, had written his story, and was selling it, through a firm of reputable solicitors in Australia, for the benefit of his children. Should we buy it?

I thought we should. I also thought that if the story was worthwhile, it would be proper to let the police at Scotland Yard see the manuscript. In due course, the manuscript arrived in London, and the office of the Commissioner of Metropolitan Police was invited to send down one or more senior officers to receive it, and to be told about the circumstances in which it came into our possession.

There was only one copy of the manuscript, and this was at all times in the safe custody of *The Sun* or with the Metropolitan Police. The first call to the Commissioner's office was referred to the office of a CID Commander. As a result two officers called at lunchtime one day, at 2 p.m.

Calling on the editor of a morning newspaper at 2 p.m. is likely to be a fruitless task. Finding me, unsurprisingly, out, the officers decided to return to the Yard. A second call to the Yard resulted in Commander Wallace Virgo, the officer in charge of murder and special crimes, paying me a call. He was accompanied by a junior officer.

Until this moment the manuscript had been locked in the

desk of Assistant Editor Norman Baitey. From this copy he and leader writer Henry Douglas had prepared a serialisation for *The Sun*. When that was completed, that, too, was locked away. The original manuscript was handed to Commander Virgo. What I wished to know was whether the thumbprint and signature on each page of the manuscript was that of Ronald Biggs, whether the Yard had any objection to the publication of the series, and whether they had any further comment which might lead to the recapture of the man. Commander Virgo took the manuscript and promised to return with the answers as soon as possible.

Within a very short time, the Editor of a rival newspaper stopped a member of *The Sun* staff and said: 'I hear you're going to publish Biggs's own story.' The closely guarded secret was out.

When Commissioner Virgo returned to my office with the manuscript, he was able to tell me – I had three senior executives at the meeting – that the thumbprint on each page was genuine; that the Yard had no reason to believe that the signature was other than Biggs's own, although, unlike the thumbprint, it could have been copied; and that the Yard had no objection whatever to the publication of the memoirs. When I quizzed him further about this, Commander Virgo said: 'That is a matter for your newspaper.' The manuscript had been seen, he said, by ex-Detective Chief Superintendent Tommy Butler, the man who tracked down the Great Train Robbery gang. And his view, according to Virgo, was that it might well renew interest in Biggs among the general public and lead to new public interest in tracing him and aiding his recapture.

As I said, I had three colleagues at the meeting. I was determined to make sure there was no possibility at any time of any misunderstanding about what was said.

The first criticism came from the London *Evening Standard*. In the Londoners' Diary, a gossip column much read in Fleet Street at the time, appeared this comment: 'Scotland

Yard views with great concern the publishing of Biggs's exploits. They feel that criminals who achieve notoriety this way will only get the idea that the bigger their crime, the greater their chance of making money out of their stories.'

When I complained to the Editor of the *Standard*, Charles Wintour, pointing out the facts, he took this line: 'The opinion of Scotland Yard officers actually entrusted with the task of catching Biggs is quite different from the alleged views of the "very senior officers" mentioned by Mr Lamb.

'Further, it is the opinion of Sir John Waldron that the publication of such stories involving fees paid to criminals and their families, is an anti-social act. Finally, the action of *The Sun* is contrary to the spirit of the Press Council ruling: "The Council deplores publication of personal articles of an unsavoury nature by persons who had been concerned in criminal acts or vicious conduct."'

The always holier-than-thou *Sunday Times* quoted a Scotland Yard spokesman as saying: 'The Commissioner has expressed his concern in the past at senior criminals being seen to profit from crime. That comment can be taken as applying in this case.'

Dog eating dog is healthy enough, but here was a hint of rabies. It became clear that Sir John Waldron, the Commissioner, did not even know that *The Sun* had provided the Yard with the Biggs manuscript in advance. Nor did the anonymous Yard spokesman. And Wintour did not know that it was Virgo who called on me, and that Virgo was in fact one of the 'very senior' officers actually entrusted with the task of catching Biggs. So each of them, instead of ascertaining the facts, had merely leapt upon the *Sun*-bashing bandwagon.

I was rather sad about Wintour. A good editor himself, in a headmasterish sort of way, he was over-fond of treating the rest of us like juvenile delinquents. Perhaps he, and the other critics, would have been better employed trying to solve another mystery: what happened to the Biggs manuscript? The Great Train Robbery was less puzzling than the Great Manuscript Mystery. There was only one copy. That had gone to the Yard and been returned, after checks by fingerprint, handwriting and other experts.

Immediately before we began serialisation, the *News of the World* announced the 'great crime scoop' and said: 'Tomorrow our sister paper, the lively young *Sun*, begins the serialisation of the memoirs of Great Train Robber Ronald Biggs. And already the jackals of Fleet Street are yapping at our heels. Newspaper groups who have failed to obtain the series are suggesting that it is somehow 'antisocial' to publish it.

'At the same time, certain papers, with supreme hypocrisy, are busy carrying long 'spoiling' stories alleged to be based on the Biggs manuscript. Let them be warned. The public is not easily fooled.'

But what a *brouhaha* there was. The *Daily Express* said it 'has not – and would not – pay any sum of money to either Biggs, his family, or associates for the right to publish his story'. The story was so disgraceful that the *Express* then said, 'turn to page 7,' where they published alleged extracts from the oh-so-naughty story. It was wrong to pay for it, but all right to steal it, apparently. The *Daily Express* made no mention of its stablemate, the *Sunday Express*, who paid out money for master-spy Kim Philby's memoirs, written from Russia, where he was out of the range of the law. No one tried to explain why it was so much more wicked to publish a train robber's story and give the money to his children, than to publish those of a traitor, ensuring that the money went to him via his Paris agents.

Others joined the outcry. Maurice (dial-a-quote) Edelman, Labour MP for Coventry North, himself a journalist, put down a question in the House of Commons, calling on the Home Secretary to 'make illegal, as being contrary to the public interest, the publication of the memoirs of living criminals, either for personal gain or for the financial benefit of relatives or others designated by them'. He clearly believed that the sins of the fathers should be visited on the children.

The National Union of Journalists in conference at Harrogate carried an emergency motion deploring the publication, and decided to report the paper to the Press Council. Mr Denys Tuckett, chairman of the union's ethics committee, agreed that the union owned Murdoch a debt for saving *The Sun* and the jobs of many of its members, but he added: 'He must realise that if he works in Britain he must respect our standards and our basis of journalism.'

John Gordon, the *Sunday Express* columnist, took a different view. He said, *inter alia*: 'My fellow journalists, acting corporately as the NUJ, pass a resolution condemning the publication. A predictable decision on a rather emotional matter. But I don't agree with it.

'Personally, I think the story has two things in its favour. It proves that crime doesn't pay, even for the biggest criminals. Which is a sound moral lesson. It proves also that the robbers were a collection of thugs who deserved every year of the sentences they got.'

Whatever they all thought, it was a highly successful series. Together with *Love Story*, the oh-so-pure story of American college love which we ran around the same time, the Biggs story was a sensation.

With police combing the four corners of the world for him, the thirty-eight-year-old criminal produced the first blow by blow account of the Great Train Robbery. In incredible detail he told how he had been going straight when he bumped into Bruce Reynolds, another robber, who asked him how he would like a very nice piece of business, with at least £40,000 as his whack. Then, everything – the planning and execution of the robbery, the search, the arrests, the trial, his dramatic escape from prison and his years on the run.

A week after the train raid, detectives searching for

Reynolds called on Biggs. As they searched his house, Biggs's own share of the loot – well over £100,000 in used notes – lay hidden under a pile of coal in the coal shed. Biggs also told of three men who went free because they kept their gloves on, of how a man then in prison as one of the train robbers was not guilty, of his own underworld route from Wandsworth jail, via a plastic surgery clinic in Paris, to freedom in Australia, of the man who on his way to help steal the fabulous £2,500,000 was worried to learn that the Land-Rover in which he was riding to the big hit had itself been stolen. And, for the first time, Biggs, whose share had risen from £40,000 to £100,000, revealed that the haul was much, much bigger than any of the gang had dreamed.

Sadly, two days after the series in *The Sun* began, gang-buster Tommy Butler died from cancer. He knew he was dying, and he had chosen to go into Westminster Hospital, and out again, whenever he pleased, knowing that there was no hope. When he learned that *The Sun* had delivered the Biggs manuscript to a Yard officer, the retired superintendent left the hospital and went round to the Yard. He studied the document, made notes, and returned to his death bed. There he died without achieving his ambition. He had vowed he would not rest until he had all the gang behind bars. And the dream which had driven him on for fifteen months beyond his retirement, was the recapture of Biggs. He had recaptured some of the most elusive robbers and his legendary crime-busting activities were aided by a phenomenal memory, which led one colleague to describe him as a 'walking criminal records office'. He had publicly warned Biggs that his pursuit had not ended.

Knowing he was dying, Butler raised no objection to *The Sun* keeping Biggs in the public eye. He knew that his prodigious memory, always at the service of the Yard, might have been aided by any clue, however small, in the Biggs memoirs, or from information which arose out of them. Nor did he raise any objection about money from the Biggs story going in trust to the children of the robber, which I had insisted upon. For the 'Guv'nor', as Butler was known, was always the first to help the innocents in a crook's family. At the end of his trial, train robber Reynolds instructed his lawyer to thank Butler publicly in open court for the 'kindness and courtesy' he had extended to his wife and child.

None of these facts was taken into account by any of the critics, certainly not by the Press Council, that shrivelled fig-leaf which, it is widely, if not altogether accurately, believed, newspaper proprietors invented themselves to cover their more disgraceful excesses. A body without teeth, it can only uphold complaints or reject them, and admonish or condemn the guilty parties. They had found nothing wrong with the wives of two train robbers, Reynolds and Edwards, writing their stories, but had condemned the publication of stories by Wilson's wife. Why? Because the Press Council found them 'sensational'.

My argument about *The Sun* series was that no payment was made to Biggs. On the contrary, elaborate arrangements were made to ensure that he was unable to benefit directly. The crime was of a wholly exceptional character, and there was no doubt that it aroused a demand for serious information among the public at large. Secondly, no attempt was made to 'sensationalise' the Biggs story. On the contrary, apart from certain deletions on the grounds of taste, the story was told exactly as he had written it. As *The Sun* had been at pains to point out, the real lesson of the memoirs was the futility, rather than the glamour, of crime. The Great Train Robbers were revealed for what they were, a set of bungling, small-time crooks, most of whom were behind bars. And Biggs himself, though still on the run, was in constant fear of arrest.

The Press Council relied heavily on the Establishment's dislike of the very word 'sensation' – even though they clearly didn't know the meaning of it. If the story is big enough it is by definition sensational. Even though what we printed were Biggs's words, the Council said *The Sun*'s offence was aggravated by the 'sensational' nature of the display, headlines and text. They meant we had done it properly. The article should have been written, they said, in a way that did not glamorise the crime or the criminal. Presumably, if *The Sun* had printed a toned-down story, and run it under boring headlines with tedious display, no offence would have been committed.

Curiously, the Press Council did not take up the case of the *Daily Sketch* and the Great Manuscript Mystery. The only copy of Biggs's story, kept under lock and key, except when it was in the possession of the police, was duly returned to *The Sun*. But on the day the series began, the *Daily Sketch* also began publishing extracts from the story. Even parts of the story which *The Sun* had deleted, on grounds of taste, were included.

Further, on the hypocritical pretext of condemning Biggs, and of throwing doubt upon his story, they persuaded Sir Ranulph 'Rasher' Bacon, the former deputy commissioner of Scotland Yard, to provide a dissection of the series. They did not, alas, explain how Sir Ranulph, a shrewd policeman, even in retirement, came into possession of the document on which he was commenting, or whether he asked the *Sketch* how they came to have it in their hands.

I point no fingers here. I make no charge. I have no evidence. The Great Manuscript Mystery remains just that.

Mr Murdoch and I took – or, more precisely, sought – legal advice on what was clearly an outrageous breach of copyright. But the distinguished lawyer we consulted – Lord Hailsham, no less – was of no help. He was so shocked by the whole thing that he advised us to halt publication of the series. I am sure his advice was well intentioned. But what we were looking for was a way of stopping the *Sketch* from publishing it.

In fact, their 'spoiler', and that in the *Daily Express*, did us no harm at all. Our calculations showed that we put on around 170,000 copies during the Biggs period, the *Daily Express* remained in rapid decline and the *Sketch* moved closer to its inevitable doom.

What other memorable series did we carry in those early, heady days? *Who Killed Hanratty?*, a brilliant account by that well-known socialist worker, Paul Foot, of the celebrated A6 murder; the shooting of Valerie Storey, the killing of her lover, Michael Gregsten, the arrest, trial, conviction and hanging of James Hanratty, and the almost inevitable conclusion that there had been a grave miscarriage of justice, we ran at considerable length.

We did the deal with Paul in the Café Royal Grill. Paul neglected to wear a tie, but did not allow his principles to stop him eating and drinking expansively and expensively, with every appearance of enjoyment. The fee was high, for that time. Years later, Paul was to write disparagingly of journalists who 'fed at the Murdoch trough'. It would be charitable to assume that the occasion when he fed there himself had slipped his memory.

In the very early days one of the braver things we did was to run a series of articles by Liz Prosser on cervical cancer, 'The Women who die of Embarrassment'. It is hard to believe nowadays, but in 1970, both 'cervix' and 'cancer' were dirty words – and certainly had no place in the pages of a family newspaper.

Liz tackled the job with conviction, style and flair. So much so, that the Women's National Cancer Control Campaign reproduced the series, together with our leading article on the subject, as a leaflet which was distributed to hospitals and maternity clinics nationwide.

The Sun said:

There is just one smear campaign that *The Sun* is ready to support. The campaign to persuade more and more women to take the two-minute cervical smear test that can save their lives. Read, in our centre pages, the pathetic story of women

who have died of embarrassment, because they thought there
was something not quite nice about the test.

Or other women who are dying of embarrassment because
they think there is something not quite nice about treatment
they know they need.

Read about them. But don't add to their numbers.

Cancer is an emotive word. There are still people who would
rather not know. And cancer of the cervix is especially
intimate and especially difficult to talk about. Or even to
think about.

. . . More women are taking the test now. But there are more
still who should and don't.

The test can be arranged through a family doctor, a hospital,
or a clinic. It costs little or nothing. It takes only a couple of
minutes.

Women owe it to themselves to take this test. They owe it
to their husbands and families too.

Commented Professor Hugh McClaren, head of Obstetrics
and Gynaecology at the University of Birmingham: 'Excellent. In good taste, whilst still getting the message across.'
Said gynaecologist Josephine Barnes, Chairman of the
Women's National Cancer Control Campaign: 'It was cour-
ageous and far-sighted of *The Sun* to express contemporary
medical thought in this fashion.'

Mind you, not all *Sun* series delighted the Establishment.
The Sensuous Woman, by Jane Garrity, an American how-to-
do-it book on how to get, please and keep your man, was
somewhat explicit in the pleasing him area. So much so,
that the copies I had asked for from New York were seized
by the Customs people at Heathrow and impounded until
such time as they had read the book and decided whether
or not it was pornographic.

A second consignment, ordered the same day from our
New York office, slipped through the net. The eagle-eyed
Excise men had not thought of this cunning ploy. And they
were still reading the first batch when I sent them page
proofs of *The Sun*'s serialisation to save their time! Their

silly behaviour, of course, gave the series, and the newspaper, masses of free publicity.

The indescribably boring *Guardian*, whose news columns, then as now, were full of opinion, and whose opinion columns were full of cotton wool, called it a 'lurid sex manual' and accused us of having 'Bowdlerised' it.

The Sun said at the time: 'There are sections of this book which are not suitable for publication in a family newspaper. These sections will not appear in *The Sun*. But it's the book that every woman will want to read. It's the book that could change your life. It's the book that could save your marriage.' I know, because of the hundreds of letters I received over the next few months, that *The Sun*'s serialisation of *The Sensuous Woman did* change lives, and *did* save marriages.

There were many other great series over the years, some light, some heavy, some sexy, some not. What became clear very early on was that how-to-do-it books, and especially how-to-do-it-in-bed books, were guaranteed to put on sale, much of which stuck. There was clearly a hunger for knowledge about these things which no one had previously sought to satisfy. *The Sun*, obligingly, stepped into the gap.

CHAPTER TWELVE

There's Always More FUN in The Sun

No news is good news. That is why, when well-meaning souls have, from time to time, tried to produce newspapers full of good news, they have invariably fallen flat on their faces. For the fact is that newspapers – national newspapers, anyway – are not in business to record the norm. Death and disaster are the media's bread and butter.

Good news on a staggering scale – say, for example, a Super-power agreement to scrap a whole armoury of nuclear weapons – will not sell a copy of most newspapers. But a major disaster – Lockerbie, Clapham Junction, the M1 jet crash are fresh in the mind as I write – sends sales shooting up even when, as often happens, the news has received saturation coverage on the box throughout the previous evening. Such coverage, in fact, far from depressing newspaper sales, actually seems to stimulate them.

But even whilst dealing with major tragedies in as much detail as the occasion demanded, we always used to insist that, on most days, there was a deliberate injection of FUN in the paper.

I had for years carried around in my head, whilst I worked on the *Daily Mirror* and elsewhere, a fairly clear idea of the kind of newspaper I would like to produce. I think every journalist has such an idea. I was lucky enough to meet the man with the money – and the vision – to help me test my theories.

And an essential part of the pattern in my mind was balance. If the leads on Pages Two, Four and Six were 'hard' news, and they often were, we looked for something more light-hearted on Three, Five and Seven. Most other newspapers, it seemed to me, were much too dour. It didn't ever stop us giving all the big news – and giving it saturation treatment when it was necessary – but it did ensure that on most days it was hard to turn a page without finding something to smile at.

There was no dearth of mirth in the Soaraway *Sun*. Perhaps the best example of the newspaper's impudent, cheerful, bumper-full-of-fun-book approach was the story of Sowerby Bridge.

If Sowerby Bridge is neither known nor remembered for anything else it has a very important place in newspaper history. It achieved that historic niche the day Stanley Robinson, the town's librarian, discovered that the then new tabloid *Sun* newspaper would not readily fit the rods which held newspapers in the public reading room of his library. It could therefore be easily stolen.

He dutifully reported this to the chairman of the Library Committee, Councillor Cecil Grenshaw, who, with an eye on the ratepayers' money, noted that the paper cost 5d before decimalisation and would probably cost three new pence after D-for-decimalisation-Day. Besides, he had been choosing books for the people of Sowerby Bridge for thirty-nine years, and at the age of seventy-eight, had come to the conclusion that *The Sun* was too sexy for the local inhabitants. As a result, with the committee's approval, the newspaper would be dismissed from the public reading room.

Our local reporter thought the story worth a couple of paragraphs. But it was a quiet night, and we decided to have some fun with it. At evening conference we evolved the headline: 'The Silly Burghers of Sowerby Bridge'.

We rushed a story into the paper, backed up by quotes from as many interested parties as we could contact. We wrote an indignant leading article. And on impulse, I switched the paper's star reporter, Jon Akass, from Spandau

Prison in Berlin, where he was waiting to interview Rudolf
Hess, off to the West Riding, where Sowerby Bridge nestled
sleepily on the banks of the Calder, in blissful ignorance of
the storm which was about to break.

The first night's story said:

> Your Super, Super *Sun* has been banned from the public
> reading room at – wait for it – Sowerby Bridge, Yorkshire.
> Why? Because, apparently, it is the wrong SHAPE to suit
> the librarian, Mr Stanley Robinson.
> And because, according to the chairman of the Library
> Committee, Councillor Cecil Grenshaw, it 'places too much
> emphasis on sex'.
>
> Well, well, well . . .
> The ban was approved by the council after Councillor Gren-
> shaw said: 'The practice of boosting the sex side influenced
> both the librarian and me.
> 'We are getting far too much of these things nowadays,' the
> 78-year-old councillor added.
> At his home in Luddenden Foot, near Halifax, last night,
> he said: 'The basic reason for not taking *The Sun* is the cost.
> 'But I was asked by the librarian whether I thought it carried
> too much sex and, quiet frankly, I had to agree.'
> Mr Robinson, who actually recommended the ban, ex-
> plained: 'I showed the committee six sample copies and they
> agreed with me that it is not the sort of paper they want. It
> is rubbish.
> 'Also,' he added, 'the shape of tabloids is wrong. They will
> not fit on the special rods and they can easily be stolen.'
> . . . Still, they're not all silly burghers in Sowerby Bridge.
> Local MP Mr Douglas Houghton, chairman of the Parlia-
> mentary Labour Party, criticised the decision. Library com-
> mittees are 'servants of the public' he said.

In a leader headed 'The Price of Freedom' we poured scorn
on the Silly Burghers. 'Fortunately,' we said, 'there are
plenty of newsagents in the Calder Valley. They sell *The
Sun*. They sell more copies than ever before. 'Fivepence is
the price of freedom.'

Akass waded in next day.

We should be thrown out of better places than this. Sowerby Bridge, the town that has banished *The Sun* from its public library, is a glum pimple on the face of the Pennines.

It is a sad place with a bankrupt Co-op, two derelict cinemas, and a café that closes sharp at 6.30 p.m.

. . . The only jeweller's and watchmaker's shop is about to shut. Every year at least 3 per cent of the population move out, mostly the young. It is a town with a bad case of hardened arteries.

The people, mind, are nice. But the place is run by know-it-alls who stare blankly at barren hills while you talk to them on their frigid doorsteps.

These councillors seem firmly opposed to sex – perhaps due to the snow, the cold and damp, and the general austerity of their surroundings.

There are occasional excitements. In the winter they cover the municipal swimming baths and make it into a dance hall. On December 18, they had a dance there. The Youth Council refused to push a request for a drinks licence. About 50 sober people turned up and there were two fights.

Nothing much has happened in Sowerby Bridge since then, except that they have banned *The Sun*.

I don't wish to exaggerate this, since I clearly have an interest, but the people of Sowerby Bridge do appear to be genuinely and spontaneously indignant about the ban.

. . . Two local millworkers, John McCreery, aged 29, and James McPartling, aged 28, this morning went to the library and offered to donate *The Sun* for free, if the library would accept it.

The chief librarian, Stanley Robinson, agreed to recommend to the Library Committee that the offer be accepted.

Mr Robinson is a chummy man. When reporters came in out of the cold he gave them mugs of Bovril.

He is a nice, stooping, scholarly man who has not heard of Philip Roth or *Portnoy's Complaint* and thinks London is provincial.

Today he abandoned the pretence that the banishment was

enforced because tabloid newspapers do not fit on to the rods in the reading room. Other libraries have had no trouble with similar mechanics.

What he told me today was: 'The business with the rods was nonsense. What we wanted here was a balance. *The Sun* did not have this balance. There is nothing political about this. We still take the *Morning Star*.'

The council chairman, Councillor Walter Turner, has a small moustache and is wrapped from head to foot in tweed.

He lives in a house called Gordon Bank on a steep chill hill and he said: 'The Library Committee have made their decision and that's that. I have looked at *The Sun* and the first three pages were all sex. We do not need this in Sowerby Bridge.'

Sowerby Bridge council is famous locally for its eccentricity. This Tuesday, for example, they rejected an invitation to join the Yorkshire and Humberside Clean Up Campaign, a scheme designed to clear away the muck. Undoubtedly the place could have done with a wash.

. . . If you want a town that is opposite to dynamic, try Sowerby Bridge.'

It was vintage Akass – illustrated by pictures of five pretty, laughing, mini-skirted girls, all from Sowerby Bridge.

The Silly Burghers refused to budge – and we refused to give up. First, we offered to pay for library copies of the newspaper. Then we offered to buy suitable filing rods to prevent it being stolen.

Then we announced a new contest – Win a Free Weekend in Sowerby Bridge (Second Prize, Win a Week in Sowerby Bridge). And we asked the readers to say, in not more than a hundred words, just why the town fathers had been wrong to ban the paper.

The Silly Burghers took it in good part. They were ready to roll out the red carpet for the winner. She was a lady who lived in Lichfield, Staffordshire, and she declined the prize because of a remarkable coincidence. To the amusement of Fleet Street, if not the Calder Valley, she explained: 'Don't

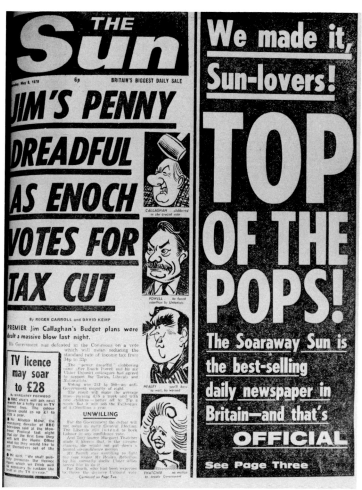

WE MADE IT! The page that says it all. After more than eight years of blood, sweat and tears, *The Sun* finally topples the *Daily Mirror* from its perch, having for the first time outsold its rival every day for six months.

COMING SOON! Rupert Murdoch at a pre-launch Press
Conference in October, 1969. On the left, author Larry Lamb, not in
disguise, but struggling to cope with an eye infection. On the right,
Deputy Editor, Bernard Shrimsley.

ON THE STONE: Compositors assemble hot metal type in *The
Sun's* Composing Room. The bench on which they are working was
traditionally made of stone. This area of a modern Composing
Room – even now that hot metal, too, has vanished from the scene –
is still known by the old name.

WHOSE FINGER ON THE BUTTON? Anna Murdoch pushes the control which should have started the presses on launch night. Such was the power of the Press unions at that time that Anna had formally to be made an honorary member of NATSOPA before the brethren would permit the owner's wife to push a button in their machine room. When she did push it, the presses didn't start.

MUCH, MUCH LATER: Rupert and Anna at the Anglo-Australian Bicentenary Ball in 1988. As a distinguished guest, with automatic access to the VIP door, Rupert characteristically insisted on joining the queue.

TOP PEOPLE'S PERSON: January 1981 – and Rupert has just made his bid for *The Times,* the paper his father once declined to edit. As ever KRM contrives to look remarkably unperturbed.

YOUR MOVE, MUM: Dame Elisabeth Murdoch, Rupert's mother, starts the presses at the launch of the Digger's latest venture, the *Sunday Australian,* in Sydney, in 1971. Dame Elisabeth still exerts a strong influence on Rupert's 'up-market' activities in Australia.

WHERE WE WERE: The front steps of *The Sun* and the *News of the World* offices in Bouverie Street, London EC4. The building was erected on the site of an ancient monastery.

ALL TOGETHER NOW: Sir Larry Lamb (*right*) with Industrial Editor Keith Mason, Prime Minister James Callaghan, and the General Secretary of the TUC, Mr Len Murray, at the Trades Union Congress of 1977. Considering the abuse the newspaper had so often heaped on the heads of these two luminaries, it was good of them to pose for this picture on the occasion of Keith's last Congress, owing to impending retirement.

END OF THE ROAD: Premier Harold Wilson, with his wife, Mary on the night of his disastrous General Election defeat in June 1970. *Sun* photographer Arthur Steele grabbed this brilliant shot as he overtook the Premier's car on the M1 at 70 m.p.h. (honest!).

WHO'S A PRETTY PUSS, THEN? Vivien Neves, possibly the greatest topless model of them all, clearly never heard that one should not take the stage with children or animals. This was the shot used for the legendary 'Win Vivien Neves' contest. Lovely kitten, isn't it?

GLITTER GIRL: Jeweller's daughter Gillian Duxbury was a great favourite with *Sun* readers – and with *Sun* photographers. Always smiling, always helpful, always fun – and as close to the male concept of the perfect shape as any woman has a right to be.

LADY IN WAITING: Vivien again – very much with child, and demonstrating beyond all doubt that women really do glow when happily pregnant.

TOP PEOPLE'S PIN-UP: Long before *The Sun* made the phrase
'Page Three girl' part of the English language, readers of the Top
People's Paper, *The Times*, had been treated to – or infuriated by –
this sensational picture of Vivien Neves. It wasn't in the editorial
columns, however. It was in a full-page advertisement. For
fertilisers!

THE Sun

Thursday, May 3, 1979   7p   TODAY'S TV: PAGES 12 and 13

The first day of the rest of our lives

THIS IS D-DAY. D for Decision. The first day of the rest of our lives.

The Sun today wishes particularly to address itself to traditional supporters of the Labour Party, and to those people who have not hitherto had the opportunity to vote in a General Election.

We are particularly well qualified to do so.

The roots of The Sun are planted deep among the working class.

We are proud to have a working class readership. The LARGEST working class readership of any daily paper.

We are equally proud of the fact that we have more young readers than any of our contemporaries.

Both young people and traditional Labour Party supporters tend to be idealists. And The Sun is an idealistic newspaper.

We firmly believe in that system of Government which offers the

PAGE ONE OPINION

greatest good to the greatest number.

That is precisely why, on this momentous occasion, we firmly advise our readers to **VOTE TORY.**

The Sun is not a Tory newspaper.

Indeed, alone among popular national newspapers, it can safely lay claim to being independent.

We have, at various times, advised
CONTINUED ON PAGE TWO

A message to Labour supporters

VOTE TORY THIS TIME

IT'S THE ONLY WAY TO STOP THE ROT

It's Maggie by a whisker, say the polls   PAGE THREE

D-FOR-DECISION DAY: Page One of *The Sun* on May 3, the date of the 1979 General Election. Not everyone in the organisation thought we were striking the right note. Many people forecast that it would cost *The Sun* many readers. It didn't.

be daft, lad. Why would I want to go to Sowerby Bridge? I was born there.' In the circumstances, we were happy to provide a cash alternative.

Sowerby Bridge was unrepentant. Despite all our efforts – and we returned to the subject from time to time – they kept the paper out of the library for sixteen months. It was restored, ironically, when the Conservatives were swept from office in the council elections of 1971.

Here is how we told the story:

> *Phew!* The Sun *shines again in Sowerby Bridge*
> *Home of the not-so-silly burghers*

The Sun came back to Sowerby Bridge yesterday.

It was the end of a 16-month ban on the paper at the Yorkshire town's public library.

The ban had been imposed by the town council when it was controlled by the Conservatives.

They said the paper was too sexy. They said it was too dear. They even claimed it was the wrong size.

And *The Sun* called them 'silly burghers'.

But despite protests, they kept *The Sun* out of the reading room.

Then Labour swept to power in this year's council elections. They decided that what Sowerby Bridge wanted was – *The Sun*.

The council's chairman, Councillor Allan Pettengell, said yesterday: 'We want the public to be free to enjoy its contents, because it is a newspaper both readable and highly informative.'

At the time of the ban Councillor Pettengell had protested on the ground that he thought it – the ban, that is – politically motivated. It is always possible that the decision to restore it was made on similar grounds!

The Silly Burghers were not the only people with whom we had fun. When the Right Honourable Lord Longford gave up hope of ever achieving high governmental office, he went into the business of morals. First, he recruited a committee of fifty-two 'names', and then had published, as a 'truly collective effort', The Longford Report on Pornography. Although it was produced by a publishing house other than his own, it was still very much a private enterprise – an unofficial, uninhibited and unbalanced catalogue of the naughty things in life which should never be mentioned in popular newspapers but which were all right if one could spare 60p for the paperback report of the noble Lord.

Not surprisingly, Lord Longford, playing King Canute on the shore of the vast sea of permissiveness, cast his net wide and far. He publicly toured Soho's sleazy bookshops, was photographed with a copy of the *Encyclopaedia of Spanking*, flew to Copenhagen and saw for himself, with cameras in attendance, the supermarkets of orgiastic equipment. In London, he took in *The Dirtiest Show in Town* and the musicals *Hair* and *Oh! Calcutta!* He read *Fanny Hill*. Then he took a sideswipe at that popular organ of public opinion, *The Sun* newspaper.

His 'truly collective' report declared: 'The Press Council, though it may have here and there restricted journalistic excesses, has, after all, not prevented *The Sun* and the *News of the World* from thriving on the uninhibited presentation of Mr Rupert Murdoch's particular Antipodean blend of erotica.'

Nothing to do with pornography, mark you. Just another gratuitous piece of *Sun*-bashing, the kind of smearsault – assault by smear – which appeals to the professional knocker. What was more curious, however, was why Longford had chosen this particular butt among his vast and nasty array of ugly, corruptive and dangerous magazines and books. He had been courteously received by myself and the Chairman when he sought our views, and invited to point to anything remotely pornographic in either newspaper: he failed to do so.

We decided to have a gentle go at His Lordship. Faithfully

we summarised the report, including the reference to Anti-podean erotica, whatever that meant. The next day we had a picture of a naked lady upside down. The Sunbird from Down Under. 'It's that old Antipodean erotica again,' said the caption.

Then we promised a special bonus. 'Don't miss your Antipodean Erotica Kit,' we said. 'You can win it only in *The Sun*, tomorrow.' At that time we didn't know what the kit would contain. We just promised it, as with so many things, knowing that if we were irretrievably committed the ideas would come.

Next day, we had a picture of another naked lady on a splendid four-poster bed. The bed – not the lady – was offered as a contest prize together with black linen sheets, a musk candle, champagne, oysters, sunbed, stereo with bedside controls, a two-month supply of vitamin pills and much, much more.

Whilst Lord Longford was still brooding about the precise wording of his letter of complaint we upset him even further, with a special offer of pillow-cases with a picture of the then fashionable heart-throb Donny Osmond, under the headline: 'Go to bed with Donny Osmond'.

So great was his indignation that he couldn't wait to write to me about this one, and telephoned. As patiently as I could, I explained that it was a very small joke, and in my considered opinion a perfectly harmless one. His Lordship refused to be appeased. 'Be warned, I am watching you,' were his final words. He had watched *Oh! Calcutta!*, too, but it didn't seem to have done the show any harm.

We seemed to be making a habit of offending members of Their Lordships' House. One day, up popped Lord Beswick, a former Captain of the Honourable Corps of Gentlemen at Arms, and at the time chief Labour spokesman in the Lords, to declare: 'I do not now include *The Sun* among my morning newspapers.'

'Never mind, folks,' we chortled happily, on Page One,

'we'll just have to soldier on without him. All umpteen million of us.'

Later, with the usual Saturday morning list of the following week's goodies, we addressed an open letter to his Lordship.

> Dear Lord Beswick,
> We know you don't read *The Sun*. You said so in the House of Lords the other day.
> May we suggest that you abandon your penance next week. Just for a week. Because next week *The Sun* really will be even more special than usual.
> And after a week, we don't think you'll be able to kick the habit. We are going to serialise *Who Killed Hanratty?*, probably the most sensational book of the decade. We also have a significant series which will set every woman talking. The series is called 'The Virgin Wives'. It's a cracker. You can also play *Sun* bingo. There's a super new plan for getting rid of excess weight without going hungry. And there's a bargain tights offer. See the *News of the World* tomorrow for more exciting details. We'll be glad to have you aboard.

As usual there was something for everyone in the package. One would have had to be a very dull Lord indeed not to find FUN in *The Sun*.

CHAPTER THIRTEEN

Sex and the Soaraway Sun

You will have heard the story about the patient who was asked by his psychiatrist for a verbal reaction to three drawings, one a straight line, one a circle and one a triangle. Each time he responded immediately: 'Sex.'

'You're sex-mad,' said the doctor.

'*I'm* sex-mad?' replied the patient. 'What about you and your dirty pictures?'

In serious tests, I have known psychiatrists who showed patients a picture of a pretty girl in a state of undress side by side with a volume of the *Encyclopaedia Britannica*, which happened to be the same size, and were surprised to find that normal women, as well as 'normal' men – the kind *The Sun* used to call red-blooded – looked at the picture first.

The Sun was in many ways fortunate to be born in an age of permissiveness. Society needed a newspaper which recognised it and was a part of it – without ever being ahead of it. *The Sun* recognised the permissive society, acknowledged its existence, but was never obsessed by it. It was the critics, not *The Sun*, who were obsessed with sex.

This outspoken new newspaper, unlike its predecessor, genuinely born of the age we live in, was staffed entirely by people who remembered a time when it wasn't done to mention in a newspaper such topics as contraception and abortion. When even the prettiest girl did not have a bosom. When the word 'rape' was among the four-letter words banned by most newspapers. But these are issues of considerable interest and importance. And the pages of a popular newspaper are a perfectly proper place in which to raise them – not least because very often people who most need to be informed read nothing else.

Of course, we tried hard to be amusing as well as informative. Sex is a serious business, but it deserves to be laughed at. I recall medical reporter Leslie Toulson approaching the News Desk in high excitement on Day Three of *The Sun*'s existence. He had unearthed a story concerning a group of doctors in Edinburgh who had established beyond doubt that men are better lovers in the morning.

'Page One, Column One,' I said at that evening's conference. 'White on black headline: "Men are better lovers in the morning – official".' As Toulson himself said, it would have been hard for him to get the story into the old *Sun* in any form, let alone on Page One.

The story itself was saucy but informative. And it was to set a new pace in medical reporting, persuading stuffier rivals to lift their unspoken bans on the publication of explicitly sexual medical information. Wrote Toulson:

> Never mind the music and the moonlight. The best time for romance is the morning – and that's official. For when a man wakes up he is at his best for sex, say scientists. While his loving ability is lowest at eight in the evening – the traditional time when a young man's fancy turns to courting.
>
> This remarkable discovery, which could become the latest excuse for being late for work, has been made at the Clinical Endocrinology Unit, Edinburgh, after experiments. And the experiments were carried out with the help of doctors and – wait for it – monks.
>
> . . . Regular sex can step up the potency of men, but experiments with volunteer monks showed that it is not necessary to have sex to be a he-man. Indeed, nine of the eleven monks tested had a higher than average level of male hormone.

Sex was news. The paper did not invent it. Discussion of sexual matters had become publicly acceptable, therefore the paper had a duty to publish it, with taste, and a sense of proportion. We set out to discover why men and women 'turn on' members of the opposite gender, and who turned on the readers most. Were men more sexy in the south? What do the top people think about sex? Prince Philip, Lord Hailsham, Mrs Mary Whitehouse, and Brigid Brophy, and more, were all quoted on the subject. And the critics continued their charge that the paper, and presumably the paper alone, was obsessed with it.

The truth was that sex was dealt with in the paper with adult responsibility. There was no room for the leer, the sneer and the snigger. As leader writer Henry Douglas pointed out in an editorial: 'It's easier to stay innocent about sex if you know about it. Otherwise it becomes a taboo and an obsession – as it became for many parents who weren't told enough soon enough.'

Douglas was the perfect answer to the wilder critics on questions of sex and permissiveness in *The Sun*. He hoisted the ensign of parental responsibility when he penned this opinion on a particularly way-out book about teenage sex which caused a great stir at the time.

The voice of our teenage children speaks loud across the generation gap: 'Dad, may I borrow the car?' Old hat, say schoolteacher authors Maurice Hill and Michael Lloyd-Jones. What our teenagers ought to ask is 'Mum, may we borrow the double bed?' And what we ought to reply is: 'Of course, dear'.

Well you can count me out on that. Maybe I am a stuffy fuddy-duddy by the lights of the National Secular Society, who publish the Hill and Lloyd-Jones 5s. booklet, *Sex and Education: The Erroneous Zone*. But at least I do have five children, aged between eleven and 18. Maurice Hill is 46 and unmarried, Michael Lloyd-Jones is in his twenties, married and childless.

Schoolmasters they may be. But I decline their teaching that I ought to encourage my daughter to be somebody's mistress. I think the booklet is liable to do a great deal of

harm to teenagers. And I question whether it has any literary
merit.

There will never be a last word on sex. Even in *The Sun*.
But as long as experts talked responsibly about sex and
sexual problems, the newspaper would, as a matter of duty,
report them. Letters to the Editor, problems put to the
paper's advice bureau, indicated to a growing degree that
the people often found comfort, and the end of needless
anxiety, when reading *The Sun*'s frank reports. And this in
the paper so often attacked for its attention to the subject.

If they had bothered to read the paper, the critics might
have noticed that as it entered the seventies, Elizabeth
Prosser, top woman's writer, later to become Woman's
Editor, welcomed the decade with this attitude towards
permissiveness:

> A little more love and a little less sex. That's my maxim for
> the Seventies. But those who have been caught up in the
> demanding Permissive Society may find it difficult to re-
> adjust if they want to stop and get off. Many do.
> I believe people are getting sick of a society which has made
> emotional and physical demands on people whose minds and
> bodies are too unformed to cope.
> . . . The danger today is that people, lacking a sense of
> security in their personal relationships, will either become
> more materialistic or swing away from the liberating trend
> in the opposite direction. It must be recognised that the
> hearts of men and women as well as their sexual needs have
> a place.
> If the best of the permissive and authoritarian systems can
> be welded to give the next generation a better understanding
> of the recipe for human happiness, then neither will have
> been in vain.

What was that they said about *The Sun*? Debased, obsessed,
and irresponsible?

CHAPTER FOURTEEN

Sport with Four Rows of Teeth

From the outset sport was big in *The Sun*. It was run by a big man, rumbustious Sports Editor Frank Nicklin ('I am 46 and still ambitious').

Frank, who is built like a bull and prone to behave like one, in that from time to time he puts his head down and charges, had a remarkable record in the Second World War. Flying Kittyhawks for the RAF he was twice shot down. On the second occasion in Yugoslavia, he linked up and fought with a group of Yugoslav partisans before he was eventually captured and imprisoned. 'If I'd escaped I'd only have been shot down again,' he says philosophically. 'The RAF wouldn't have wanted me back anyway. I was losing too many aeroplanes.'

On Day One of the Murdoch *Sun* I asked Frank to write to the readers about his plans for the future. He promised them 'Sport with four rows of teeth'. The address is worth recording:

> This is it, folks. The shining new *Sun* Sports Service that will leave all its rivals trailing like a bunch of selling-platers.
> The sporting paper that will be bright, punchy, probing, provocative, courageous, critical, witty – and honest.
> The sporting paper that will give full and free rein to a brilliant, hand-picked team of writers, reporters and specialists.
> In fact, the paper that cares about sport.
> The paper that will not fob off its readers with space-filling trivia, small talk, hypocrisy and great dollops of sporting codswallop. Like some papers we could mention.

I am the proudest team boss in sports journalism. I have good reason to be. And this I promise:

. . . WE SHALL HAMMER those in high places and those who hide behind the Establishment. Without fear of reprisals.

WE SHALL EXPOSE the fiddlers, the scroungers and the ponces who give British sport a dirty name.

WE SHALL DESTROY the cheats, the rogues, the villains. We shall never, ever lack the courage of our convictions.

In return, *Sun* readers, I invite you to let us have your ideas, criticisms, queries. Please write – we will be pleased to publish your views – and show that you also care for the paper that cares for sport.

Today we have ten exciting pages of sport. Big. Bold. Breezy. Because that's the way it's going to be.

. . . let me leave you with a little story about the late Harry Storer, the toughest guy I've ever met in football.

Harry had just signed a new centre-half, a real ox of a man. I questioned his toughness. 'Tough?' barked Harry. 'Believe me, this feller's got four rows of teeth!'

The new *Sun* Sports Service will also have four rows of teeth. And its bite will be as big as its bark.

I promise you.

We often used to address the readers as folks – usually in apologies for lateness or for having been off-sale the previous day, for which the stock heading was 'Sorry, folks!' *The Times* made gentle fun of Frank's 'folks' line in a third leader. He immediately sent round a letter by hand which said: 'Dear Folks, I read with great interest and amusement your third leader. I am ordering six more copies of this issue to send to the old Sirs at home.'

It was unfortunate that Frank had referred briefly in his address to racing writer Don Cox who, as it happened, resigned in the first few days over the following incident.

The front page of the first issue carried a story under the heading 'Horse Dope Sensation', an exclusive about a racehorse trainer, the first one to confess to doping his horses to make them go faster. It was the greatest sports scandal since the 1964 soccer bribes exposé. (Sports Editor Nicklin had already recruited Peter Campling, the key man in that famous investigation.)

The sports staff were already depleted. John Kendrick, an experienced sub-editor with some knowledge of horses, had never worked as a specialist on racing before, but he was made the first Racing Editor. He was very short of specialist staff. Disastrously, on Day Three, Don Cox walked out, supposedly over the dope scandal.

His reason was that 'people of authority in racing circles expressed considerable doubts as to the credibility of some of the statements made', and he felt that his 'reputation and integrity as a fair-minded, accurate reporter of racing, established over many years, was being seriously jeopardised'. This was dangerous rubbish as well as pompous humbug. What followed was worse.

There was a disgraceful attempt to have *The Sun* debarred from the Turf. Lionel Cureton (Templegate) *The Sun*'s Number One tipster, had mingled with all his racing journalist colleagues at Kempton Park during the first week of the new paper. But no one had mentioned to him the plot which was afoot. It was only when he read a copy of the *Racehorse*, twelve days after the first issue of *The Sun*, he learned that Clive Graham (The Scout) of the *Daily Express*, who also commentated on racing for BBC TV, had been behind the conspiracy.

As Chairman of the Horserace Writers' Assocation Graham wrote that, at their meeting at Kempton Park, 'My personal feeling that Press badges granted to any racing journalist employed by *The Sun* should be withheld was over-ruled by a considerable majority. I still believe though in the old axiom: Who is not with us is against us.' It was the most amazing confession imaginable from an experienced journalist. Before he knew the truth, before ex-Flying Squad Chief Superintendent Bob Anderson, then serving the

Jockey Club, had investigated the matter, before the trainer concerned had relinquished his licence, before the Jockey Club had disqualified him for five years, Graham was willing and anxious to have *The Sun* warned off.

Why? For exposing someone who was crooked? For performing a public service? It did not seem to strike Cox, or Graham, that it was the dopers, not *The Sun*, who were bringing the sport into disrepute. And how revealing is that 'Who is not with us is against us'. With who, for God's sake? Against who? They were supposed to be *with The Sun* and *with* the *Daily Express*. They were supposed to be *in* the business of exposing graft and corruption.

This was a classic example of the danger of allowing specialists to get too close to their subject. They tend to forget who is paying their wages. In this case, it certainly wasn't the Horserace Writers' Assocation – or the Jockey Club.

Meanwhile Templegate, who was to become a huge asset to the new paper, began in fine style by tipping four winners at Nottingham, at prices of 6–5, 7–4, 6–4 and 8–1, and in the next few days gave six out of seven winners at Kempton Park (the very place where there was an attempt to bar him and his colleagues), and later four out of six winners at Wincanton. This bookie-bashing (a phrase which was to be widely copied) brought a telegram from a leading bookmaker:

> CONGRATULATIONS. EXCELLENT PAPER. OUR CLIENTS PRAISE SUN RACING. SO DO WE. BUT CAN'T YOU SACK TEMPLEGATE? HE'S TOO GOOD. REGARDS. JOE CORAL.

In spite of his boasts about the strength of his team Frank was desperately short of staff, especially on the production side. He was later to write: 'It would be untrue to say that the staff on the Murdoch *Sun* throbbed from Day One. In fact the sports staff was a rag-bag collection of mercenaries who had failed to get on the lifeboat to more secure berths elsewhere. I spent most of the 72 hours in the run-up to the launch press-ganging freelance sports subs to come in to help shift up to ten pages a night – and to bring their own pencils.'

On the Friday before the launch I sent Frank round to the office of the *Greyhound Express*, a loss-making publication which had been part of the *News of the World* empire, and which Rupert had decided to close. The Chairman wanted to know if there was anyone there who would be useful to *The Sun*.

Frank recalls: 'I signed three of the eleven people there, plus one freelance writer. They were John Hardie, who was later to succeed Templegate, Stan Vickery, who became the country's leading greyhound tipster, and a sub-editor called John Bathe. Rupert said we had to have him because he'd been there twenty-six years and we couldn't afford the redundancy pay.

'The freelance was Claude Duval, who became one of the finest racing writers in popular journalism. I signed him mainly because he claimed to be an off-spinner.

'I always signed cricketers when I found them – and looked at their cuttings and CVs *after* they had signed. Because of this policy, ultimately *The Sun* beat the *Mirror*, the *Mail* and the *Express* out of sight at cricket, as well as everything else.'

Whatever the strength of his team – and I am sure Frank would agree that there were at least a handful who could properly be exempted from his 'mercenaries' charge – he seemed to strike the right note from the outset, in spite of his formidable problems. Printing only in London, we were at first unable to get reports of night football to soccer-mad Tyneside, or even to Manchester, Leeds and Liverpool. So we filled the football pages with yards and yards of features, columns, personality pieces, nostalgic articles about great sportsmen of the past, and readers' letters. This formula worked so well that when production improved, and we were able to get running reports of late matches into some parts of the north, the readers complained about missing their 'fix' of football gossip and chit-chat.

Says Frank: 'It was a fluke, really. We had the right kind of streetwise knock-about reporters . . . but we also had a touch of class. Our soccer coverage, overall, succeeded entirely by accident. On Sunday nights, because our production and distribution was so erratic, we covered *all* Saturday's big matches in style, and had a story on *every* League game in the country, simply because we didn't know who the hell was getting what. The readers loved it. And the *Mirror* soon started to copy it, believing that we were doing it on purpose, when in fact we were hugely envious of their ability to regionalise.'

In Week One, Frank shouted loudly about 'A Million Pounds' Worth of Soccer Talent' who would be writing for *The Sun*. He meant that our own estimate of their combined transfer fees would amount to a million. And 'writing for' was a bit of a euphemism. Some of them couldn't have written a cheque without help.

Among them – and not, I hasten to add, in the latter category – was Britain's, and probably the world's most skilful footballer of that time, Ulster and Manchester United's wonder-boy, George Best. His first column, believe it or not, actually did include the phrase which was to become the notorious soccer-players' cliché, 'Sick as a parrot'.

It also said he wanted to be a millionaire by the time he was thirty. Didn't we all? I don't know whether George Best achieved this ambition or not, but he was a sad example of someone being blessed with great talent without the ability to cope with fame.

Apart from his footballing talent, George was, of course, a hearth-throbbing glamour-laden attraction for young ladies. He wanted to write about them, too. 'Some blokes notice a girl's face first,' his column opined. 'Some her hair, others her bust. Me. I'm a leg man.'

George did not survive long. Although happy to draw what was then a considerable sum in exchange for our right to put his name on an article written by someone else, he was not willing to work for it. When he told reporter Frank Clough to go away, somewhat more tersely, when Frank was merely seeking material for his column, I decided that *The Sun* could manage without George. Sir Matt Busby and the board of Manchester United came to the same conclusion some time later. It was very, very sad. The young Mr Best was both hero and genius. And when I first met him, when I was Northern Editor of the *Daily Mail* in Manchester in 1968, he was also both charming and diffident.

Brian Clough, outspoken manager of Derby County at the time of the launch, phoned Frank in the early days. 'If you are going to give football a big shout like that,' he said, 'I'll write for you myself.' And he did.

We got Cloughie out of bed one night, when he was on holiday in the Scillies, and his team were 'resting' in Majorca, to tell him they were League champions. Derby County had finished their League programme and gone away on holiday. On the night in question the only two teams who could have beaten them to the top themselves failed to win. Leeds were beaten 2–1 at Wolverhampton. Liverpool, who could have won the Championship with a single goal, failed to score at Highbury. And we slipped several pages, with a late, late spread, and exclusive quotes from the Derby boys, twenty-four hours ahead of the pack.

Our obsession with Derby County sprang partly from the fact that Frank himself was from that fair city, and that the then Deputy Editor, Peter Stephens, was also a Derby supporter. When they were on duty together I had to fight hard to prevent them from leading the paper on Derby's exploits.

We did football pools in a big, big way. Peter Campling, of soccer bribes fame, understood the pools better than any man before or since. He handled this section of the paper with tremendous success. One of his permutations, Sunplan 40, is still the biggest pools moneyspinner of them all – bigger by far than all other newspaper plans combined.

Sunpools, devised and edited by Campling, brought sacks of mail whenever a new plan was launched. Hundreds of readers owed their early retirement to Peter Campling – and wrote to tell us so.

Apart from the soccer pools and racing, *The Sun* covered big cricket in a major way – much more seriously than any other popular newspaper. Cricket is, of course, my own particular enthusiasm. 'You were the only Editor I ever knew who knew what a leg-bye was,' said Frank.

The gentlemen at Lords were astonished when we published full scoreboards for all the big games, just like the *Daily Telegraph*. And when we gave our elegant cricket-writer Clive Taylor the space he deserved they were also astonished to realise that we understood the game, and cared about it, every bit as much as the so-called up-market newspapers.

There is a sad story about Clive Taylor. He was in Melbourne for the Centenary Test in 1977, following a tour of Pakistan, when I began to worry that he was filing highly uncharacteristic copy.

Discreet inquiries – I had excellent contacts in Australia, of course – revealed that he wasn't filing at all, that he had been smitten by a mysterious ailment, and was confined to bed in his hotel, having arranged with his friends on rival newspapers to cover for him. Of course, we arranged to have him flown home as soon as the doctors said he was fit to travel, and subsequently booked him into a London hospital specialising in tropical diseases, assuming, because of the timing, that the bug was more likely to have been picked up in Pakistan than in Melbourne.

Clive wasted away and died without the illness ever being properly diagnosed. He was a great loss to us. Though many people wrote splendidly about cricket for *The Sun* in the years to come, none of them had his touch. I often thought that I would like to write about cricket myself, when editing became too great a burden, but I do not think I would have written half as well as Clive.

We were close to Geoffrey Boycott at one time. He came from my own birthplace of Fitzwilliam, in the West Riding of Yorkshire, and regarded me, together with another professional Yorkshireman, Mike Parkinson, as a sort of guide whose job it was to lead him through the media minefield.

I admired Boycott. Not the most talented of cricketers, he became through sheer dedication the hardest batsman in the world to get out. He helped us with a number of series, especially one we called the 99 Club, about the great batsmen, himself included, who had been dismissed one short of the magic century.

We discovered Ian Botham, too, and signed him up long before England recognised his talent. We paid him £100 a week for his column. Twelve years later he fell out with my successor and tore up a contract worth £50,000 a year.

The Sun was concerned not only with the major sports. Hurricane Higgins wrote for us about snooker long before it became television's favourite (low-budget) sport. I introduced a twice-weekly fishing column. Nicklin, a sporting traditionalist, said that fishing was not sport and that the column should go on the news pages. I said we could hardly pretend that the biggest participating sport of all was not really sport, and Frank had to make room for it, protesting noisily the while.

Our first fishing writer was Charles Wade, a delightful Northumbrian from Ashington with a Geordie accent one could have cut with a blunt knife. He was a great enthusiast. Apart from his contribution to the newspaper he taught me to fish (albeit badly) and he taught my boys to fish, too.

From time to time I took a couple of chums from the paper to a remote Northumbrian lake where Charles had exclusive fishing rights. We frightened more trout than we caught, and drank a lot of whisky in the fishing hut, because it rained a great deal. They were days of pure magic for me, as I was by then Group Editorial Director, overseeing the *News of the World* and working seven days a week most of the time.

Sometimes, we went hunting for salmon, surely the most exciting fish of all, on the Tweed, which divides Northumberland and Scotland. Salmon fishing is an expensive business. Once I calculated that the fish I had caught, in twenty years of intermittent and desultory attention to the sport, had cost me in the region of £100 an ounce. The fact is, that I don't really like killing fish. But I do love muddy river-banks.

Frank Nicklin was a great opportunist, and a great competitor. He took a savage delight in scoring off a rival newspaper. Once he heard that the *Daily Mirror* was about to launch a major series about sporting giants of the past entitled 'Where are they now?' They planned to run one a week. Gleefully, and in great haste, Frank assembled no fewer than a hundred such stories, and we ran them all in one week – the week *before* the *Mirror* launched their series.

We ran many successful promotions involving sport. For several years Frank and I and our wives entertained contest winners in a *Sun* box at Epsom on Derby Day. One told us with some pride that he read only the *Daily Mirror*, and had seen an entry coupon for *The Sun* contest in a paper left in the lavatory at work. This was the one, who, having won a free trip with his wife to London, first class, a chauffeur-driven Rolls to Epsom, a £1 bet on every winner of the day, an early evening trip to the theatre and a late night date at the Savoy's Derby Day Ball, produced a bill for a new shirt he said he had been obliged to buy for the occasion and asked who was going to reimburse him!

In co-operation with the *News of the World*, we helped to save the Grand National by pumping in a big subsidy over several years. Often, my wife presented the cup. We saw

Red Rum's three famous victories, and Bob Champion's heroic performance on Aldaniti in 1981.

Frank was always good company on these occasions. But I remember him best at work. He had enormous stamina, and seemed to get better as the night wore on. I have in my mind's eye a picture of him, as I often saw him, seated in the centre of the Sports Desk late at night having returned from the pub, full of pints and pies, determinedly remaking his pages for the late London edition, his brow furrowed, his left hand fiercely driving his thick black pencil across his make-up pad. He never thought of leaving till the job was done.

There is a story about Peter Batt which perhaps illustrates better than any other the magnifcient eccentricity of Frank's four-rows-of-teeth department. Batt, no mean eccentric himself, went walkabout for a week immediately after winning the title Sports Writer of the Year.

Unable to capitalise on this triumph in the unexplained absence of his star writer, Frank stuck a huge white-on-black headline across the back page on the Saturday morning. 'WHAT IS BATT UP TO?' it shrieked. 'See *The Sun* next week!'

The Sun, of course, did not have the slightest idea what he was up to. But it worked. A somewhat incoherent and hugely indignant Batt telephoned Frank at home before 9 a.m. to protest. But he filed a piece which was pure poetry for the following Monday.

Yes, Sunsport was a mad, mad, mad, mad world. But I often wished that Frank would bite some of my other generals.

CHAPTER FIFTEEN

The Sun *and Politics*

In the issue of 3 May 1979, I wrote: 'This is D-Day. D for Decision. The first day of the rest of our lives.' What followed was probably – as Rupert Murdoch pointed out – the longest political article ever to appear in *The Sun*. It was certainly the longest leading article in Fleet Street that morning.

Like so many of our major policy statements, it was the work of several minds. I had asked some of my senior colleagues to put in writing what they thought the newspaper should be saying, and I welded these views together. On one issue we were unanimous. We should tell the readers – and we did: 'Vote Tory This Time. It's the only way to stop the rot.' Rupert had significant reservations about it. He asked me to substitute 'This Time' for my own preference, 'Today' – on the ground that it would suggest that we were not committed to the Tories for all time. I agreed. It seemed a small price to pay.

Because the arguments in the leader are as valid now as they were then, they are well worth recalling:

> *The Sun* today wishes particularly to address itself to tra-
> ditional supporters of the Labour Party, and to those people
> who have not hitherto had the opportunity to vote in a
> General Election.
> We are particularly well qualified so to do.
> The roots of *The Sun* are planted deep among the working
> class.

We are proud to have a working-class readership. The LARGEST working-class readership of any daily paper.
We are equally proud of the fact that we have more young readers than any of our contemporaries.
Both young people and traditional Labour Party supporters tend to be idealists. And *The Sun* is an idealistic newspaper.

We firmly believe in that system of Government which offers the greatest good to the greatest number.
That is precisely why, on this momentous occasion, we firmly advise our readers to VOTE TORY.
The Sun is not a Tory newspaper.
Indeed, alone among popular national newspapers, it can safely lay claim to being independent.
We have, at various times, advised our readers to vote for Labour, to vote for the Tories and to vote for the best man regardless of party. No other popular newspaper can properly claim to have judged the issues over the last ten years as they have arisen.
. . . Why do we advise a vote for the Tories?
Because *The Sun* is above all a RADICAL newspaper.
And we believe that at this time the only radical proposals being put to you are being put by Maggie Thatcher and her Tory team . . .

Do you really want the next five years to follow the dismal pattern of the last five?

The choice you have to make today is quite simply the choice between freedom and shackles.
FREEDOM to run your life as YOU want to run it. Or to be shackled by the bureaucrats and political bully boys . . .
FREEDOM to work, with or without a union card – or to be shackled to a dole queue in a declining economy.
FREEDOM to spend your money or save it – or to be shackled to an endless cash crisis because the taxman has sliced away your money before you've even seen it.
. . . FREEDOM to live life YOUR way.
. . . Once upon a time, as we have said, we urged our readers to vote Labour.

So why the change? What has happened to cause *The Sun* to switch its stance?

What has gone wrong is that the Labour Party has gone wrong.

Like the many distinguished political figures who have been writing in our columns in recent days, we believe we have not left the Labour Party, but that the Labour Party has left us. Its idealism, its passions, have given way to equivocation, to cheap parliamentary manipulation.

Its authority in government has become a grotesque pretence. The special relationship it claims with the trade unions has been shown to be a sham.

The party has become the refuge of militants, Marxist bullies, and class war warriors.

. . . PRICES soar. Labour says it has an agreement with the unions to cut price rises by half within three years.

An agreement with the unions?

Tell that to the Marines (whilst we still have a few).

INFLATION runs at double figures. The Government seeks credit for 'getting it down' to 10 per cent.

For God's sake! THEY got it UP to 25 per cent!

. . . TAXATION cripples us all. Lower tax at source and higher taxes on goods would give each of us more money in our pocket.

TRADE UNION leaders have lost control of their members, are no longer in touch with them.

. . . And the forces of law and order are allowed to run down at the very time when they need unprecedented support and strength.

THE GOVERNMENT, hungry for votes, spends public money like a drunken sailor. YOUR money. OUR money. On nationalised disasters. On the lame ducks of industry.

. . . But there is another, and overwhelming reason why this Labour Government must go.

Because it has all but destroyed the spirit of Britain.

THERE IS a Crisis of Spirit.

THERE IS disillusionment at the way the politicians have handled our affairs.
THERE IS cynicism about the ability of any party to put things right.

. . . We have become the nation of the promise not kept. The job half done. The truth half told. We have adopted the philosophy of 'I'm all right, Jack.'
We have a Health Service that cannot look after the sick.
We take not enough care of the old. We do too little to ensure the right future for the young.
We know what is wrong with us as a nation. We see it about us – every hour of every day.
We are in peril of losing the will to do anything about it.
That is the heaviest charge to lay against this Government.
That it has contrived to destroy Britain's belief in itself.

. . . The Labour Party no longer carries any torches. It does not excite. It does not inspire.

. . . So will it all be different overnight with the Tories?
OF COURSE NOT.
A nation in crisis, like Britain today, is not going to achieve prosperity for all in weeks or months.
The years ahead will be turbulent.

But we believe that, under new leadership, the will to make Britain proud again can be revived.
That is what matters. THE WILL . . .

To argue against a woman as Prime Minister is no argument at all – if the passion, the will and the ability are there.
With Jim (What crisis?) Callaghan we looked into the abyss.
With Margaret Thatcher there is a chance for us to look again to the skies.
. . . *The Sun* says: Vote Tory. Stop the Rot. There may not be another chance.

As often happened, when the print union activists didn't like what we were saying, this article very nearly didn't get published. First time round, it came up set in the wrong measure and in the wrong type size. The body type, mysteriously, was in 12-point – that is, one-sixth of an inch deep – as opposed to the 8-point and 10-point requested.

The result, as those responsible must have anticipated, was that the article would not fit, even in the three pages allocated. When I went out into the Composing Room to see what was going on, substantial and arbitrary cuts had been made which completely destroyed the sense of the piece.

I refused to have it cut, and ordered it reset. In consequence, we were very late, though not, fortunately, disastrously so, and the saboteurs, since they were on piece-work, got paid twice for their efforts.

This article, totally unequivocal in its support for Mrs Thatcher and the radical solutions to the country's ills which she was advocating, represented a complete volte-face over the ten years of *The Sun*'s existence. In 1970, we had supported Harold Wilson with reservations. By 1979 we had pulled the paper – built on the ashes of the old *Daily Herald* – right across the political spectrum.

Politics don't sell newspapers, but they cannot be sold without them. Tony Shrimsley's brilliant organisation of *The Sun*'s coverage of the 1970 election was rounded off by publication of one of the best political photographs of all time. Cameraman Arthur Steele was packing up his equipment at Huyton, Harold Wilson's constituency, after the Prime Minister had conceded defeat, when the office, on his checking-out call, asked him to follow the Prime Minister in case there were any more picture opportunities.

It was in the wee small hours. Steele had no transport, but he scrounged a lift in the office car of a rival newspaper. As their car sped southwards on the motorway to London, behind that of the defeated Premier, Steele set up his camera. There was the exhausted Wilson resting his head on the shoulder of his wife, Mary, in the back seat of their chauffeur-driven Rover. As the photographer's car sped past the PM's at well over 70 m.p.h. Steele took his picture. *The*

Sun published it over a caption, 'Harold Wilson – tragedy of the man who fooled himself'.

'Cruel, but not callous; news and therefore necessary,' said the UK *Press Gazette*. The *Sunday Telegraph* paid *The Sun* the compliment of reprinting the Steele photograph, recognising its brilliance as a news picture.

In the first General Election of 1974, we supported Ted Heath. Later that year, we found ourselves uncharacteristically equivocal. Rupert and I both tended to think we needed a middle-of-the-road government, involving a coalition of some kind, though we saw little hope of getting one.

I toyed for a while with an election campaign based on the slogan 'Vote for a GOAT' (Government of all the Talents) or a GNU (Government of National Unity). Rupert thought this kind of sloganising trivialised the situation. He was probably right.

In the end, without much pride, and feeling as though I was being required to walk the proverbial tightrope between right and wrong, I said that *The Sun*, if it had a vote, would vote not for the best manifesto, but the best man or woman regardless of Party. We did, however, put the issues very clearly.

'There are only two that matter,' we said. 'Galloping inflation and the sinister and ever-growing power of a small band of anarchists, bully-boys and professional class-war warriors. Or, to put it another way, we're flat broke, and our democracy is in real danger.'

Wilson, of course, increased his tiny majority, and Labour, under Wilson and Callaghan, and protected in the later stages, by the infamous Lib–Lab pact, stayed in office right up to, and through, the Winter of Discontent. That, incidentally (with apologies to Shakespeare), was *The Sun*'s own label, though it was to be widely adopted.

Since we had also, some years earlier, when she was at the Ministry of Education, called the new Prime Minister 'Thatcher, Milk-Snatcher', no one could accuse us of political consistency. Indeed, we would have been offended if anyone had. No one did.

Neither Rupert nor I had reached this political standpoint without pain. He was very much a socialist at Oxford. His father is once said to have told Hugh Cudlipp that he was very concerned about Rupert's left-wing views.

My own father, a former colliery blacksmith who had been gassed on the Somme, and an NUM official at one time, was old-fashioned Labour Party through and through. His views coloured my political thinking for years. Indeed, I suspect they still do.

But during the seventies Rupert and I both began to feel that socialism was not the answer to anything. In particular I began to sense, in the words of Labour's former Deputy Premier, George Brown, that it wasn't so much a question of my leaving the Labour Party as the Labour Party leaving me.

I was in good company. Former Cabinet Ministers Lord Shawcross and Dick Marsh, former Coal Board Chairman Alf Robens, Lord Chalfont, Reg Prentice, and later the Gang of Four – Roy Jenkins, Shirley Williams, David Owen and Bill Rodgers – all felt the same way. I often wonder what would have happened in British politics if a few more significant Labour figures – Dennis Healey or Merlyn Rees, for example – had felt able to tear themselves away from the party they loved when it became clear that it was no longer very lovable.

Of course, there were factors other than the ever-leftward drift of the Labour Party, or its increasing involvement with the politics of malice and envy, which helped to affect our thinking. Not least of these was that it became perfectly clear in the seventies that the poor and the underprivileged were better off under the systems put in place decades earlier in France and West Germany by de Gaulle and Adenauer, than they were in Britain's welfare state. The trade unions had a lot to do with it, too. Especially the print unions.

Anyone who had suffered as we had, physically, financially and emotionally, at the hands of the politically motivated thugs who, though few in number, had dominated so many Fleet Street branches for so long, could hardly be expected to support a political party which more and more seemed dedicated to the proposition that the trade unions were themselves an arm of government. The Fleet Street print unions could probably claim to have unmade more socialists than all Labour's prime ministers put together.

There is much speculation about how much influence newspapers have on the voters. In my view, not normally very much. Oddly enough, in my experience, it is politicians, rather than newspapermen, who tend to exaggerate the power of the Press.

I think, perhaps, there is a case to be made for citing 1979 as an exception. On that occasion, I believe it to be distinctly possible that we helped, albeit to a limited extent, to put the Callaghan government out of office – though Callaghan himself had helped a great deal, by declining to go to the country in the autumn of 1978, when he was in with a chance, and thereby exposing us all to the Winter of Discontent, when militant trade unionists were declining to bury the dead and rats were photographed among the uncollected rubbish in the streets of London.

In 1979 *The Sun*, addressing itself to an essentially working-class audience of around 13,000,000, was probably talking to most of the people who could be persuaded to switch their political allegiance. After all, what difference did it make if the *Daily Telegraph* supported the Tories, or the *Guardian* did not? They were preaching only to the converted.

Elections are sometimes won or lost on swings of only 1 or 2 per cent. If *The Sun* succeeded in convincing only 1 or 2 per cent of its vast readership that – in our own words – a vote for the Tories was the only way to stop the rot, then its influence could have been critical, if not decisive.

Certainly Mrs Thatcher thought so. I have a charming
letter from her thanking the paper for its support – and
saying that she would strive to be worthy of the confidence
placed in her by *The Sun* and its readers. I think this worth
recording, if only because humility is not one of the qualities
for which she is normally given credit.

Outspoken as we were, we made many friends in politics,
on both sides of the House. Most of them, I am glad to say,
are still my personal friends. It is not always easy, or wise,
for journalists to have friends in politics. Inevitably the time
will come when it becomes the newspaper's duty to criticise,
and those of one's political friends who do not really understand these things will feel betrayed.

Equally, there is a very real danger that journalists who
get too close to those upon whom they are supposed to be
keeping a beady eye will fail to expose what they should be
exposing, or be offered, 'in confidence', information which
should be published, as a means of preventing its publication.

So it is better, in a purely professional sense, to keep one's
political friends at arm's length. However, I know of no
editors who do not have friends in politics. It is essential for
a professional communicator at editor level to know what is
going on behind the scenes at Westminster as well as what
is on the record. And many politicians will divulge important
background information more freely in the presence of an
editor than when talking to a Parliamentary correspondent.
So the relationship is rarely easy. It involves a bit of a
balancing act on both sides. Most of those involved seem to
believe that it is a tightrope worth walking.

I made a habit of going to Party Conferences, partly
because, except in highly exceptional circumstances, they
provided most of the day's hard news when they were in
progress, and partly because they offered opportunities to
meet and talk to senior politicians away from the immediate
stresses of Westminster and Bouverie Street.

Once, when I was entertaining Willie (now Lord) White-law, then Secretary of State for Northern Ireland, in the River House at Blackpool, I was annoyed because my usual table was occupied by two men I didn't know. Only when they stood up and politely escorted from the room another diner, who came to our table and began to harangue Willie, did I realise how naïve I had been.

At my choice of table the Secretary of State would have had his back to the window. And that did not seem like a good idea to his bodyguards, who persuaded the proprietor to change my seating arrangements so that only *they* provided an easy target. I found the cost of their dinner on my bill, too. Fortunately, it was modest.

Years later, when I was Editor of the *Daily Express*, my wife and I were to dine with Cecil Parkinson and his wife in the same restaurant on the historic night before the Sarah Keays letter to *The Times*, and Cecil's dramatic resignation. On that occasion I had asked the proprietor to rearrange the seating, to keep us well away from representatives of the *Daily Mail* and the BBC, who were listed in the reservations book. Alas, we made a mess of that one. We were seated by accident alongside a local reporter, a young man unknown to anyone present, and much of our highly confidential conversation became public knowledge the next day.

We saw quite a bit of Harold Wilson when he was in office. He came to lunch from time to time in the Chairman's dining room, in an eyrie reached by a spiral staircase at the very top of the Bouverie Street building.

Once, he invited a few of us to lunch at Downing Street. I recall that he served excellent burgundy, but drank only beer himself. It was Federation Bitter, specially brewed for working men's clubs in the North-East, which some MPs had demanded should be made available in the House of Commons.

Harold was quick to take offence at criticism, and defended himself and his government fiercely. I could scarcely blame him for that. I felt the same way about the newspaper. But he was always good company, just sufficiently indiscreet to be entertaining.

His wife, Mary, who had thought she was marrying an Oxford don, never really took to the political hurly-burly. I recall that we once did a centre spread on extracts from a book of poems she had written. Her publishers later wrote to demand a much bigger fee than the one we had agreed upon, on the curious ground that we had treated the subject with much more prominence than they had anticipated.

I lunched with Anthony ('Call-me-Tony') Wedgwood Benn in his office when he was Energy Minister. He wore a holey cardigan, and served warm hock with a limp salad, but I enjoyed his company. Though we attacked him fiercely, sometimes savagely, in the paper, he bore no malice. I admire him still, for his passionate dedication to justice and fairness, though I think him hopelessly misguided.

Ted Heath visited us once or twice. And once or twice I visited him, at his request. Once I was rude enough to light a cigarette without asking permission when he chose to meet me in the Cabinet Room at Number Ten, having forgotten that he was supposed to have banned smoking there. I realised my mistake as soon as I saw there were no ashtrays, but I decided, probably wrongly, to brazen it out. I smoked on, though Ted's disapproval was heavy enough to be felt. Curiously, I cannot recall how I disposed of the cigarette end.

He, too, was hugely sensitive to criticism. Once, at lunch in Bouverie Street in the Chairman's dining room, he accused me bitterly of running a 'Powellite' newspaper, because we had carried a couple of articles by Enoch. Clearly, Ted used to think *The Sun* mattered.

In 1973, following a leader headed 'For God's Sake, Stop', which claimed that the government's expansionist, boom-boom programme was leading the nation to disaster, he dispatched the amiable Robert (now Lord) Carr to persuade me of the error of our ways. Bob, who had done his homework, took me to one of my favourite restaurants, Boulestin in Covent Garden, and tried earnestly for hours to convince me that all was going well. I remained unconvinced. Afterwards, *The Sun* continued to say that go-go wasn't working, and that Chancellor Tony ('The Demon') Barber should take his razor to government spending in all areas. I suspect that Bob Carr, privately, agreed with us.

We saw quite a bit of Mrs Thatcher, after her election to the leadership of the Tory Party, and during the 1979 election campaign. She came to my office one night to meet my colleagues, accepted a glass of whisky, kicked off her shoes and engaged us all in spirited debate for several hours. We were all impressed, not least by the fact that she listened.

In the run-up to the election campaign I went to see her at her home in Flood Street, Chelsea, to talk about the kind of campaign she planned, who she felt might emerge as the star performers, and which members of her team we should stick close to. She was most helpful. Indeed, I have never found her less than helpful, even at those times when whichever newspaper I happened to be editing was most critical of the government's activities.

Of course, the chat at Flood Street was not all one way. I was convinced that the return of a union-dominated Callaghan government would be disastrous for Britain, and I offered all the advice she asked for about popular communication. Some of her other advisers in this field – Gordon (now Sir Gordon) Reece, and Tim Bell, then Chairman of Saatchis, were personal friends of mine, and I guess we were all three saying much the same thing.

It is sometimes suggested that Mrs Thatcher and her advisers 'used' the media at that time – that newspapers in general, and *The Sun* in particular, were merely her tools. This is the exact reverse of the truth. The fact is that there were a great many patriotic Britons, including many life-long socialists, and not a few influential newspapermen, who recognised that Britain had gone a long, long way down a wrong, wrong road, and were desperate for change. To that extent, Mrs Thatcher was *their* tool.

Now, ten years or so down the track, I sometimes have considerable anxieties about Thatcherism. In particular, I have anxieties about the way the Prime Minister seems to be, even after her mid-term shuffle, surrounding herself with Thatcher clones. Can any government, I ask myself, afford so recklessly to dispense with people of the calibre of Francis Pym, John Biffen, or Michael Heseltine?

I well understand how tempting it is for people in big jobs to surround themselves with yes-persons. Abrasive colleagues, one sometimes feels, are the last thing one needs. They irritate. They slow up the decision-making process. As an Editor, however, I used to surround myself, by design, with abrasive people, for all the obvious reasons. I tend to think that Mrs Thatcher would have a stronger Cabinet had she adopted a similar strategy. At the end of the day, though, I am driven to the conclusion that, in the Prime Minister's own words: There is no alternative to the Tories.

It would be better for all of us if there was. For the government's record is in many ways undistinguished. Elected three times in a row on a tax-cutting platform, they have managed to ensure over ten years that most people are paying slightly more in taxes than they were in 1979.

Government spending, in spite of all Labour's hysterical nonsense about 'cut-backs', has gone up, not down. Unemployment, though falling consistently, remains at unacceptably high levels. So does inflation. So do interest rates. The quality of life, especially in our inner cities, is diminished. London itself is being slowly strangled because of the government's failure to tackle the transport problem. Lager louts – and soccer hooligans – continue to multiply. Violent crime, in particular crime involving violence to women, seems to increase in direct proportion to the number of extra policemen deployed.

In one area alone can the Tories claim credit for a job well done: they have, at least up till now, slowed the frightening march of trade union power. We hear few union leaders nowadays threatening to take the class war to the streets because they had been frustrated at the ballot box.

The Sun was never reluctant to give advice, usually unwelcome, to whoever was in power. But it was rarely *bad* advice. We thought about it, talked about it, consulted experts. We did not pontificate from a platform of no knowledge.

When I was finally able to bring myself to vote Tory, for the first time, in 1979 – I had abstained in some earlier elections – I was quite convinced that that There *Was* No Alternative.

Years later Tony Rees, who had returned to continue his career in Australia, wrote to me saying:

> I am still amazed at the legions of allegedly intelligent people who wrote about *The Sun* who completely missed its hard political edge.
> I used to get very angry with those of our media peers who could not see past the pretty girls and the bezazz, who did not realise that *The Sun* was a product of enormous complexity.

Some critics scoffed at *Sun* political leaders because, they claimed, they were usually in very simple language. They certainly were. I insisted that everything in the newspaper should be capable of being understood by a child of twelve – a firm rule on the *Daily Mirror* in its great days.

It is a far harder task reducing complex issues into simple language than it is merely to write down the words which come into one's head. Throughout my career I felt that the best journalists I worked with on popular papers, like *The Sun* and the *Daily Mirror*, could transfer readily and painlessly to the so-called 'quality' newspapers, the 'unpopular' ones. Many of them did. But the same was not true in reverse. The gift of utter simplicity in assembling words is not given to everyone. But 'Jesus wept' is popularly supposed to be the most powerful sentence in the English language. The Gettysburg Address was pretty simply written. So was the Twenty-third Psalm.

CHAPTER SIXTEEN

What The Sun *Said:*

The importance of Page Two

I have quoted former Education Minister Sir Keith (now Lord) Joseph in an earlier chapter, when he told the House of Commons: 'Page Two of *The Sun*, the editorial page, is a very valuable page for the country.'

This view may, of course, owe something to the fact that we often reflected the minister's own prejudices. But whether or not anyone, other than Sir Keith himself, was listening, *The Sun* certainly did its share of shouting the odds.

There are those who claim that leading articles in popular newspapers are rarely read. Indeed, there are those who believe that newspapers should not have views, and should be required to present political issues only in a 'balanced' way, in the way that the BBC or ITV are supposed to present them.

For my part, I enjoy leading articles. I enjoy reading them, and I have, from time to time, enjoyed writing them. And I think strong opinions, expressed with conviction and verve, are an essential part of the newspaper mix. Contrary to some opinions, it doesn't much matter whether the readers agree with one or not. To preach right-wing economics, day after day, week after week, to an essentially working-class audience, as we did in *The Sun*, would, on the face of it, be calculated to drive the customers back into the arms of the *Daily Mirror*.

Of course, it did nothing of the kind. They may not have supported wage restraint, tax relief for the better-off, and

169

massive cuts in government spending, all of which we advocated ceaselessly. They wrote in their thousands to complain. But they didn't desert us.

The Sun was, I suppose, Thatcherite pre-Thatcher. We had been preaching the virtues of good housekeeping, the need to curb the ever-growing arrogance of some sections of the trade union movement, the need to provide tax incentives to high-fliers, and the need to stamp upon government, and local government, extravagance long before she came to power.

We said it often, sometimes noisily. But we were not concerned solely with the economy and trade union powers. We were concerned with all the things with which our readers were concerned. We were interested in all the things they were interested in.

Not only in politics, but in beer and skittles.

In bread and circuses.

In life and death.

And in love.

Here is a preface I wrote to a collection of *Sun* leading articles published in 1979:

In this booklet we have brought together a representative selection of *Sun* leaders. Here are *The Sun*'s views on the topics of the day. They range from the economy to Europe, strikes to hanging, Ulster to Concorde. They are forthright. Sometimes clamorous. And, we like to think, more often right than wrong.

Everyone has heard of Page Three. The phrase is now part of the language . . . But Sir Keith is right. To the people who read *The Sun*, and the people who write it, the voice of Britain's liveliest newspaper is every bit as important as the other ingredients in *The Sun*'s top-selling package.

And Britain's political, industrial and business leaders know that the message of *The Sun*'s well-argued editorials is a major factor in the way the nation forms its opinions.

The Sun is not only entertaining. It is well informed, ahead of the news and strongly opinionated.

The Sun never hesitates to speak its mind, sometimes crisply, sometimes at length.
Again and again its warnings and predictions prove justified.
The Sun puts the interest of its readers before those of any government. No political party can count on its automatic support.
What *The Sun* says appears regularly on Page Two. We think Page Two is important – so important we sometimes put it on Page One.

We did indeed sometimes put it on Page One. On a dull news night Page One Opinion, always clearly so labelled, often enabled us to give the newspaper an extra dimension. It was a technique I had learned from the master political pamphleteer, Hugh Cudlipp, on the *Daily Mirror* years before.

Here are some of the things we said: in June, 1970, under the heading 'Why it must be Labour':

In the past few weeks *The Sun* has kept its promise to bring you all the Election news. Our coverage has been, as we promised, detailed, analytical, and non-partisan. We also promised that we would tell you, when the time came, which way *The Sun* would vote. The time has come, and *The Sun* would vote Labour. Not because the Government has been a scintillating success. It hasn't. But because, all things considered, we believe that Harold Wilson has the better team. Not only the better team, but a team which is more concerned about ordinary people. Concerned, too, about things like social justice, equality of opportunity, and the quality of living. These are the things *The Sun* cares about. *The Sun* believes that Edward Heath cares about them, too. But we feel they are more likely to be lost sight of under a Tory administration. For Mr Heath is not the Tory party. And *The Sun* is not convinced that the Tory leopard has changed its spots.

We didn't persuade enough people. We backed the losing side. And we backed the losing side again in February

1974 – only this time it was the other side. Under the heading 'The Devil and the Deep Blue Sea' we wrote:

> In our view Mr Wilson is incapable of inspiring that sense of national pride and purpose which alone can save us. A Labour Party led by the moderate Jim Callaghan while it sorted out its own long-term internal problems might just get *The Sun*'s vote. A Labour Party led by Roy Jenkins might well do so. A Labour Party led by Harold Wilson cannot.
> Another factor bearing heavily on *The Sun*'s decision is that today's Tories look less likely than Tories have traditionally been to lose sight of justice, fairness and social democracy along the way.
> They get our vote – just. But your vote is your concern.

Again we backed a loser, though by the narrowest of margins. Not until 1979, when *The Sun* was ten years old, did the nation finally vote in accordance with our recommendation. We could never properly be accused of having trimmed our political sails to catch the prevailing wind!

Most *Sun* leaders on the economy, irrespective of which government was in power at the time, demanded cuts in government spending. Both the government and the people, we said, had to stop spending money we had not got and were not earning.

We said it in September 1973 in the leader which caused Ted Heath to dispatch Bob Carr to see me. We were still saying it in June 1975 when Harold Wilson was in power. In a long, dramatic leader entitled 'The Bells of Hell' we said that Britain was broke – and getting broker. 'We are living on borrowed money, and paying ourselves more of it,' we proclaimed.

> Production is stagnating. The dole queue grows by the hour.
> The pound in your pocket is dwindling by the hour.
> Even the staid and cautious Bank of England is demanding tough new measures to deal with our 'critical' rate of inflation.

We ended with an appeal to the pipe-smoking Prime Minister to take urgent action. 'We plead with the Government to govern,' we said. 'Stop puffing. And get cracking.'

Apart from the economy, we believed that the other critical issue of the seventies was Britain's membership of the EEC, the Common Market, and the Wilson government's referendum in June 1975. *The Sun* was emphatically *for* membership. We had backed Ted Heath unequivocally when he took us in, and we argued unequivocally for staying in – even when the polls seemed to suggest that most people wanted out.

Rupert was supportive on this issue, though I don't think he was quite as enthusiastic about it as the rest of us. His view was inevitably tempered by his Australian background. There were many Australian producers who saw long-prized markets disappearing, and cast Britain in the role of a nation prepared to desert its friends in the Commonwealth family of nations to join an association of 'foreigners'.

We repeatedly explained, campaigned, chided and championed over the issue of British entry into the Common Market. When Harold Wilson was trying to negotiate entry *The Sun* gave unflinching support. And when Wilson, in opposition, found reasons for denouncing the terms which the Tories had succeeded in negotiating, *The Sun* offered equally unflinching criticism:

> There is nothing unconstitutional about the Labour Party coming out against the Common Market. *The Sun* considers the decision misguided, muddleheaded and wrong. But the choice must be that of the Party itself. What Mr Wilson's sell-out demolishes is his own standing as a national leader.
> It is the opinion of *The Sun* that Harold Wilson's conduct of his Common Market Policy is *DAMAGING* to Mr Wilson, *DAMAGING* to the integrity of British politics, *DAMAGING* to the reputation of the Labour Party and *DAMAGING* to Britain.

Was Mr Wilson pleased by this verdict? Mr Wilson was not.

On the eve of the referendum, we made a rousing call for a big 'YES' vote, ending with these words:

> It is not enough, in this referendum, for Britain to give the right answer. It must also be a decisive answer.
> We cannot afford to be half-hearted about Europe. That is why it is crucial to vote. Apathy is dangerous. *The Sun* urges you to vote to keep Britain in Europe. Because, baby, it's cold outside.

Britain voted to stay in. And it was a much bigger vote than anyone had anticipated.

On this issue, as on others, *The Sun* believed that its job was to make sure its readers had a complete newspaper which would enable them to be well informed about the things which were going to matter to them. *The Sun* gave its own views. But it gave facts in a form which made them understandable.

Nowhere was this better illustrated than the way in which we tackled the complex and volatile issue of Northern Ireland. Political Editor Tony Shrimsley had over the years of this bloody crisis written thousands of words about the problems facing the governments of Britain, Ulster and the Irish Republic. But on 16 March 1972 the whole appalling situation was summed up on a centre-page spread, under twelve main headings, with all sides of the case being laboriously put. One senior Tory commented the next day: 'We could have circulated it as a Cabinet paper just the way it was.' *The Sun*'s chart seemed to underline the lesson that only the abolition of the Stormont Parliament and direct rule from London could offer any hope of a breakthrough.

Direct Rule was, indeed, a course which *The Sun* had been openly advocating since the autumn of 1971, when it demanded 'End this Bloody Farce Now'. On 21 February 1972 we reported:

> The Truth about the Ulster deadlock today is this: There is almost more in common between Heath and Dublin than between him and the immovable men of Stormont.

174

On 16 March came *The Sun*'s chart. On 23 March came the headline, 'Ulster: It's the Crunch', as Stormont Premier Brian Faulkner faced Edward Heath in Downing Street. On 24 March *The Sun* said that Faulkner was quitting and Direct Rule would be announced that day. It was. So, incidentally, was the appointment of William Whitelaw as Secretary of State – news which *The Sun* had been able exclusively to predict the previous November.

The Sun's outspokenness on Northern Ireland and its repeated references to the IRA as politically motivated thugs brought a number of threats to the paper, and some to me in person. One was particularly chilling.

At that time I drove, or was driven in, a blue Mercedes with the number plate SUN 1. I had also been able to secure NOW 1 for my colleague, Tiny Lear, on the *News of the World*. We were neither of us particularly flamboyant people, but we thought this a modest conceit. One day I received a letter addressed to the Editor in a barely literate scrawl which said, in effect, we know where you live and we know which is your car and we are going to get you.

We passed the letter to Scotland Yard who, of course, immediately said that we should get rid of the number plates.

My own instinct would have been to paint SUN 1 on the side of the car in letters two feet high. But it wouldn't have been very sensible. As Alick McKay, who had the most compelling reason for being sensitive about number plates, pointed out, I would never forgive myself if someone threw a bomb in to the front hall, or into my block of flats, whilst the car was parked outside.

So we took them off. I still have the original plates. The number was transferred to a company van in the Midlands. And we continued to attack the IRA as vigorously as ever, whenever the occasion demanded.

Situations such as these – Ireland, the Common Market, Pay and Prices – enabled *The Sun* repeatedly to show that as well as being the most entertaining and readable paper in Britain, it could take the lead in serious popular journalism. Politicians watched its rapidly growing readership, its trenchant comments and its capacity to reveal the news and explain it too, and realised that here was a paper they dare not and could not ignore.

They wrote to it and they wrote for it. They talked about it. They talked to it. Edward Heath, Harold Wilson, Enoch Powell, Reginald Maudling, Peter Walker, Jeremy Thorpe . . . *Sun* readers knew what they were up to, what they thought, and what *The Sun* thought of them.

The Sun had succeeded in turning away from the shackles of a 'unique relationship' with any political party and developing a 'unique relationship' with its readers. It was a paper with a mind of its own – like them.

When *The Sun* decided to go for somebody it went for them tooth and claw. Look at this attack on Len (now Lord) Murray, the General Secretary of the TUC, in April 1976:

> Consider, if you will, the astonishing case of the arrogant Mr Murray.
> Mr Lionel (Len-to-you) Murray does not agree with the Chancellor's sums about pay rises and tax reliefs. He says: 'The TUC found a figure last year and made it stick. We will do so again.' How's that for a frightening piece of cheek? Lofty Lionel, the chief clerk of the TUC, the bureaucrat who represents no one, lays down the law on how much you should have in your pay packet. The Chancellor will not decide how much tax you pay. The Government will not decide it. Mr Murray will.

But for simple invective it would be hard to beat *The Sun*'s farewell to President Nixon. The heading was 'Nixon Deleted'. And we said:

> Nixon was your President, too.
> For the man in the White House is the leader of the free world, whether we like him or not.
> Nixon, we did not like.

He was the shabbiest, most squalid, deceitful, ruthless, mendacious, double-dealing, conniving, sanctimonious, hypocritical twister that great office will ever know.
There is but one verdict history will accord him:
'Expletive Deleted'.

In 1976 critic Bill Grundy, one of the many pundits who would have applauded a gallant failure but could never forgive *The Sun* for being right when they were wrong, wrote that we had no serious leading articles, and 'very little Parliamentary reporting'. Well, we had lots of serious leading articles. And we had more people reporting Parliament than *The Times*. Dear Old Bill. Which newspaper can he have been reading?

CHAPTER SEVENTEEN

Letters To – and From – the Editor

One of the most remarkable things about the Soaraway *Sun* was the way its immediate rapport with the paying customers was reflected in the Editor's post-bag. *The Sun* welcomed letters, of course. We encouraged them. And we got them by the sackload.

We were astonished not only by the volume of letters, which was phenomenal, but by their diversity, their warmth, and their candour. Even when the readers were being critical, which was often, they were remarkably tolerant. They complained more in sorrow than in anger. We had from Day One succeeded in making the readers feel that it was *their* newspaper, to the extent that they not only took pride in its growing success, but seemed, in an odd sort of way, to be willing to take their share of the blame when we got things wrong.

Letters were addressed to the newspaper under several different headings. The bulk of them were to Liveliest Letters. This was rather an in-joke. The *Daily Mirror* had for years run a letters column they called Live Letters. In the same impudent fashion we had adopted the slogan, 'Forward with the People' which the *Mirror* for some reason had dropped, and devised a strip cartoon called Scarth about a shapely and skimpily dressed space lady who was a sort of female Garth.

I digress. The other letters to *The Sun* in the early days came to Post Box, which was a column for letters on the serious issues of the day, to Sunsport, to the advice column run initially by the *News of the World*'s John Hilton Bureau, and to Doctor Wendy Greengross, a medical adviser to the Marriage Guidance Council.

We had very few rules on *The Sun*, but one thing I was adamant about: everyone who wrote to us got a reply. And if a letter raised a problem to which we could not reply sensibly in forty-eight hours the writer had to have an acknowledgement within that time saying that we were working on it.

The Sun had inherited from its predecessor the benign and talented Tony Field, a youthful octogenarian with a heart as big as a bus. He it was who assumed control of Liveliest Letters. He it was who helped to forge the remarkable bond between the newspaper and its readers.

Long before *The Sun* was the biggest daily newspaper in Fleet Street, Tony had the biggest post-bag – sometimes as many as 5,000 letters a week. Dealing with correspondence on this scale was a huge, and unbudgeted expense, but I never begrudged a penny of it.

Readers wrote to us as if to a family friend about what caught their eye, and their minds, what worried them, what delighted them. They wrote about their loved ones, when they were well and when they were ill, asking fellow readers to remember the sick in their prayers. They wrote about their families, their friends, their pets, their experiences. They laughed at themselves as well as others. They wrote to share their emotions, their despondencies and their happiness. Some of their letters were memorable.

Today has been such a happy day for me. I am a supervisor in a junior school playground, and I had a busy time. I stuck plasters on cut knees. I managed to wipe mud off a boy's pullover so that his Mum wouldn't grumble when he got home. Three boys gave me a kiss because they were so pleased to see me. Two told me of their birthday presents. I had a lovely hot school dinner, and then I dashed off to Hounslow. A bus driver stopped to let me get on between regular stops. Coming home I made friends with the mother of beautiful twins. They brought back memories of my own twins. We had such a happy talk about bringing up twins that we parted with a promise to have coffee together. Such a happy day! I just had to tell *The Sun* about it!

Mrs R. Rennie, Hanworth, Middlesex.

My walk to the altar was like a scene from a Carry on Film. As I approached the vicar I suddenly noticed that there was a large bee in my wedding bouquet. As I am terrified of being stung I instinctively hurled the bouquet away from me. It hit the vicar full in the face.

Mrs H.K., Poulton, Lancashire.

As I joined my bridegroom I saw that the look on his face was one of sheer terror. Before the wedding service began, however, the vicar bent down and whispered in his ear. My bridegroom's face lit up with a huge smile. What were the magic words of comfort? The local football club, of which my bridegroom was a member, were playing that afternoon, and the vicar had whispered, 'They're two up at half time.'

Mrs I. E. Tapp, Plymouth.

On the first night of my honeymoon I went to bed wearing my false teeth. Next morning they were missing. I jumped out of bed and searched for them. My husband found them – in the bed. As he handed them over he said, 'So that's what's been biting me all night!' He must have been sleeping on them.

Mrs B.M., Tower Hamlets, London.

We haven't had a holiday for 14 years because we have four dogs and a mynah bird which we cannot leave. We have separate beds because we each take a poodle to bed with us. Our life has been spoilt. I've forgotten what it's like.

Mrs M.S., Hucknall, Nottingham.

When I was in the Navy, the commander of our ship told us that unless the excuse for being late after weekend leave was new, the offender would be severely punished. The first offender's excuse was 'Sir, when I got home the wife was in the bath. It took 48 hours to dry my clothes.' Case dismissed.

F. H. Wicks, Gosport, Hampshire.

They also wrote about their children.

My granddaughter, who is ten years old, was shown a sex education film at school. When she came home she threw her books down and exclaimed 'That's the end. When I get married I'm adopting two children. I'm not having any of that lark.'

G. N. Gofton, Wallsend, Northumberland.

A motorist I know drove to a friend's house with his wife and five-year-old daughter. Their host asked the little girl 'Did you have a nice journey?' 'Yes,' she replied. 'This time we didn't meet any bastards.'

Maxwell Lincoln, Edgware, Middlesex.

And from a very young reader:

I wish that the batteries of my toys would never run out. I wish I could have a big tin of spaghetti all to myself. I wish my big sister would leave home.

Robert, aged 9, Blackpool.

The everyday behaviour and off the cuff sayings of ordinary people were, and remain, the theme of a large proportion of the mailbag.

Two women were sitting behind me on the bus. One said, 'Well, my top's false but my bottom's my own.' It didn't dawn on me immediately she was referring to her teeth.

Mrs Sally Ellis, Blackpool.

An elderly lady was in trouble with her luggage at the station, so I stepped briskly up to her and offered, 'Let me carry these for you.' 'No,' she said. 'I don't want you to . . .' 'Don't mention it,' I interrupted, and strode out of the station with her luggage. She followed, still protesting. When she caught up with me I asked 'Shall I call you a taxi?' 'No,' she almost shrieked. 'I was going *into* the station.'

M.C., Newham, London.

Daydreamers and dream-makers wrote to Liveliest Letters, too.

My boyfriend was kissing me goodnight at our garden gate. He broke off, and gazed up thoughtfully at the sky which was crowded with stars. 'What are you thinking, darling?' I asked. 'I was just thinking,' my boyfriend replied, 'that if your father turned the TV aerial a bit, he'd get a much better reception.'

Miss E.L., Farnborough, Hampshire.

I have my favourite daydream every time I hear The Stripper record. I am standing in the glare of the spotlights at a famous night-club. My Raquel Welch figure is wriggling and writhing its way out of the skimpy, spangled costume. The audience is spellbound. Slowly the last piece of clothing is dropped from my lovely body, and I stand proudly there, while the audience cheers . . . Ah well, back to my slimming exercises.

Mrs M.D., Horbury, Yorkshire.

My mother used to tell me that my trouble was that I had a millionaire complex. Maybe I have. I am 64, and work for a low wage as a labourer. But, once a month, I enjoy myself like a millionaire. I put on my best – my one good suit, rolled umbrella, the lot – and go to a good hotel in Cardiff. I have a few double brandies, listen to the subdued hum of conversation and, when invited, join in. I thoroughly enjoy myself, away from life's realities. I feel wonderfully relaxed, and return cheerfully to the grindstone.

D.C.P., Caerphilly, Glamorgan.

Being late for work, celebrating a birthday – whatever the occasion – they all prompted 'Dear Sir . . .' letters.

I was late for work, and rushed into the lift. To my horror it contained the boss. 'Late again!' he exclaimed. I was confused and stammered, 'Yes, sir. So am I.'

H. E. Waite, Wirral, Cheshire.

On my wife's birthday I took her to a show and then to dinner in a West End restaurant. There were soft lights and sweet music. A violinist wandered about playing gipsy music. As we were having our main course he came to our table and played to us. It was so perfectly romantic that there were tears in my wife's eyes. Still playing, the violinist bent down to my wife and whispered in her ear. When he went away I asked her, 'What did he say?' I shall never forget the expression in her face as she told me, 'He asked me what the chips were like.'

H. Collin, Harlesden, London.

Few letters gave more pleasure than thank you letters from people who had asked for help and been helped. From a lonely British forces outpost in the Persian Gulf two soldiers wrote:

> Thank you for publishing our letter asking for some of the bright girls who read the brightest paper to write to letter-hungry soldiers here. Christmas will be brighter for us as a result. We received almost 500 letters in two days. Reading them, we know that the brightest girls read *The Sun*.

Stew and Joe, HQ, BTS, Sharjah, BFPO 64.

Dr Wendy's heart-to-heart column dealt with readers' emotional and marital problems with wisdom and sympathy. More advice came from the company's John Hilton Bureau, which was based in Cambridge, and had a large and expert staff. They received more than 100,000 letters a year asking for specific advice or help with problems ranging from consumer complaints, welfare problems, redundancy payments, the rent laws, and matrimonial difficulties. So highly regarded was the Bureau that, when the Law Commission, the government's permanent body of Law reformers, set out to amend the laws relating to family property, Mr Justice Scarman, the chairman, called in the Bureau chief to discuss the problems which beset ordinary people. The judge said later that the Bureau which served the *News of the World* and *The Sun* 'has its finger on the public pulse'.

As Editor, I not only received a lot of letters, but I wrote a lot. This was partly because I had a bit of a persecution complex about the newspaper, and reacted angrily to criticism, but more often because I saw an opportunity for free publicity. Thus, early in 1970, to the Editor of *The Times*, I wrote:

> Your contributor, Robert Jones, is quite wrong to suggest that *The Sun* has in any way failed to meet its obligations to advertisers.
>
> The initial guaranteed circulation of this newspaper was not 1,500,000 as Mr Jones reported, but 1,000,000. This figure has been handsomely exceeded. The current guarantee is for 1,250,000 copies, which will be exceeded.

Mr Dennis Hackett was another critic who was careless with figures. He was a former executive of the International Publishing Corporation, and media guru on the *Spectator*. In a letter to that publication I wrote:

> Dennis Hackett says the estimated circulation of *The Sun* is 'said to be' about 2,080,000.
>
> Said by whom? The published, audited Audit Bureau of Circulations figure for June (1971) is 2,352,126. The average daily sale so far this month (July) is in excess of 2,380,000. If Mr Hackett wants a reliable estimate of *The Sun*'s circulation he can get one every week for the cost of a phone call.

Hackett must have forgotten, for just twelve months later, I had to write again.

> Poor Mr Hackett has it wrong again. *The Sun* is not now selling 2,600,000 copies a day. It is selling more than 2,750,000. For the second time in a year [he] has chosen to give an outdated six-monthly average figure, without saying that it was a six-monthly average, rather than the up-to-date figure which was available to him for the price of a telephone call.

Nearly twenty years later, I am prepared to give Dennis the benefit of the doubt. But I wonder if he would have used out-of-date figures had *The Sun*'s circulation been going down?

When the *Sunday Times* sniffily tilted at *The Sun* for 'baring their 17th nipple in nine days', I reached for my pen and dashed off another 'Dear Sir'. This time I said:

> It was fascinating to learn that the new *Sun* had bared 17 nipples in nine days. We hadn't been counting. We had been counting those in the *Sunday Times*, however. Your score in nine issues – 22. *Sun* readers need not despair. It is clear that they are still fractionally under-privileged, but the situation is not irretrievable.

The Newspaper of the Year Award which we won in 1971 greatly exercised a Mr Desmond Albrow, then Editor of the *Catholic Herald*. He said in a letter to *The Times*, *inter alia*, that the success of *The Sun* caused the *Daily Mirror* to 'reduce its sights' – a silly theory which was popular among pundits at the time, though the idea was as insulting to my friends at the *Mirror* as it was to me. I wrote to *The Times* as follows:

> Mr Albrow's opinions are too superficial to merit serious attention. But even he must accept some responsibility for getting the facts right.
>
> To suggest that the *Daily Mirror* carries, or has carried, more serious and literate material than *The Sun* is nonsense. Mr Albrow does not need to take my word for that. All he needs is a ruler.

CHAPTER EIGHTEEN

The Sun *and the Pundits*

At the launch of the Soaraway *Sun*, everyone in sight, but especially those journalists who had adopted punditry as a profession, was anxious to tell us that we hadn't a hope. All of them were equally anxious, after the launch, to tell the world that what we were doing was wrong, wrong, wrong.

And as the months went by, and the sale went up and up, they got more and more hysterical, more and more unreasonable, more and more publicly contemptuous. But their contempt, quite clearly, was based on anger and envy; we were constantly making nonsense of their predictions, and we were doing what so many of them, throughout their careers, had failed to do – we were winning. Just listen to the prophets of doom:

> I had control of *The Sun* for a number of years. I'm afraid I had no success, and I don't anticipate that anybody else will have more success than I had.
> Cecil King, former Chairman of the Mirror Group, September 1969.

> If Rupert Murdoch succeeds, I shall be the first to applaud.
> Hugh (now Lord) Cudlipp, architect of the IPC *Sun*, September 1969.

> I wish Rupert Murdoch every success. But I would sooner it was his money than mine. I have been saying all along that there are too many national papers, and some will have to go. *The Sun* is a very obvious one.
> Lord Thomson of Fleet, Chairman of the Thomson Organisation, then owner of *The Times* and the *Sunday Times*, September 1969.

We were never to be forgiven for proving them wrong.

Of the real journalists who indulged in punditry from time to time, not all were to sneer. Hearken – as he would have said – to John Gordon, the sage of Fleet Street, in April 1971:

> Annually the International Publishing Corporation (*Daily Mirror* etc.) picks a Journalist of the Year. This year it bestows the honour upon Mr Alistair Hetherington, Editor of the *Guardian*. A good editor of an excellent newspaper.
> But could I choose a journalist who better deserves the title? I could. Mr Larry Lamb, Editor of *The Sun*, who in one year has raised his lively paper from the point of death to be a new force in journalism to the admiration of Fleet Street.
> That is the achievement of the year without a doubt. Though not I expect to the prize-giving IPC who sold *The Sun* because it couldn't do anything with it and now finds its own *Daily Mirror* caught in the back blast.

I was less impressed with another bouquet which came my way earlier in 1971 when we won Granada Television's 'What the Papers Say' award as Newspaper of the Year. The Savoy luncheon at which it was presented was a humiliating experience, with presenter Brian Inglis falling over himself to make it clear that they wouldn't have given it to us if they hadn't felt that they had no choice. Just to emphasise the fact, they made a 'special award' to the *Financial Times*. I had, and still have, a great admiration for the *Financial Times*, and its then Editor, Gordon Newton. But they did nothing special in 1970. It was made abundantly clear that this award was a sop to those who had not agreed that *The Sun* deserved the prize.

I have been patronised by better men than Mr Inglis. I felt like walking out in the middle of his address, and I now feel, with hindsight, that I should have done so. Since the experience was so excruciating, I should have played it for maximum publicity, as some sort of compensation.

In the event we didn't do too badly for publicity: I put

the story at the bottom of Page Four, two paragraphs only. Everyone who hadn't won the award carried the story with more prominence, and my own derisory treatment of it became a story in itself and ensured us a second day's exposure.

'We didn't pay any attention to them when they were sneering and jeering, week after week,' I said. 'Why should we think they are more deserving of notice now they're giving us a reluctant pat on the back?'

Apart from the publicity – all stories about *The Sun* were good stories, in our book – the best thing to emerge from the luncheon was the information that cartoonist Paul Rigby, columnist Jon Akass and photographer Michael Brennan would all have been strong candidates for awards in their own classes had the newspaper not scooped the top prize.

Needless to say, I accepted no further invitations to that event, though it was subsequently put to me, on more than one occasion, that I would hear something to the paper's advantage if I chose to attend.

One of the paper's noisier critics was Mr Bill Grundy, who was associated with *What the Papers Say* as well as writing for the *Spectator* and the *Daily Sketch*. His grasp of the newspaper business may be judged by his assessment, in November 1969, that the new paper posed no threat to the *Daily Sketch*. *Sketch* readers, he thought, 'are a different race of beings altogether'. So different that when the *Sketch* was forced by *The Sun*'s success to merge with the new, tabloid *Daily Mail* a year or so later, *The Sun* put on close to 500,000 and the *Mail* none at all.

Six years, and many thousands of even sillier words later, Grundy was still demonstrating that he didn't even begin to understand the newspaper he was so fond of sneering at. 'Rupert Murdoch's *Sun* made no attempt to be serious,' he prattled. 'The result: it put on circulation faster than any other newspaper this century.'

Not serious? Ask Ted Heath. Ask Harold Wilson. Ask Margaret Thatcher. Count the column inches. Or listen to Sir John Hunt, of Everest and, more pertinently – in this context – the 1976 Royal Commission on the Press, who said he was 'greatly impressed with *The Sun*'s serious content'.

Tom Baistow, a newspaperman who had been an executive on the *News Chronicle*, the *Daily Herald* and the IPC *Sun* before all three papers bit the dust, also felt himself qualified to sneer and jeer, in the pages of the *Statesman* and elsewhere. High on his list of things better left unsaid must have been his potty prediction, in May 1971, that *The Sun*'s circulation would level off 'around the two million mark'. But he did once have the grace to write – having repeatedly accused us of trivialisation – that over a three-week period he had monitored himself we had far more 'serious' page leads than the *Mirror* or the *Daily Sketch*.

Another pundit, former *Mail* Editor Mike Randall, was more objective than most. Writing in the *Sunday Times* in 1970 on the 'Battle of the Tabloids' he said that there was 'far more substance in Lamb's *Sun* than his critics have allowed'. He also said that the *Mirror* was 'so far ahead of the tabloid field it must be only marginally challengeable for a long time to come'. I supposed it all depends what one means by a long time.

We would not have sought objectivity from Mr Michael Christiansen, son of Arthur, who succeeded Lee Howard as Editor of the *Daily Mirror*, and we were not disappointed. In 1970 he launched a totally unprovoked attack on Murdoch and his newspapers – the *News of the World* in particular – in the following terms:

> From the popular newspapers' point of view I think that Murdoch's arrival in Fleet Street was the worst thing that could have happened. The clock of journalistic standards has been put back ten to fifteen years, and it now seems that what has happened on my paper is that one's major

consideration every week is whether you should have a picture that shows off pubic hair.

I had three or four years of editing the *Sunday Mirror* on the basis of trying to improve the subject matter of its features. Then came Murdoch, and his reversion to the most primitive judgements in terms of Sunday newspaper journalism.

The consequence is that each week the production of a Sunday newspaper has become a job of looking over one's shoulder at the opposition.

I asked my deputy, Bernard Shrimsley, to deny the charge that *The Sun* forced the *Daily Mirror* and *Sunday Mirror* to publish pictures showing pubic hair: there had been no such picture in *The Sun*.

I did not think it worth drawing attention to the absurdity of the claim that the *Sunday Mirror* had been at any time and in any way 'intellectual' – or that Michael had ever attempted to improve the 'subject matter' of his features. I knew. I did a long Saturday shift there for years whilst he was in charge.

Hugh Cudlipp, who might have been forgiven for not being too pleased with us, was really quite kind. After telling his executives on launch night that the new *Sun* was 'nothing to worry about' and giving us six months to live, he went on to say, at the end of January 1970: 'I don't want to say anything disrespectful about *The Sun*. I rather like Mr Murdoch, and I think that the Editor is quite excellent. But the competition with the *Daily Mirror* is still not enough for anybody to be concerned about.'

Hugh, at least, could fairly claim to know what he was talking about. It was, after all, he who said the new newspaper was 'breezy, not sleazy', a slogan later to be adopted by Eddy Shah's ill-fated *Daily Post*. Mr (now Sir) Alex Jarrett, who succeeded Cudlipp as the head of IPC, then the world's biggest publishers and our own biggest rivals, did *not* know what he was talking about. 'I think it's fair to

say that *The Sun* doesn't try to be serious,' quoth Mr Jarrett
in 1972. That old chestnut.

A day or two later I had a platform from which to reply.
I was able to tell the Annual Conference of the Institute of
Journalists, in Luxembourg:

> Mr Jarrett was a highly respected civil servant. (He had
> gone to IPC from Whitehall.) He is said to be an adept
> administrator. I am even prepared to believe, since I have
> never met him, that he is a remarkably nice chap.
>
> But he is certainly a remarkably naïve publisher. When he
> has been around just a little longer I trust Mr Jarrett will
> appreciate that there is no more serious newspaper on earth.
>
> . . . There is no more serious business than providing a
> thousand jobs at a time when another vast unemployment
> queue was about to be formed in Fleet Street.
>
> And there is certainly no more serious business in Fleet
> Street than the daily planning, projecting and publishing of
> *The Sun*.
>
> If Mr Jarrett, whose company publishes among other
> things the *Sunday Mirror*, the *Sunday People*, and *Reveille*,
> still doubts whether *The Sun* is a serious newspaper, let him
> take a long close look at the respective circulation figures of
> *The Sun* and the *Daily Mirror* in November 1969 and on
> Monday of this week.
>
> I suspect he will find very little evidence of undue frivolity
> on our part.
>
> . . . Some time ago *The Sun* suggested to one critic, who
> also alleged that *The Sun* carried no news, no serious and
> literate material, that he picked up a ruler and checked.
>
> Humbly, I make the same recommendation to Mr Jarrett.
> I look forward to receiving his apology in due course.

Another member of the prattling classes was one Clive Irving,
who wrote of the first issue, that *The Sun*'s 'poor quality' copy
was made worse by 'maladroit layouts and dated typography'.
For typography which was dated to begin with, it is wearing
remarkably well, and still being widely copied.

In a later article he said that the layout 'owed much to

Murdoch's Australian tabloids'. It didn't. No one who had anything to do with the design of the new paper (Mr Murdoch didn't) had ever seen an Australian tabloid. But *they* now owe much to *The Sun*.

Still later Irving was to write: 'For the first few years Murdoch edited *The Sun* himself on a day to day basis.' He didn't. It is inconceivable that Irving received this prize piece of misinformation from anyone who was in a position to know. Certainly he made no attempt to check it with Mr Murdoch or myself.

But Irving was finally forced to concede – when *The Sun* on the way up met the *Mirror* on the way down – that the toppling of the *Mirror* 'is certainly the most remarkable *disturbance of the market* among the popular dailies since the war'. Disturbance of the market, indeed! They had another name for it in the *Mirror* building.

Irving wrote for the advertising trade paper, *Campaign*. So, too, did Rex Winsburg. Once he said, with unconscious humour, that *The Sun* was brash, breezy, self-confident and 'free from sanctimoniousness' – but he, Winsburg, didn't read it. Clever chap, Mr Winsburg. He should have been a film critic. There would have been no need for him to waste his employer's time in the cinema.

We all rather liked the punditry of Bryan ('Scruffy') Roberts, Editor of the *Sunday Telegraph*. 'Tomorrow *The Sun* rises under your auspices,' he wrote, in an open letter to the Chairman. 'Be warned, Mr Murdoch, the British people are not sheep, fit only for an Australian abattoir.'

I met Editor Roberts a year or two later, on a facility trip (i.e. a freebie) to Hong Kong, on the inaugural flight of BOAC's new 747 service to the colony. 'We're getting a few sheep on the abattoir trail,' I joked.

Said Scruffy, always courteous, but always honest: 'It isn't quite as bad as I thought it was going to be.'

The pundits at the *Financial Times*, with which newspaper we had shared the honours at the Newspaper of the Year

Awards in 1971, always gave us a fair crack of the whip. They were led by Sheila Black, some of whose delightful mixed metaphors I will treasure for ever. 'Challenge is Rupert Murdoch's carrot,' she wrote. 'The thing that makes him tick.' And how about: 'The Soaraway *Sun* is on the crest of a wave.'

In a survey headlined 'Taking note of *The Sun*' the *Financial Times* treated its readers to both a sociological and mathematical study of the new paper. The time had come to sit up and take notice, they said, of a newspaper which had increased its circulation by something like 600,000 in the first hundred days, and which had a fair chance of reaching the 1.75 million mark by the end of the year.

They went on: 'It is not primarily a topless daily version of the *News of the World*, as some people seem to believe. Although it is widely imagined that *The Sun* has done well by printing pictures of naked ladies, accompanied by salacious text, this is not true. There has been a naked lady or so (although not so many as in some of the 'serious' Sunday newspapers) and there has been titillating text although, again, not so much as in the posh Sundays.'

The article went on to point out that we ran many more stories than the *Daily Mirror* in the two-week period under review, more 'serious' stories, (though I never know what that means) and more – though shorter – foreign stories. We also devoted more space to TV and radio and to sport. Would that everyone could have been as objective as the Pink 'Un.

When the Guild of Newspaper Editors sought the views of its members, Colin Brannigan, then Editor of the *Sheffield Star*, commented: '*The Sun* is a marvellous paper where the staff work hard. People buy it because it contains what they want.'

But his Guild colleague Jack Wiggins (Jack *who?*) of the *South Wales Echo*, was bitingly critical: '*The Sun* has revived an old recipe,' he said. 'It doesn't worry about hard news, but has sex and stuff for the cloth-capped brigade. *The Sun* has degraded British journalism.' It takes a bold man to speak of 'the cloth-capped brigade' in South Wales. Were we to assume that Mr Wiggins didn't want them as customers?

Perhaps the most penetrating comment came from Michael Finlay, then Editor of the *Kent Messenger*:

'I feel sure,' he said, 'that *The Sun* will be seen as a sudden, momentary irrelevance.' Sudden? Momentary? Irrelevant? Never mind, Mike. You can't win 'em all.

CHAPTER NINETEEN

The Sun *and the Unions:*

Eager to wound, but afraid to strike

In my father's house, the TUC-dominated *Daily Herald* was the fount of all political wisdom. For many years, like him, I was an active trade unionist. I believed, with him, that bad industrial relations were the fault of the bosses, and that one had only to treat people properly in order to be properly treated. It is one of my great personal sadnesses that it isn't, alas, true. Finding out was one of my more traumatic experiences.

In 1978 when for the first time we reached a sale in excess of 4,000,000 every day for a month, we did it in spite of a cover price increase, from 6p to 7p, major shutdowns in the warehouse and the machine room, costing many millions of copies, and a hugely depressing ten-day stoppage caused by journalists striking over a pay claim which could only be described as absurd. This was one of the very few occasions over ten years when the journalists had the courage to strike. Usually they preferred to hold 'mandatory' meetings, deliberately dragged on for hour after hour so that they would be paid in full for the privilege of stopping production. Most of the time they didn't even succeed in doing that.

Those of us who cared quickly learned techniques for getting the paper out with only a handful of people. And then, as sometimes happened, the union threatened to expel those executives who failed to attend their disruptive meetings, thereby depriving them of their livelihoods in a closed shop situation, I was even able to get the paper out single-handed, often for days at a time.

I did not do so without difficulty, of course. And I had a great deal of undercover help. Journalists, even department heads, were often so intimidated by the union that they dare not be seen at their desks when a chapel meeting was in progress. But many of them were loyal enough to sneak out to clubs and bars to scribble down information, pass on racing tips or draw rough page plans. Much of this material was smuggled back into the building by secretaries from other departments, and seemed to find its way into my in-tray almost of its own accord.

There were very few aspects of newspaper production in which I was totally unskilled, but I never really understood racing or race-cards, the meaning of many abbreviations in common use on the racing pages, or the rather specialist typography needed to cram all that information into a relatively tiny space. So when I got the appropriate information on the wire machines, I marked it 'set as style' without having the slightest idea what the style was, and sent it to the printer, who thankfully broke all the rules by marking up the style himself.

It was a tremendously exhausting business, of course. And it was impossible to produce fresh new feature material. Though I could get all the news from the agency tape machines, process it, in a fashion, and dig out library pictures, I was frequently driven to using features which had been rejected – or even, in some cases, actually published – years before.

Every day I carried an apology for the paper's rough edges, for its lack of regionalisation, for its missing columns, and so on. The readers were massively encouraging. It was not uncommon for the sale to go up during traumas of this kind.

Though the journalists tried often, on all sorts of issues, to bring the paper to a halt, they succeeded only rarely –

and then only when they could persuade the typesetters in the Composing Room to back them. If the Composing Room FOC (Father of the Chapel, traditional print union nomenclature for branch chairman) said his members were to set copy only from 'normal' sources, clearly I was lost. Not by any stretch of the imagination could I have persuaded them that I was in the habit of sub-editing every word in the paper myself.

In a situation of industrial strife so bloody, and often so pointless as to beggar belief, I found the behaviour of the journalists most wounding of all. Early in 1970, when the paper was only a few weeks old, they demanded a 10 per cent pay rise. I went to the Chairman with what was for that time a remarkably novel proposal.

'Why don't we dodge the ritual dance over pay with the journalists?' I said. 'Let us pay them their 10 per cent and promise another 10 per cent next year. That way, we won't have to waste any time wrangling, we will create a lot of goodwill and we can all get on with the job.'

Rupert demurred for a while, but was eventually persuaded, against his better judgement. He was right to be sceptical. I announced the plan to the chapel with great pride, and a lot of uplifting stuff about wanting everyone to share in our success.

An hour later a deputation came to see me to say that they had voted to reject the plan. Later I discovered that there had been a number of speeches from the floor at the chapel meeting held to discuss the offer to the effect that if Murdoch was willing to pay 10 per cent without a fight their demand had clearly been pitched too low. There was obviously more in the kitty, they said. There wasn't any more in the kitty. The infant *Sun* was doing well, in circulation terms, but struggling to get into the black.

So we despairingly took our partners for the ritual dance we had so much hoped to avoid. Many weeks, and many millions of lost copies later, we settled for increases averaging slightly more than 10 per cent – but without any guarantee for the following year.

My big gesture had been a total failure. I did not again enter the lists on the chapel's behalf, though I was, of course, empowered to raise individual salaries, pretty well at my own discretion. Rupert never quarrelled with the principle that effort over and above the call of duty merited exceptional reward.

I never understood just why some members of *The Sun*'s NUJ (National Union of Journalists) chapel were so bitter, or why so many of their colleagues so regularly lined up behind the extremists.

I knew, of course, that we had some members of the Free Communications Group – a left-wing organisation which was set up ostensibly to fight to get print and media workers a bigger say in policy matters. I knew that the first rule in the anarchists' handbook was 'Infiltrate the media'. I knew also that we had a large number of people, many so-called specialists, who had lost offices, secretaries and prestige as a result of the change of ownership. And I knew that there were a handful of people, who, whilst eager to take our money, were contemptuous of what we were doing.

But none of these things, it seemed to me, provided sufficient explanation for the unremittingly venomous fashion in which some journalists, who, without Murdoch, might well have been unemployed, tried to damage the newspaper. I suppose the moral is never to do anyone a favour.

There were some years when scarcely a week went by without a disruptive meeting of some kind. Sometimes these meetings went on for several days. Once, when a handful of journalists either refused to attend, or walked out of such a meeting protesting that it was a thinly disguised withdrawal of labour, the chapel had them 'disciplined' by the union's National Executive, which graciously decided that they should merely be cautioned on this occasion.

The journalists concerned – there were five of them – were not, however, disposed to accept this ruling. Nor was I. We challenged the union's right to discipline its members in this fashion on this issue, took the case to the High Court and won. It didn't do much for relations between the chapel and the management, but they were at rock-bottom anyway. And it did encourage those members of the staff who did not care to be press-ganged into unofficial stoppages, to defy the chapel next time a similar situation arose.

Journalists were by no means the only source of trouble. The immensely powerful print unions had held sway in Fleet Street for many years. Not a line of type was set, not a truck moved, not a light bulb was changed, if one of the Street's union commissars decreed otherwise.

When my office television set broke down, members of the Electrical Trades Union – then Communist-dominated in Fleet Street – took it to pieces and couldn't put it together again. Since they refused to allow into the building anyone who could, I had to buy another set.

Outrageous though this kind of behaviour seemed at the time, we did not, in fact, have a great deal of trouble with the electricians who, once having done a deal, tended to stick to it. We had a number of far more significant and far more intractable union problems.

First we had a 'mixed' machine room. In Bouverie Street, in the old *News of the World* days, the presses had been crewed by members of NATSOPA – the National Society of Operative Printers. But the machine crews who crossed over from Endell Street, from the old *Sun*, were members of the National Graphical Association.

Thus we started off with a situation where one half of the staff in the machine room was at the throats of the other half. And, indeed, where one half – the NGA half – regarded themselves as superior and were constantly demanding that their 'differentials' should be maintained. The issue was never totally resolved.

We also lost many millions of copies through another inter-union dispute. Members of the NGA used to set type in Bouverie Street. Because of the kind of paper we were, however, with lots of display and lots of big pictures, we made great use of the process department, staffed by members of SLADE – the Society of Lithographic Artists, Designers, Engravers and Process Workers.

The NGA, who were paid piece-rates, claimed that SLADE members were depriving them of income. SLADE in turn demanded parity of earnings with the NGA, and evolved a piece-work scheme of their own called a 'block count'. Between them, out of sheer wanton destructiveness, these two unions ruined page after page, and edition after edition, night after night, as they struggled for supremacy. It was quite common for us to go away hours behind schedule with huge holes in the paper, either because SLADE hadn't made the block properly or because the NGA had refused to put it in the page.

I can illustrate something of the absurd lengths to which they were prepared to go with the story of the typewriter type. Early in the history of the new newspaper I devised a system of subliminal 'puffs' – little pieces of boastful self-advertisement like 'There's always more NEWS in *The Sun*' – to go across the top, or sometimes across the bottom, of pages otherwise lacking in eye-appeal. I found it added visual contrast, and visual urgency, if I had these typed on an ordinary typewriter, photographed and made into a block in the same way as we made a picture.

Journalists set the type, and the blocks were made by members of SLADE. Militant members of the NGA, however, claimed that type of all kinds was their business. Since they couldn't make the blocks, they insisted on being paid for *not* making them. And when I refused, they refused to put the blocks in the paper.

In despair, I ordered a new, hugely expensive and quite unnecessary fount of type which was designed to *look* as though it had been done on a typewriter, so that it could be used by the NGA. Promptly and predictably SLADE demanded payment for the work *they* were not doing every time it was used. The issue was ultimately fudged during a general in-house revision of the pay deals we had with each union, both of them, in effect, getting paid extra for work which was perfectly routine.

So vicious, and so fatuous, were some disputes of this kind, that even the unions themselves, at national level, despaired of their London branches and effectively washed their hands of them. The Fleet Street unions in the seventies were not so much 'lions led by donkeys', as someone or other once described Arthur Scargill's miners, but donkeys led by suicidal maniacs.

They broke agreements without compunction; held up the paper for hours without cause, then demanded overtime payments to catch up. They insisted that they needed another press, or presses, but when the point was conceded, declined to operate the additional machinery, saying that they would 'volunteer' to share the wages of the crews who *should* have been operating it.

As the sale of the newspaper leapt up, some unions agreed to accept extra staffing and substantial bonus payments for printing 4,000,000 copies a night, then failed for many months to complete the print order whenever it reached that figure. They kept a whole new line of presses, capable of printing more than 250,000 copies an hour, idle for two years whilst making nonsensical demands for compensation for bringing them on stream; once the new units were printing, print workers stopped or delayed the paper night after night for months on end on the wholly spurious pretext that the new presses, the finest in Fleet Street at that time, were 'unsafe'.

When they were not complaining about health and safety they were complaining about being undermanned. Undermanned! The truth is that if everyone who was paid to work

in the machine room had turned up when he was supposed
to do so I doubt if we could have fitted them all into the
building.

This overmanning led to the pernicious practice of half-
nights, whereby, instead of working throughout the production span, from, say 8 p.m. to 4 a.m., many workers
would leave the building, ostensibly on a supper break, at
around midnight and march across Fleet Street into the
machine room at the *Daily Telegraph*. Their places in Bouverie Street would be taken by men who had worked the
first half of the night on the *Telegraph*. Thus hundreds of
print workers maintained two jobs and drew two wages –
complaining the while that noise, paper dust and ink-fly
made working conditions so unpleasant that they should all
have shorter shifts and longer breaks. For more pay, of
course.

There was massive overmanning, too, in the warehouse,
staffed largely by members of SOGAT, the Society of
Graphical and Allied Trades. Unless, that is, the London
branch wanted to teach us a lesson of some kind, in which
case they sent us far too few people to do the job.

Either way, we had to take what they sent. All labour of
this kind was supplied by the union. So that, even if staff
had worked in Bouverie Street, before and after Murdoch,
for thirty years, they regarded the union as their real employer, and had no vestige of product-loyalty. And if more
men were available at the London branch office than Fleet
Street required on any one night, then selected newspapers
had no choice but to take on some they didn't need – or
they wouldn't have got any at all.

This situation became so absurd that if, because of wrecking tactics by other unions earlier in the production schedule, we missed a train, and needed, say, six extra drivers to
take three trucks to a West Country wholesaler in Exeter,
the London branch office would say blandly that they had
twelve drivers without shifts that night. And if we insisted

we needed only six (already twice as many as we really needed), then those six would mysteriously fail to appear.

Ironically, one key production area, the Composing Room, was always chronically *under*manned, so that we had tremendous difficulty in getting the paper away on time. This was because the typesetters worked a piece-work pool system, and would never allow us to recruit enough people to do the job properly because that would have reduced their very substantial earnings, which sometimes exceeded £650 a week. In consequence we were always struggling to beat the clock, except, ironically, on really big news nights, when there were usually enough craftsmen of the old school around who were willing to make a special effort to see us through.

When we equipped a new office in Glasgow, preparatory to making our first big onslaught on the Scottish market, members of SOGAT kept it idle for years. Though SOGAT represented mainly unskilled workers in London, in Scotland SOGAT members set type. Provoked by some ardent trades unionists on the Scottish *Daily Record*, the Scottish end of the *Daily Mirror* empire, they insisted that *The Sun* could not be allowed to publish in Scotland unless all the type in the newspaper was set there, by their members. They knew, of course, that this would be totally unacceptable to the NGA typesetters in London. They also knew that to duplicate the entire operation in Glasgow as they suggested would immediately make economic nonsense of the whole project. So the Scottish plant was mothballed, and the paper's natural expansion further delayed.

A big part in the scuppering of negotiations about the Glasgow plant was played by one Brenda Dean, who, as I write, is General Secretary of SOGAT and busy projecting an image of sweetness and light. We saw her as a Luddite wrecker, though I am sure she believed that she was merely protecting her members' interests. At the time, she was the union's regional organiser in Manchester.

Like all other print unions, SOGAT bitterly resented the fact that *The Sun* had demonstrated that it was possible for a national newspaper not only to survive, but to flourish, without duplicating the entire operation in Manchester. Ms Dean's view – of which she made no secret – was that if we were permitted to print in Scotland, from which we could easily serve both Ulster and Eire, then any lingering hope that we might ultimately be forced to open up shop in Manchester would disappear, and the inevitable end of Manchester as a major newspaper centre would be brought that much closer.

So Brenda pursued the interests of those of her members in her own patch with skill and vigour. She found ready allies among SOGAT members in Glasgow, who, well briefed by colleagues on the *Daily Record*, could envisage the new plant employing lots of people, but very few members of SOGAT.

In the event, *The Sun*'s Glasgow plant was not up and running until after the Wapping Revolution – which did not stop *The Sun* becoming the best-selling English newspaper north of the border long before that time. The story of how the Glasgow office came into being is a mini saga in itself.

We had long been thinking that the solution to our production problems – demand for *The Sun* was threatening to blow the roof off Bouverie Street – was to open a second plant. We were determined, for all the obvious reasons, that it would not be in Manchester. Glasgow seemed to be an obvious choice. And it happened that a subsidiary company, Convoys, owned a large and little-used warehouse alongside a Glasgow ring road.

All our own presses were by then fully employed. We knew that IPC, publishers of the *Daily Mirror*, had surplus plant in an unused print shop south of the river, close by Blackfriars Bridge. We also knew that there wasn't a cat in hell's chance that they could be persuaded to sell this plant to News International.

So we bid through an agent, letting it be known, without

actually saying so, that the giant and somewhat obsolescent presses were destined for the 'Third World'. The *Times of India* was the destination most widely guessed at. In due course we were able to secure the machines at give-away prices, had them crated up and shipped up the motorways to Glasgow in a series of road-juddering juggernaut convoys. It was some considerable time before we were able to bring Glasgow on stream, and I had long since left the organisation when it happened. But the plant is now a major factor in *The Sun*'s pre-eminence north of the border, enabling the newspaper to make significant changes to accommodate news, sport and features of a specifically Scottish nature.

But back to the unions. Their outrageous and short-sighted behaviour in stopping publication on the most trivial of pretexts, their cowardice, in that they seemed always eager to wound, but rarely had the courage to strike, and the fact that inter-union disputes, which had little or nothing to do with the management, cost us millions and millions of copies every year, were perhaps, all told, of less significance than the many frightening ways in which they tried to influence the content of the newspaper, and sometimes succeeded in doing so.

They were probably, also, of less significance than the many ways in which they tried – again, not always without success – to bring influence to bear upon governments, or other employers, by stopping the newspaper to draw attention to issues in which we were in no way involved. There were many such incidents. The stories which follow do not pretend to provide a comprehensive account of these iniquities. They are merely the tip of what was a very large and very sinister iceberg.

Remember the Pentonville Five, the five dockers jailed in 1972 for contempt of the Industrial Relations Court? *The Sun* lost four nights' production over that dispute, which was nothing whatever to do with the newspaper. On this occasion, other newspapers were hit, too.

Remember Grunwick – a protracted dispute over union recognition at a north London photo-processing firm in 1977? The story ran and ran – and it became increasingly clear that the ever-growing and ever-uglier picket line was being manned not only by genuine, involved Grunwick workers but by the gaggle of industrial troublemakers known as rent-a-mob who turned up at factory gates nationwide whenever there was a hint of bother.

When Employment Secretary Albert Booth announced the setting up of a Court of Inquiry into the dispute *The Sun* asked what he, or the union involved, APEX, planned to do about the 'unofficial mobs' who had moved in on the row. The compositor assembling the leader page objected to the line 'unofficial mobs' and threw it away. I had it set again, and he refused to put it in the page. The Composing Room FOC, far from ordering him, or anyone else, to do so, took the view, and put it to me unblushingly, that any member of his union was entitled, as a working newspaperman, to refuse to assist in the publication of views with which he did not agree.

Obviously, I found this a frightening and totally unacceptable concept. I was later informed – I have no means of telling whether the information was sound or not – that the compositor had himself been on the Grunwick picket line that day.

Be that as it may, the duty Head Printer suggested that I should reword the leader. The Night Production Manager forecast that we would produce no newspapers at all until I did. I refused to do so. Eventually we went away, several hours late, with a hole where the leader should have been. We ran the offending article in full the following night, after much to-ing and fro-ing between the NGA's National Officers and the Newspaper Publishers' Association. The unions stopped or delayed us often on matters of this kind.

When the Engineers' Union – in a dispute not involving our own engineers – was fined for contempt of the Industrial

Relations Court they stopped the paper. When the NGA was in dispute with provincial newspapers over a pay deal they chose to shut down *The Sun*, the logic being that, as owners of a small provincial group based in Worcester, we would readily pay our provincial employees anything they wanted in order to keep *The Sun* in business, and that once we had broken the line, other provincial employers would have to follow suit. Happily, we did not break the line on that occasion, and our Fleet Street employees were not so dedicated to furthering the interests of their brothers in the provinces that they were willing to suspend themselves indefinitely without pay.

It was during the seventies that the print unions developed the mindless parrot-cry about the so-called Right of Reply. There is no such right, of course, though I never refused *space* for a reply to anyone who had been attacked.

But the opportunity to defend themselves was not what the print unions were seeking, since no one dared to attack them. What they demanded was the right to reply, on the night, to anything with which they disagreed. We lost many millions of copies, and some complete issues, because I took, and stuck to, the view that they had no more rights in this matter than anyone else, and invited them to write a letter to the Editor if they had a complaint. Ultimately both the Press Council and the NPA spelt out this view as their official policy. But it did not stop truculent FOCs bursting into my office almost nightly demanding space in the newspaper to quarrel with some particular political views expressed, or to ride a union hobby-horse of some kind, and threatening to shut down the presses if I failed to comply.

Union extremists attempted to influence content in other ways, too. Once, I recall, a bout of inter-union fisticuffs at Heathrow Airport was broken up by a single airport security man who happened to be a dog-handler.

The Sun's account of this modest scuffle stated that at one stage in proceedings '. . . police then set the dogs on the workers'. We could find no one in the building who would admit to having written these words.

After the dreadful happenings in Londonderry in January 1972, when troops who claimed they were acting in self-defence shot dead thirteen people in a Bogside gun-battle, I put out a series of linking headlines which simply said 'Bloody Sunday'. In the Composing Room, minutes before we were due to go away, I saw with horror that they had all been changed to 'Bloody Sunday Massacre'. And every word in the story relating to the soldiers'claim that they had been acting in self-defence had been deleted.

I was able to get back into the paper enough words to put both sides of the case, but it was impossible, without delaying the edition interminably, to get rid of all the 'massacres'. One of them was 2½ inches deep and would have involved a total remake of the page. I did, however, delay things for long enough to get quotation marks round them, which made the headlines half-way justified since the story quoted someone who had used the word. Attempts at this kind of censorship were common, and became more so as *The Sun* moved further and further away from its traditional political stance on the left.

Strongly worded leaders would often be 'lost' between the Printer's Desk and the pages, and have to be rewritten after close-copy time. It became a regular occurrence for the word 'not' to be introduced, mysteriously, into headlines where the whole sense of the story was reversed by it, as, for example, in 'Union boss found (not) guilty'.

Whenever we tried to explain to the readers the reasons for our lateness, or our absence from the bookstalls, the previous day or days, one or other of the union robber barons was quite likely to order his members to refuse to handle it, and we would lose another night's production. It was a dreadfully wearing business.

I have to say, too, that the editorial department did not always get from management the support we felt we deserved. All too often, it seemed to me, we were put up as fall guys, encouraged to take a tough stand, then let down when it came to the crunch. This was particularly true on the question of journalists' pay.

More than once, when there was a pay row in progress, I was told that the offer on the table was 'final', and that I should persuade my staff that they were wasting their time in holding out for a better deal. And more than once, when they did hold out, the offer was improved, or 'fudged' in such a way that the money I had said was not available was made available.

When this happened, I was not the only person who felt let down. For I had in good faith persuaded all my department heads to preach the 'no more' message to their colleagues, so that they, too, felt betrayed.

We were bitter enough about this sort of thing when it happened, but it is not difficult, in retrospect, to understand, and even to sympathise with, the tortures to which the proprietor and his senior managers were subject on these occasions. For a newspaper is not a can of beans. We were not printing labels in Bouverie Street. Nor were we building motor-cars. Unlike Ford's of Dagenham, we could not afford to shut down for three weeks, secure in the knowledge that we could catch up on our production targets well before the end of the year.

A newspaper lost is lost for ever. There is no sale tomorrow for today's newspapers. No amount of extra effort, extra overtime, extra advertising, will help a newspaper to make up for a copy not printed, not delivered. Not only that, but when we were not on sale, our rivals usually were. To give them a boost on the day was frustrating, but not in itself crippling. The real danger was that if we permitted a dispute to drag on for long our hard-won readers would get out of *The Sun* habit and start switching back to other newspapers.

This is why we were so vulnerable to the union bully-boys. And this is why so many of us in Fleet Street watched in despair for so many years as so many tough-talking managements fell apart when challenged.

It is hard to blame them. Neither editors nor managers get any thanks for losing an edition, or even a copy, on issues of principle. Brave words will initially be spoken in their support, but no proprietor wants to see his business collapsing around his ears on an issue of principle, or even on an issue involving only cash. If either editors or managers raise too many such issues, the whispers about their suitability for the job will begin and multiply faster than rats in a sewer.

Whenever management did contrive to present a united front the unions were pretty skilled at splitting it. Talking to the Industrial Relations Manager, or the Managing Director, they would hint: 'If only the Editor would bend a little. If only he would publish this, or agree not to publish that . . .' During pay disputes, they would say to me: 'You're losing the paper night after night for peanuts. If only John (or Bruce, or Bert) would agree to just half-an-hour's overtime we could be back at work in an hour.' Or: 'If only you could persuade the Chairman . . .'

Since all we ever wanted was to get the paper out, we gave way far too often. I was as much to blame as anyone else.

From time to time, guilt-ridden about the amount of time I was spending in the office, I would ask my wife to make baby-sitting arrangements so that we could go out together to, say, a film première, or more probably a post-première party. Such nights almost invariably turned out to be disastrous.

I remember night after dreadful night when my wife, powdered and perfumed, resplendent in evening dress and full of eager anticipation of the evening ahead, strove nobly (but without conspicuous success) to merge into the background in my outer office whilst a procession of union mini-men came and went, shouted and threatened, screamed and stamped their tiny feet.

Time after time we crept miserably home way after midnight having been nowhere at all. Sometimes a stoppage had been averted, sometimes it hadn't.

No wonder everyone, from the Chairman downwards, was obsessed with industrial relations. The astonishing thing is that in spite of it all the paper, like Topsy, just growed and growed.

CHAPTER TWENTY

The Sun *and the Press Council:*

How many lay members has the BMA?

I write as Tony Worthington's Right of Reply Bill has come to grief in the House of Commons and John Browne has withdrawn his Privacy Bill. Parliament has, in effect, given the Press 'a year or two' on probation, a period in which to put its own house in order before the clamour for swingeing anti-Press legislation becomes overwhelming.

Mr Worthington's bill would have established a legal right of reply to factual inaccuracies in newspapers. Mr Browne's bill would have allowed anyone whose privacy had been invaded to bring a High Court action for damages.

Both were superficial, sloppily drafted and virtually un-workable attempts to legislate against what are undoubtedly Press excesses. But I have to say that had they been *better* bills I would have supported them; that I see a genuine need for legislation on both issues, and that I am convinced legislation will come. When it does, newspapers will have only themselves to blame.

Tory MP Jonathan Aitken said during the debate on the Worthington bill that the 'lower' tabloid newspapers had replaced journalism with voyeurism. 'The reporter's pro-fession has been infiltrated by a seedy stream of rent boys, pimps, bimbos, spurned lovers, smear artists, prostitutes and perjurers,' he cried. Mr Aitken, sadly, is right.

Michael Corner, Editor of the *Sheffield Star* and President of the Parliamentary Committee of the Guild of British Newspaper Editors, is on record as saying that he thinks the Press Council, under its new chairman Louis Blom-Cooper, should be given time to show that it is effective. That also appears, for the moment, to be the government's view. In God's name, how much time does the Press Council need?

This absurd body, through all its wasted years under many chairmen, has totally failed to satisfy anyone at all on any issue of the slightest importance. It has left journalists feeling that it could be more properly described as the anti-Press Council, and the public believing either that it is some sort of smokescreen protecting newspapers from the consequences of their own folly or that, since it has no powers and no influence, it does not in any case matter a damn what it says or does.

All these views are valid, to some extent. And if we accept that, we must accept firstly that there is no good reason for the Council's continued existence and secondly that we have to devise an *effective* substitute. Legislation seems to me to be the only viable option.

Lest anyone should think this is merely sour grapes on the part of one who has frequently come under the Council's lash let me say that, during the first ten years of the Murdoch *Sun*, the Council recorded only *six* adjudications against the newspaper, a record of probity equalled only, I believe, by the *Financial Times*. We fought no major libel actions during this period.

I do not believe that this is necessarily a matter for pride. Indeed I am sometimes tempted to share the view expressed by Mr Murdoch, that the record shows us to have been insufficiently adventurous.

The fact is that I never *cared* what the Press Council thought or said *unless* I believed that they were right. That, surely, is the test. If I thought their criticisms justified, I worried. If I didn't, I didn't. It follows, therefore, that nothing they said or did had any effect whatever on what *The Sun* said or did. If I thought it was wrong at the time, I wouldn't do it. If I thought it was right, then the Press

Council's likely reaction would have no bearing on my decision.

The Council was set up in 1953, following the recommendations of the 1948 Royal Commission on the Press. It was then a fully professional body, composed of and financed by journalistic and proprietorial bodies. Its objectives were simple: to maintain and raise Press freedom and standards, to hear complaints and to publish findings.

The Council got off to a slow start, but gradually developed into a body which was just beginning to command respect among fellow professionals, even though it had no sanctions at its disposal beyond the voluntary agreement of editors to publish all adverse findings.

There was at one time a prospect that it might be given real powers, and possibly even meaningful sanctions against editors and journalists whose standards fell below those the public had a right to expect. At this stage, alas, a subsequent Royal Commission recommended the introduction of lay members. Throughout the sixties there were increasing pressures to strengthen the lay element, and the Council now has parity between lay and Press representatives on the all-important Complaints Committee.

Once lay members were introduced, it seemed to me, the chances of the Press Council ever being a respected and effective body dwindled to zero. Certainly I lost interest in it from that time on. And certainly that decision eliminated the budding willingness of many Pressmen to accept the Council as a body qualified to sit in judgement upon them. In consequence, it is now about as much use as a chocolate fireguard.

How many lay members has the British Medical Association? Or the Law Society? Yet these bodies discipline their respective professions with an iron hand. Doctors or solicitors fall foul of them at their peril.

As I said in evidence to the 1976 Royal Commission on the Press, I would much rather have had a ruthless and totally professional body, with powers to subpoena, fine, withdraw licences, and generally make life intolerable for rogue newspapers and rogue journalists. If we had such a body we would not need further legislation. Since we don't, we do.

Incidentally, it is worth recording that *The Sun* was not always wholly contemptuous of the Press Council's activities. In February 1976, discussing in the leader column the Council's submissions to that year's Royal Commission, we wrote, under the heading 'The Lion Roars':

> The Press Council sometimes behaves like an anti-Press Council. But it strikes some blows for freedom in its latest submissions to the Royal Commission on the Press.
> The Council firmly rejects the nonsensical idea of an Advertisement Revenue Board dispensing a newsprint subsidy.
> It calls the Labour Party's proposed Communications Council 'a machinery for the destruction of freedom of the Press'.
> It pours scorn on the widely-canvassed proposal that local authorities and Government spokesmen should have the 'right' to space in newspapers, for the publication of official statements.
> Toothless lion the Council may be, but it is nice to find that it is still capable of a relevant roar now and then.

That said, I still believe that the Council is a toothless lion, that the public would be better served, and newspapers better able to defend themselves, in court, in a situation where evidence is privileged, and it is possible to be legally represented, than before a nod-and-wink, quasi-judicial, quasi-professional body which commands little respect among Press or public. Which is why I believe we do not need the Press Council, but we do need legislation.

I have little time for those who rabbit on about the loss of Press freedom which legislation would supposedly entail. Surely that depends upon the legislation? Is it seriously argued that the Press could not lobby at least as effectively as those who would wish to see its powers dramatically curtailed? Surely we are capable of achieving legislation which does no more than compel newspapers to do that which they should be doing of their own accord? In any case, good newspapermen will always find ways of saying what needs to be said.

I never found the laws of libel or contempt particularly inhibiting on those occasions when I thought the scrupulous observance of them would not be in the public interest. Indeed I cannot remember a time when I was unable, because of the law, to say something I thought needed saying. The gagging powers of the print unions and the influence the unions had on those proprietors whose creed was to publish at all costs, were far more of a threat to Press freedom than anything the law had to offer.

The run of cases which led to increasing public demand for some kind of legislation to curb the worst excesses of the Press is well enough known. The names Koo Stark, Jeffrey Archer, Elton John spring readily to mind. Less memorable, perhaps because they were perpetrated in so-called 'quality' newspapers, and did not lead to million-pound settlements, were the outrageous newspaper harassment of the Prime Minister's son, Mark, and the publication of details from Denis Thatcher's private bank account.

Libel apart, not only did some of these cases involve wholly unwarrantable invasions of privacy, but the way in which the stories were told, or in some cases the fact that they were told at all, broke all the rules of fair reporting. There is another factor here, of course. Any or all of the people I have just named may have been badly treated by one or more newspapers. But they are all, including Miss Stark, quite big enough to fend for themselves.

What I think the public finds increasingly unacceptable is the growing tendency for newspapers to go gunning for little people, usually minor television personalities or sportsmen, over trifling sexual peccadilloes. Not everyone can afford to take the terrifying risk of a massive bill for court costs if a libel action is lost. And, of course, with the law as it stands, much that is brutally damaging is not necessarily libellous: prurient newspapers are allowed to intrude upon privacy without just cause in perfect safety.

News Group, which publishes *The Sun* and the *News of the World*, has recently shown belated signs of anxiety about this problem, and appointed an Ombudsman, Ken Donlan, to look into readers' complaints. It will be already clear that I hold Donlan in high regard. I have no doubt that his investigations will be thorough and his judgements objective. And I do not believe that Rupert Murdoch is enough of a cynic to have made the appointment *solely* for cosmetic purposes. But inevitably it will be seen in this light, and therefore, as a stratagem for turning away wrath, it is, I fear, doomed to failure.

That is not to say that much good does not come from the proper investigation of complaints. But in my experience there never was a time when complaints were *not* properly investigated on *The Sun*, or any other newspaper.

Of course, anyone can make mistakes in the hury-burly of newspaper production. Heaven knows I have made enough of them myself. And it is right and proper, in my view, for newspapers always to be pushing their luck. They are in the business of disclosure. It is their *duty* to expose many things which many people, sometimes very influential people, would prefer to keep under a stone, and it is inevitable that they will sometimes take chances in the process of discharging that duty.

But when the Press's joint bill for libel damages runs into many millions, when few days pass without some newspaper or other having to carry a grovelling apology, when newspapers set out to destroy reputations on the flimsiest of evidence, from hopelessly tainted sources, when they behave in such a way that juries feel it necessary to take it upon themselves to punish the transgressors rather than merely to compensate those sinned against, then one is inclined to suspect something more alarming than a series of simple, heat-of-the-moment errors of judgement. One is inclined to suspect a carelessness so gross that it amounts to arrogance, to a total disregard for the rights of the individual, and as such it cannot be ignored.

CHAPTER TWENTY-ONE

What Does *Make Rupert Run?*

Private Eye calls him the Dirty Digger. I have called him a name or two myself in my time. So just what sort of man is he, the boy from Down Under who now bestrides the narrow world like a Colossus, whilst we petty men walk under his huge legs?

I fear I have to disappoint those of you – including many journalists and most back-bench Labour MPs – who would like to believe that he eats babies for breakfast. The reality is very different from the public perception.

In real life, as they say, he is charming, hospitable – and shy. He is a very private person. It is not always easy to know what he is thinking. He is also a bit of a Calvinist. In spite of his reputation he was always worried, when I worked for him, that *The Sun* might be pushing back the frontiers a little too far, and a little too fast.

He sold the money-spinning soft-porn *Melbourne Truth*, as soon as he could comfortably afford to do so because his mother, Dame Elisabeth, who lives in Melbourne, did not wish to be associated with it. He has fired more than one editor because he thought they were producing 'dirty' newspapers.

Once, when I was Editor of the *Australian*, he rang up in a fury to complain about a delicate, beautifully written account of some fairly innocent schoolgirl-groping in the bicycle shed – an article, by a distinguished woman writer, which would have graced the pages of any newspaper. Yet he still produces *The Sun*, which gets closer each day to the brink of what is, or is not tolerable in popular journalism, and the *News of the World*, which is bought by millions solely because of its high titillation factor.

Years ago, in Australia, I tried, without success, to dissuade him from appearing on an Australian Broadcasting Corporation documentary entitled 'What makes Rupert Run?' Predictably, they tore him to shreds – as David Frost and a carefully briefed studio audience had done years earlier, in London. On both occasions Rupert was genuinely bewildered by the hostility he had aroused. *He* knows he means well. He is proud of the fact there are many thousands of people in work who would be unemployed without him. He believes, rightly, that many people who read his papers read nothing else, and would be significantly less well informed without him. He makes substantial charitable donations, buys pictures and is a patron of the arts. He is a good husband and father. And yet he is regarded here in the UK, in his native Australia, and to a somewhat lesser extent in his adopted country, the United States of America, as some sort of a monster.

Let it be said that I fought with Rupert often, and I did not always think he fought fairly. Furthermore, someone who has, or controls, 51 per cent of the stock, or thereabouts, starts with a significant advantage in debate over someone who hasn't.

Even so, he did not at any time *order* that something I wanted in the newspaper should be kept out, or that something I wanted out should be kept in. Nor, unlike some other proprietors I have known, did he insist during my time there upon using *The Sun* and the *News of the World* to further his other business interests. I fear he has since abandoned this principled stance. I cannot bring myself to admire Murdoch newspapers' outrageous and relentless plugging of Sky Channel at the time of its launch, whether the plugs were technically paid-for advertising or not.

It could well be that Murdoch himself did not insist upon them appearing in the way they appeared. Most editors like to try to please their proprietors, and some of the excesses may well have been due to an excess of editorial zeal.

Be that as it may, there is no doubt in my mind that I would rather have produced *The Sun* for him than for anyone else. Although he took what I regarded as an almost obsessional interest in the nuts and bolts of what we were doing, and was often very critical, it would be fair to say that he was more often at my elbow than on my back.

Above all else, Rupert is a complete newspaperman. He was not as good an editor as many of his editors, nor as clever an accountant as his Finance Director. His Chief Engineer knew more about installing presses than did Rupert, and his advertisement directors were better salesmen.

But Rupert was the only man I ever met who could carry on an informed and intelligent discussion with each of these specialists, within the field of each one's specialisation. I have worked for no other proprietor who so well deserved to be described as a newspaperman.

His knowledge is astonishing, his energy demonic. Shortly before the launch of *The Sun*, when he announced that the *News of the World* presses would have to print a tabloid newspaper six nights a week, he was told that they were not equipped to do so.

'Oh, yes, they are,' said Rupert, 'we just need the crusher bars.' A crusher bar is a piece of machinery which enables the printing press to fold the 'web' – the roll of newsprint – down the middle, printing the paper exactly half-size.

In Bouverie Street the machine room bosses said they had never seen any crusher bars. But Rupert was convinced that the presses he had – some of them older than himself – had initially been supplied with them. And it was Rupert himself who found them – bolted away in ink-blackened boxes above each press, and long forgotten.

When the weekly circulation figures didn't add up, Rupert would seize unerringly on the error. In my own department, though he rarely read anything from beginning to end, he would spot the weakness in a story before he knew what it was really all about. And, flicking through a thirty-two-page tabloid paper in just three minutes, he would tell you within 1 or 2 per cent what the advertisement revenue was likely to be.

When we met, his political views were distinctly left of centre, as indeed, were my own. We started to move to the right at the same time, and, fortunately for me, at roughly the same pace, having reached the fairly obvious conclusion that the way to achieve the greatest good for the greatest number was to encourage wealth-producers to produce wealth.

But Rupert is as volatile politically as he is in every other respect, and he likes to back winners. No government can rely totally upon his support.

He was at one time a fervent supporter of Gough Whitlam. And he had considerable reservations about my own, un-equivocal backing of Margaret Thatcher in 1979. So far is he from the power-crazed dictatorial maniac of popular imagination that some of his Australian newspapers have found themselves on different sides, with his full knowledge and consent, in General Elections there.

Physically, Rupert is fairly small. He walks in a hunched, diffident sort of way. But he is tough and fit, and – to quote his novel-writing wife, Anna, herself a former reporter – 'brave as mustard'.

He took up skiing at a fairly advanced age and bought a house in Aspen, Colorado, for Anna so as to have a base in the snow on some of his rare days off. I was with him, on a marlin-fishing trip, on the Great Barrier Reef, when he persuaded the boat boys to teach him scuba diving in waters where the dorsal fins of prowling reef sharks were clearly visible. He was fifty-one at the time. I caught my one and only black marlin on that trip. It was a wonderful experience. Rupert caught a bigger one, of course.

He swims well, walks ferociously, and plays a mean game of tennis. So much so that on his day he could give former champion John Newcombe, who worked for the group, a run for his money.

His father, Keith, a distinguished war correspondent in the First World War, had a heart attack in middle life, and Rupert, who, like many tycoons, is something of a hypochondriac, is still waiting for his. If there is any justice, it won't happen. He stopped smoking long ago, now drinks only wine, and that in moderation, and exercises regularly. Anna keeps a strict watch on his diet. He was once a formidable trencherman, with the native Australian's love of great chunks of red meat, but he now seeks out plainly cooked fish and poultry dishes.

He is often said to be mean. I never found him so, except in matters of detail. He could be very cross about the cost of paper-clips or carbon paper, but it was not difficult to persuade him to provide huge sums, sometimes as much as £250,000, for a weekend's television promotion. And he was generous with people, as individuals, however much he dug his heels in when he was obliged to deal with them as trade unionists. More than once I went to him with a hard luck story on behalf of some member of the staff, and I never came away empty-handed.

On my own initiative I used to send hard-working editorial executives who had been sick with anything worse than a bout of flu away to the sun to recuperate, at the company's expense. Rupert never questioned a single one of these bills, though there was no shortage of grey-flannel-suit men lurking in corners who would have been eager to draw them to his attention. I don't know to what extent his generosity may have been due to the cunning of Mike Nevard.

Rupert professed to have great faith in the stars, though one never knew whether or not to take him seriously. At a very early stage in proceedings Mike established his star sign – Pisces – and leant on our tame astrologer to doctor her forecasts a little. Thus, day after day, Rupert was assured that there was a good day in prospect, that he could gain most advantage from the conjunction of Mars and Saturn, or whatever, by being full of goodwill. And he was repeatedly urged to cast his bread upon the waters – to be generous in all things. I don't suppose it did any harm.

There was a strange, tripartite relationship between Rupert, myself and the Soaraway *Sun*, which quickly developed a character of its own. In Sydney, where he had made a huge success of the ailing *Daily Mirror*, he was highly regarded as a journalist, and actually involved himself in the nitty-gritty of editing. In London, he was not so highly regarded, nor so active editorially. He was critical, of course, after the event, sometimes brutally so, but he did not initiate.

It was, I think, ultimately to his advantage that the Muriel McKay situation, and the implied threat to Anna, kept him out of the United Kingdom in the first few weeks of 1970. The *Sydney Mirror* formula would not have worked in London. By the time Rupert returned, *The Sun* was already well established, and clearly headed for success.

Generously, he used to say, '. . . this is not my paper, it's Larry's.' I suspect what he really meant was that, somehow or other, he had been cheated of the chance to do in London what he had done earlier, with such conspicuous success, in Sydney. He never quite forgave us for it. But he never really understood the Poms anyway.

'Get me Wilson,' (the then Prime Minister) he said to me on one occasion. 'I want to see him tomorrow.' I knew that Rupert could summon the most senior politicians in Australia. Indeed, I had seen him do so. But when, after talking to the Prime Minister's office, I fixed a date for a meeting only three days hence, he clearly thought I had failed him. In vain did I point out that Prime Ministers in England did not jump when publishers cracked whips.

Still, as I said, I never felt that he really understood us, though he tried. Like many Australians, he was very ambivalent about us. Sometimes he seemed almost to resent the Brits in a twisted sort of way. Especially the English. Presumably because of his Scottish background he exempted Scotland from his general strictures about the UK and claimed that North Sea oil was Scottish oil.

He quite seriously regarded the Poms as 'colonialists' in Ulster, and never quite came to grips with the paper's policy on that unhappy land. All Poms were whingeing Poms, in Rupert's book. Anyone in receipt of any kind of state aid was a dole-bludger. Anyone who smelt of after-shave was a poofter.

He was obsessed, to what I sometimes regarded as an alarming degree, by what he chose to call the 'English' class system. It was futile to tell him that there is little difference between the class system here, and in New England, for example, where 'family' means everything. It was futile to point out that class systems based upon race and income, as in most of the United States, and most of Australia, are often more pernicious than those based upon ancestry. And it was even more futile to tell him that the country where the great aristocratic, ancestral barons still held overwhelming sway over most of the countryside, where forelock-tugging was still the norm, was not England, but Scotland.

When he appeared on television on the evening of the launch of Sky Channel, he was accused by the interviewer of wanting to take British television 'down-market'. He reacted, rather foolishly, I thought, by describing the question as 'typically English'. 'Why are you so concerned about this up-market down-market nonsense?' he demanded. 'This is a class-conscious thing.'

Now it may well be true that the whole up-market, down-market concept is foolish. But it is certainly not true that it is particularly British, or English, foolishness. And class consciousness has nothing whatever to do with it. It wasn't the Brits who first made tabloid into a dirty word. It was those eager, egalitarian young democrats from the New World.

But it was of small use striving to unseat Rupert's prejudices. One of the jokes he was gleefully fond of repeating was that *The Sun* never set on the British Empire because God didn't trust the Brits after dark. It was funny the first time. Some of us found it all amusing, some of us found much of it hurtful. And some of us merely tried to put it in perspective.

I found the Chairman's attitude to my homeland easier to take than his attitude to the paper. In the early days, after his return to the UK, we got the impression that he did not think too highly of *The Sun*, or the editorial mix which we had devised. He was often bitterly critical of what we were doing, and it was sometimes difficult, after a painful early morning session with him, to prevent my despondency from showing itself at my own morning conference.

I was fiercely protective of the newspaper, which I was convinced was the best thing of its kind, and I resented all criticism of *The Sun*. But I found criticism from Rupert much more wounding than that from any other source.

My wife recalls an occasion when she was seated next to him at a formal dinner. Some idiot made the usual vapid observation about tits and bums. As it happened, I was the next speaker. And I took him apart with much more vigour than the occasion demanded. 'What's eating Larry?' said Rupert to my wife.

'Look, Rupert,' she replied. 'I know it's your newspaper. But to you it is only a newspaper. To Larry it's a baby.'

I think that was true. I was so dedicated to *The Sun*, so fond of it, so proud of it, that my judgement may often have been warped when I faced the critics.

In particular, I was frequently over the top when arguing with the Chairman, the critic whose views I most cared about, and I acquired a reputation for being difficult, for

being straightforwardly bloody-minded, which was probably justified, but which wasn't really me. On these occasions he used to call me, with some justice, a 'prickly
Pommy bastard'.

I won more of these debates than I deserved to win for
one very good reason: *The Sun* itself was winning. Day after
day, week after week, the sale went up.

'Why did you print this dreadful rubbish?' Rupert would
say.

'Because I thought it might put on 25,000 readers,' I
would reply, knowing full well that he knew the latest figures
would show a 25,000 rise.

'Why all this crap about poofters?' he would say, speaking
of the most fleeting reference to homosexuals.

'Because they all pay threepence,' I replied.

We fenced in this fashion for a long time. But eventually
we reached an unspoken truce. He ceased to be so unrelentingly critical, and I tried harder not to take offence when
he was. Outside his office, and the often agonising interviews
which took place there, Rupert was all charm – an engagingly
boyish host, and a good companion.

On the rare occasions when he was able genuinely to relax
he could be delightfully mischievous. Once, at an exclusive
and very expensive island restaurant off the Côte d'Azur,
approachable only by sea, we were having a pre-lunch drink
by the pool when Lady 'Bubbles' Rothermere, wife of the
owner of the *Daily Mail*, strolled in with a very bronzed
young man in startlingly tight blue jeans, and sat at a table
some distance away. The boy could have been a family
friend, or her ladyship's nephew, for all I knew, but Rupert
decided to create some mischief.

He dived into the pool, swam under water until he was
directly opposite her table, then leapt out of the water like
the Demon King springing through a trapdoor in panto-
mime. She clearly had not expected to see anyone she knew,
let alone another Fleet Street proprietor, so far from home,

but she absorbed the shock well enough, and chatted in a composed and friendly fashion until it was time for lunch.

This trip was one of the few occasions when I remember thinking that Rupert was relatively wound down. He had organised some time off and gone with his family to Cap Ferrat to stay in the home of his friend Paul Hamlyn. My wife and I spent an enjoyable weekend with them. Though I had gone primarily to discuss a projected cover price increase Rupert referred to the subject only once, and that briefly.

One day a huge yacht rounded the headland as we sat on the terrace of the house at Cap Ferrat, and anchored in the bay. Rupert recognised it immediately as the floating headquarters of impresario Robert Stigwood, of Bee Gees fame. Stigwood had once been a print-worker at Rupert's plant in Sydney, and they were later partners in the making of the film *Gallipoli*. *Gallipoli* was, of course, of particular interest to Rupert because it was his father's searing dispatches from that battlefront about the incompetence of the British High Command which made him famous as a war correspondent – and may well have had something to do with Rupert's own attitude towards the Poms.

Anxious to get in touch with his old friend, and furious that the French telephone system seemed unable to connect him immediately, Rupert simply plunged into the sea and swam out to the yacht. Some minutes later a nervous secretary approached Stigwood.

'There's a Mr Murdoch . . .' she began.

'Put him on,' said Stigwood, reaching for the ship-to-shore telephone.

'He's not on the phone,' said the secretary. 'He's on deck. He just climbed over the stern.'

I got what was probably my first taste of top tycoonery on the way home from that trip. Rupert was returning, not to London, but to New York. And in style. We flew from Nice to Paris in a private jet, and landed alongside a scheduled Air France Concorde which was waiting on the runway. Rupert and family walked down one gangway and up the next, luggage was swiftly transferred and the Concorde took off. At Rupert's invitation we took the private plane on to Heathrow, where I discovered that both Customs and Immigration formalities can be less of a problem than most of us usually find them.

Rupert was often amusing, and sometimes embarrassing, in restaurants, where we tried, whenever possible, to prevent him seeing the price of anything, because he was always accusing us of extravagance. On one occasion, in Boulestin, he ordered a bottle of the house claret. Guillaume, the wine waiter, was shocked. 'Oh, no, sir,' he said, recognising me, but not Rupert, 'Mr Lamb wouldn't like that!' Who needs enemies?

In New York, at La Grenouille, at a dinner where five or six News International directors were present, Rupert asked me to choose the wine. I made my stock joke, asking whether he wanted a bargain or an experience, and compromised, as usual, with the latter. There are no 'bargains' on the wine list at La Grenouille!

When the bill arrived we were all at great pains to stop Rupert seeing it, but it was so huge that no one was anxious to sign it. So it was passed furtively round the table until it came to rest with George Viles. 'Jesus Christ,' said George. 'We could have dug up Escoffier for that.'

On another occasion in New York, when Rupert was driving, he pulled up outside a swish Fifth Avenue restaurant and gave a dollar to the doorman. 'Can you park this?' he asked.

The doorman returned his dollar. 'I'll park it, bud,' he said. 'But I don't park for a dollar.' Since the going rate was at least five dollars I would have been mortified in Rupert's shoes. But he was in no way abashed. He was delighted that he had saved a dollar – and may well have been encouraged to buy an extra bottle of Krug in consequence!

It was at Boulestin, which had been one of his father's favourite restaurants, where we celebrated late at night with champagne and lobster the birth of his two sons, Lachlan, who is now sixteen, and James, fifteen. Both were born at St Theresa's, Wimbledon, where two of my own children were born.

Rupert's belief that I knew something about wine was based entirely upon a subterfuge on my part. Once we were flying to Australia together. It was Rupert's custom on this painfully long trip to spy out a row of three empty seats in tourist class to which he could retire after dinner to sleep. I was in the lavatory when I heard him returning from such a foray, and addressing the chief steward just outside my door. 'My colleague will probably ask for a glass of champagne before dinner,' he said. 'Give him Great Western, but make sure he doesn't see the label.'

In the office at this time there was a great deal of *badinage* between English and Australian directors about Australian wines, and in particular Great Western 'champagne', which was anything but, but was always carried by Qantas, the Australian national airline, for patriotic reasons. We used to say there was no such thing as Australian champagne. The Australians used to accuse us of being wine snobs, and genuinely believed that we couldn't tell the difference. Of course, knowing the plot, when served with a glass I was able to say with complete confidence: 'Take this stuff away. I ordered champagne.' Rupert's eyes opened wide. I never thought it necessary to confess, before now.

The Chairman was hell to travel with. On an Australian trip he would take a handful of sleeping pills after dinner, go to the rear cabin and sleep as far as Singapore. Then, just about the time I was thoroughly exhausted, and had champagne bubbles coming out of my ears, he would take a stiff dose of wake-up pills, return to the First Class cabin and open his briefcase ready for work.

If I have so far painted a portrait of a thoroughly nice,

occasionally difficult but basically easy-going family man, that is because there is just such a man. But as we have seen, there is another side to Rupert, as all those who have worked for him and all those who have challenged him have discovered.

He is enormously single-minded in his pursuit of the immediate objective, and can be not only fierce, but ruthless. When he sets his sights upon a target, however distant, woe betide anyone who gets in his way. He is also capable of blind, unreasoning prejudice. I have known more than one journalist who claimed that his career was unfairly blighted because Rupert had taken an irrational dislike to him. This kind of irrationality also works in reverse. There are journalists who have been guilty of indolence, incompetence and the most blatant disloyalty who survive and flourish under the Murdoch umbrella.

In business, and in politics, above all else, he likes to win. In consequence he has more than once paid too high a price for something he coveted. Unlike some other Australian entrepreneurs – Alan Bond, for example, or Robert Holmes à Court, Rupert is not primarily a money-manipulator. He is a creative entrepreneur. He buys to build, and rarely buys to sell.

He gets bored very quickly. In conversation, his attention span is extremely limited. One can sense his mind leaping ahead to the next thought before the person he is talking to has finished a sentence. I have known him to leave a board meeting, without explanation, whilst someone was still speaking. I am sure he was not being deliberately rude. It was just that a new idea had driven all other thoughts from his mind.

In business, he does not have a lot of time to spare for anything which is working well. As soon as the wheels turn when the appropriate buttons are pressed he is looking for something new to do, something else to buy, usually in the communications business.

Those who may be puzzled at his involvement with Australia's Ansett Airlines, and the TNT transport giant may not know that he acquired them almost by accident. His real target was a moribund television station in Melbourne which happened to be owned by Reg Ansett, a crusty old boy who refused to sell it, even though it was a loss-maker, and a tiny part of the group's activities. Thwarted, Rupert then found a partner, Sir Peter Abeles of TNT, to help him mount a bid for the whole shooting match.

Robert Holmes à Court, in Perth, was also involved and there was a great deal of to-ing and fro-ing before Robert finally offered Rupert the shares which he had acquired, thus enabling the Murdoch–Abeles combination to win the day. Rupert quite enjoyed playing at aeroplanes for a while after that triumph.

By a coincidence I was staying at Cavan, Rupert's country home near Canberra, when Holmes à Court called to offer the key package, and I answered the phone. It is difficult to get to a phone before Rupert, if he is in the room. Indeed, he seems affronted if one fails to ring when he passes it. On this occasion, however, he was nursing a torn ligament acquired in a joust with John Newcombe and I beat him to it. This was the first time I had spoken to, or even heard of, Mr Holmes à Court. It was not to be the last.

In many ways, I suppose the acquisition which gave Rupert greatest satisfaction must have been Australia's Herald and Weekly Times Group, which he secured in 1987 after a bloody battle lasting several weeks – and after having been defeated on a previous occasion. Holmes à Court, too, had bid for, and failed to acquire, a controlling interest in the group, Australia's biggest publishers. But this time Rupert was determined.

The *Melbourne Herald* is often thought of as his father's paper, but Keith Murdoch, though what we would nowadays call Chief Executive, was, in fact, a salaried employee. His legacy to the young Rupert was not the *Herald*, but a big chunk of the *Adelaide News*, the paper upon which Rupert's empire was founded.

Even so, Rupert, and even more so his mother, the charming and gracious Dame Elisabeth, tended to think that the *Herald* should have been theirs by right. And if Rupert decided he wanted to buy the Taj Mahal it would be a brave man who would dare to say it was beyond his reach. I think the determination with which he pursued the *Herald* – acquiring dozens of other newspapers in the process – is the strongest single indication of what drives him.

It is Keith, who was once invited by Northcliffe to edit *The Times*, who makes Rupert run. Some people live for ever in the shadow of distinguished fathers. Whatever else, Rupert was always determined that he would cast the longer shadow.

By the time he bought *The Times*, the paper his father had declined to edit, no one doubted that he had succeeded. But by then, of course, he couldn't stop running. And by now his friends, with increasing concern, are wont to say that he isn't running the business, but the business is running him.

For all his wealth, and what is perceived to be his power and influence, Rupert is in many ways still extraordinarily modest and unassuming. He lived in New York for years before his colleagues persuaded him that he should have a chauffeur, hiring cabs off the street as he needed them, and often driving himself. He cares little for clothes, is most comfortable in well worn business suits, and needs to be reminded when his shoes need repairing.

He likes to think of himself as an ordinary sort of chap, though, of course, he is anything but. When he lived briefly in a lovely old house near Epping Forest, he told us all that he planned to come in to work by Tube. 'You bloody Pommie journalists are always buzzing about in taxis,' he said. 'You don't know what the people are thinking.'

I suspect some of us were rather closer to the people than

Mr Murdoch. Be that as it may, his devotion to the delights of the Central Line was short-lived. Within days his secretary was overheard making inquiries about the possibility of landing a helicopter somewhere closer to Blackfriars Bridge than Battersea heliport, and we heard very little more about Tube trains.

Helicopters, of course, are not always to be relied upon. Once, when he and I had agreed to take our wives to Luxembourg, where I was making a speech, there was thick fog at Epping, and the helicopter which was to take the Murdochs to Heathrow was unable to land on his lawn. It was too late to call for a chauffeur. Rupert, in no way perturbed, threw the luggage into his wife's BMW, raced all the way round London to the airport in fog, on the appalling North Circular road, parked the car, and arrived at the departure gate with a minute to spare. He wasn't even breathing hard.

He has never played the Big Shot, though Big Shot he undoubtedly is. He has never been very attracted by the trappings of power.

A few months ago my wife and I were in a slow-moving queue of people waiting to get into a ball organised by the British Australian Bicentennial Committee in honour of Bicentenary Year. Rupert and Anna were special guests, due to sit at the Royal table with the Duke and Duchess of Kent, and for them there was a special door, where a uniformed escort waited. Rupert at first refused to use it, and joined the queue. Only the combined pressure of Anna, my wife, myself, and the doorman persuaded him to change his mind.

Though he has never sought the trappings of power, he has inevitably attracted them. I chanced to be in Sydney (there was a Test match in progress) when Rupert flew in from New York to mastermind the *Herald* takeover battle, and we had dinner together. As usual, he had got his appointments book in a terrible mess.

'We could do with Dot,' I said, referring to his phenomenally efficient, globe-trotting personal secretary.

'She'll be here tomorrow,' he said. '*She's on my other plane.*'

CHAPTER TWENTY-TWO
I Did It Their Way

And so we come to the final curtain. I am tempted to write: 'I did it my way.' (A cliché is only a cliché because it says something effectively.) But the fact is that I did it everyone else's way. At all stages along the way I sought, and often took, advice from my wife, from my children, from my colleagues and even, *de temps en temps*, from Mr K. (for Keith) Rupert Murdoch.

I never lost an idea because I was too busy to listen to it. The Soaraway *Sun*, possibly the most dramatic success in newspaper publishing history, was the product of many minds and much blood, sweat and tears, by no means all of it mine.

I am often asked why *The Sun* has become the best-selling daily newspaper in the English language. What is the formula? they cry, as though making newspapers was like making axle grease. What are the magic ingredients? I cannot offer a formula, but I think I can offer a kind of philosophy – a philosophy which will be already clearly understood by the reader who has stayed with me thus far.

It is a simple philosophy. Always encourage the reader to feel part of the team. Never talk down to him. Never feel superior. Always remember that, in these days of multi-channelled broadcast information, it is no longer a newspaper's duty solely to inform.

One must at the same time aim to stimulate, educate, coax, coerce, cajole – shock when necessary – but, above all, to entertain. No newspaper, and no newspaperman, should ever be ashamed to entertain.

As I have suggested earlier, I believe it to be a fundamental error, which many so-called up-market newspapers make day after day, to believe that what is dull must be important, that news from abroad is somehow more significant than news from home, and that what interests the man in the street must of necessity be trivial. My advice to the national newspaper editors of the 1990s would be this: Never believe that it is irresponsible to be interesting. Never tailor the product in order to pander to the prejudices, real or imagined, of the paying customer. But never patronise him either.

In the same way that we did not have an easy-to-define formula at *The Sun* in the seventies, we did not have a lot of rules. We did not, for example, have a style book – a sort of book of house rules which was traditional among newspapermen at that time. I refused to have one. Years earlier, on the *Daily Mirror*, I had been infuriated many times by a silly house rule which was that 'jail' had to be spelt 'gaol'. One does not need to have served a print union apprenticeship to see that 'jail' takes up less room than 'gaol'. And night after night, it seemed to me, I was writing scintillating headlines in which 'jail' would fit, and 'gaol' would not.

So, in Bouverie Street, no style book. And not many rules. On the Murdoch *Sun*, flexibility was all. I reasoned that the first time I laid down a rule about the way something should be done would be the night I myself had good cause to break it.

Just as I had firm ideas about the editorial mix, though, I had firm ideas about how the job should be tackled. I insisted that the newspaper should be comprehensive. Never invite the reader to buy another newspaper to find out what is going on, I said. If it was on Page One of *The Times*, or the *Daily Telegraph*, I wanted it somewhere in *The Sun*, even though it may sometimes have been told in two paragraphs as opposed to two columns.

I expressed my how-to-do-it philosophy in a memo to back bench executives in November 1971, after we had just recruited a crop of new ones. 'We aren't the only people making newspapers,' I said.

> Competition is what it's all about – and the Back Bench is the nightly spearhead of that competition.
> To keep *The Sun* shooting to the top, the Back Bench must always be sales-conscious, efficient, opportunist.
> Most new readers are, and will continue to be, people who buy us INSTEAD OF – not AS WELL AS – their former paper.
> Inadequate, apathetic pages will lose them.
> 'It wasn't in my *Sun*,' is a death sentence.
>
> Our readers are the people who matter most.
> We want more than their threepences: we want their confidence.
> If you can see the holes in the story, so can they.
> If you can't make sense of a story, neither can they.
> If you think a headline is dirty or a picture is tatty, so will they.
> If you think a page is dull, so will they.
> . . . The Back Bench must seek constantly to improve and polish and up-date everything in the paper.
> Never be satisfied.
>
> Glamour captions should never be written for men. Cut out nudges, winks and leers.
> Always have second thoughts on stories about the jockstrap world of men only.
> . . . avoid so-called glamour pictures that make women say 'Ye-uck!'
>
> Cecil King once said that both young and old will read about goings-on among the young, but neither is much interested in the world of the old.
> Cecil King was right.

Most of the rest of the memo is too technical for reproduction here. But one further instruction was absolutely explicit. Under the heading *!*!*!*!* I wrote: '*The Sun* does not print dirty words or dirty pictures.' Nor did we. Saucy ones, certainly. Sexy ones, often. But I like to think that we were at great pains to avoid *nastiness*.

I had three children of varying ages. Most of my senior staff were family men, too. Whenever we considered the problem of what it was right and proper to print I used to say that it shouldn't be in the paper if we didn't want our children to read it.

Pictures of naked girls caused me no anxiety on this score. Nor did the serialisation of sexually explicit how-to-do-it books. As I said earlier, we didn't invent the permissive society. We were merely in tune with the times.

We saw no reason to keep from our readers – or our children – what was really going on in the world. No *topic* was banned in *The Sun*. We did not accept the standards of a different era.

Some *things* were banned, however. Some ways of writing. We did not bring our big guns to bear upon tiny targets. We did not set out to wound people, let alone destroy them. We did not encourage our reporters to write fiction, or invent interviews. We did not exult in the slaughter of Britain's enemies. There are some newspapers which now-adays seem to regard all these crimes as the journalistic norm.

Lord Cudlipp has said that we are living in the Dark Ages of popular journalism. Though Hugh has a gift for hyperbole, I certainly know what he means. It is clearly not possible to exempt *The Sun* from these general strictures, and it would be hypocritical to try to do so. The record speaks for itself. Yet it is easy for me to pontificate, and it may well be that *The Sun* today is more in keeping with the mood of the country than its detractors allow, as was *The Sun* of the seventies.

After all, though I was able to take the paper to the top of the hill, my successor has been required to keep it there. Perhaps his was the harder task, the greater burden. It is certainly more fun storming the battlements than defending the hill-top. And Kelvin MacKenzie has certainly performed his own task, and carried his own burden, with flair and distinction. I am not foolish enough to suppose that the editor of a newspaper which is read by more than 13,000,000 people is not getting most things right, most of the time. I salute him. He is a professional.

I hope people say that of me, too. A year or two back in a radio interview my old friend Derek Jameson asked me whether I would prefer to be remembered as the man who invented Page Three or the man who helped Mrs Thatcher into Number Ten.

'I'm not sure I would like to lay claim to either of those titles,' I told him. 'If I am remembered at all I would like it to be just as a professional newspaperman.'

So where does the industry go from here? Is there journalism after Wapping?

Are newspapers, in this electronic age, destined to lose power and influence in direct proportion to the speed at which the satellites crowd the skies?

Has the so-called 'new' technology made technocrats of us all?

Will Rupert (Sky Channel) Murdoch, like the late Lord Thomson, come to regard balance sheets as his favourite reading?

And have we really seen the end of The Street? Or is Fleet Street, as I like to believe, more of a way of life than a map reference?

I do not pretend to know the answers to all these questions. But I do know that I am distinctly unhappy with the way the industry seems to be moving. New technology has not given us better newspapers, or even faster newspapers, except in some highly specialised areas, like City prices. It has not raised standards in any way at all that I can see. What it does do, and that is why it has been necessary to embrace it, is dramatically to reduce labour costs, by eliminating, however sadly, whole swathes of once-proud and highly paid craftsmen.

In the process, it seems to me, much of what some of us feared might happen, has happened. Management pressures to cut costs still further, to keep it simple and change it not at all, if possible, have become stronger and stronger.

Thus we get – and by no means only in the popular Press – more and more headlines, even in late London editions, which are either boring, misleading, inaccurate, or simply fail to tell the story. We get in all newspapers hordes of literals (typographical errors) which no self-respecting printer of the old school would have permitted in his newspaper; we get sloppy spacing, tortured type, badly scaled pictures and stories which have clearly been chopped off in the middle.

I like to think that this is an interim period, and that newspapers will return, in time, typographically and in every other way, to the higher standards of an earlier age; that they will restore some of the checking and cross-checking, honing and polishing, doubting and questioning which seem to have been largely abandoned with the onset of editing on the small screen.

Those who are fortunate enough to work for newspapers owe it to themselves to love them and nourish them and cherish them. They should strive to produce them with ever more meticulous attention to detail, but at the same time with style and confidence, brevity and wit. Then, I promise, they will find in them a never-failing source of pride and wonder, satisfaction and delight.

I remember Alan Coren (*Punch*, the *Listener*, et al.) once wrote about children that they were bound to one's calves 'with hoops of titanium'. That is the way I feel about newspapers – but particularly, of course, about the Murdoch *Sun*.

Years after I left it, when I was Editor of the *Daily Express*, *The Sun*'s first edition used to drop on my desk at around 9 p.m. I actually *worried* if it was late. And not infrequently, if I saw something I did not like, or something I did, I would reach instinctively for the telephone, eager to administer praise or blame.

I have never been able to rid myself of this instinct. I am furious when I hear people sneer about the paper, and even more furious on those occasions when I believe their observations to be justified.

This much is beyond doubt: whether *The Sun* is being outrageous or irresponsible, witty or boring, exciting or tedious, whether it is getting things wrong, or, as is more often the case, it is being cruelly misrepresented by those who cannot be bothered to read it, I shall never cease to bleed for it.

About the Author

Sir Larry Lamb has had a varied and distinguished career in the newspaper world, having edited a variety of newspapers here, in Australia and in the United States.

He now runs a modest media consultancy business '. . . more as a hobby than anything else', and divides his time between a Cotswold cottage and an apartment in South Kensington.

'Generally, nowadays, I prefer to be in the country,' he says, 'but my wife gets withdrawal symptoms outside the Harrods van delivery area.'

Sir Larry has three children – '. . . 2s., 1d. as *Who's Who* so charmingly puts it' – all now pursuing successful careers.

'They are quite different, but all interesting, caring people,' he says. 'That is the biggest achievement of all. But it is more my wife's achievement than mine. I was never home long enough.'

Sir Larry has few interests outside his family. He enjoys fishing, but doesn't much like killing fish. He likes mountains, but a battery of constantly slipping discs restricts his enjoyment of them. He loves wine, '. . . but mainly the kind I can't afford'. And, as befits a Yorkshireman in exile, he loves cricket.

He was knighted in 1980, for services to journalism.

Index

Picture Acknowledgements

The publishers are grateful to the following for permission
to reproduce photographs in the plate section:

Michael Boys, vii
Camera Press (photo: John Kelly), vi (above left and below)
The Hulton Picture Company, iv (above)
Desmond O'Neill Features, iii (below)
Popperfoto, 2 (above)
The Sun/News International PLC, i, ii (below), iii (above),
iv (below left and right), v (both), vi (above right, photo:
Beverley Goodway), viii